Rednecks, Queers, and Country Music

The publisher gratefully acknowledges the support of the Manfred Bukofzer Endowment of the American Musicological Society, funded in part by the National Endowment for the Humanities and the Andrew W. Mellon Foundation.

Rednecks, Queers, and Country Music

NADINE HUBBS

University of California Press

BERKELEY   LOS ANGELES   LONDON

University of California Press, one of the most distinguished university presses in the United States, enriches lives around the world by advancing scholarship in the humanities, social sciences, and natural sciences. Its activities are supported by the UC Press Foundation and by philanthropic contributions from individuals and institutions. For more information, visit www.ucpress.edu.

University of California Press
Berkeley and Los Angeles, California

University of California Press, Ltd.
London, England

An earlier version of chapter 3 appeared in *Southern Cultures* 17, no. 4 (2011): 44–70, under the title "'Redneck Woman' and the Gendered Poetics of Class Rebellion."

Library of Congress Cataloging-in-Publication Data

Rednecks, queers, and country music / Nadine Hubbs.
    pages cm
    Includes bibliographical references and index.
    ISBN 978-0-520-28065-6 (cloth : alk. paper)
    ISBN 978-0-520-28066-3 (pbk. : alk. paper)
    1. Country music—History and criticism.   2. Country music—Social aspects—United States.   3. Homosexuality and popular music—United States   I. Title.
    ML3524.H78   2014
    781.642086′640973—dc23

                                                    2013049681

23 22 21 20 19 18 17 16 15 14
10 9 8 7 6 5 4 3 2 1

For the Krebs twins, Jerrie and Janet,
and in memory of Jack Hubbs and Mike Cavanaugh

Contents

Illustrations

Acknowledgments

"I got friends that I owe" is a line that resounds convincingly in "Here I Am," a 1997 track by the hard-living country and roots artist Steve Earle. He continues, "I ain't namin' names / Cuz they know." Surely my friends, like Earle's, "know," too. But namin' names in these acknowledgments is something I have looked forward to for a long time. I relish the chance to do it now.

I am grateful to colleagues and staff in the University of Michigan Women's Studies Department for supporting me and my work and helping me to find the time and resources I needed to bring this book project to fruition. Department chairs Valerie Traub and Liz Cole, department managers Sandra Vallie and Karen Cox Diedo, and staff members Shelley Shock, Vanessa Criste, and Donna Ainsworth contributed generously and crucially to my efforts.

The Center for Lesbian and Gay Studies (CLAGS) at City University of New York provided generous support for this book through its 2009 Martin Duberman Fellowship. Important thanks go to Michigan's College of Literature, Science, and the Arts (LSA) and Dean Terry McDonald for a sabbatical leave that allowed me to write full-time in fall 2011 and to LSA and the Office of the Vice Provost for Research for a Michigan Humanities Award that allowed me to write full-time in winter 2012.

From 2004 through 2013 I presented portions of this project in various venues, and I am grateful to all the audiences who inspired me with their engagement and sharpened my arguments with their critique. I am especially grateful to those who hosted, organized, and facilitated my speaking opportunities: Lisa Withers at Emory & Henry College, Kathleen Berkeley and Bill McCarthy at University of North Carolina–Wilmington, Carol Boyd and Terri Eagan-Torkko at the University of Michigan Institute for Research on Women and Gender, Megan Jenkins and Richard Kramer (on separate occasions) at City University of New York Graduate Center, Rachel Maine and Inna Naroditskaya at Northwestern University, Louis Bergonzi and Bruce Carter at University of Illinois at Urbana-Champaign, Ryan Powell and John Howard at King's College London, Sharon O'Dair at the University of Alabama, Robert Caserio at Pennsylvania State University, Daniel Party and Bettina Spencer at Saint Mary's College, Jin Cao and Qian Wang at Fudan University, and Fangfang Gao and Adel Wang Jing at Zhejiang University. I am also indebted to those colleagues who organized conference sessions at which I presented parts of this work: Melissa De Graaf, Scott Herring, Heather Love, Jocelyn Neal, and Fred Whiting. And I am grateful for the stimulus and input of copanelists and respondents, including Michael Bertrand, Greg DeNardo, Lisa Duggan, Jen Jack Gieseking, Mary Gray, Lydia Hamessley, Scott Herring, Colin R. Johnson, Emily Kazyak, Heather Love, Kris McCusker, Jocelyn Neal, Sherry Ortner, Diane Pecknold, Ricky T. Rodríguez, Kathryn Bond Stockton, and Eric Weisbard.

This is my second book with University of California Press, and it has been gratifying to work once again with Mary Francis as my editor. I have been buoyed by Mary's enthusiasm about this project since the earliest stages and by her steadfast engagement and support in our dialogues and meetings over the past decade. Kim Hogeland has been terrific as editorial assistant, keeping an eye on crucial production details and pulling things together at just the right moment. I am grateful to managing editor Kate Warne for her superb handling of the publication process and to copy editor Sheila Berg for her many improvements and elucidations.

I have received help and support from Library staff at the University of Michigan, including Women's Studies librarian Beth Strickland. Thanks to Mick Buck and Tim Davis of the Country Music Hall of Fame for searching their photo archives and providing many of the images used here. Jina B. Kim was ideal as research assistant, and this book has benefited greatly from her smart and diligent work in uploading my bibliography, locating images, and securing all the copyright permissions. I am grateful and fortunate that Phoebe Gloeckner, an amazing artist who is also an admired writer, so generously shared her time and expertise to create my author's photo.

In 2009–12 I worked through many of the sources and arguments of this book with sharp, musically and politically engaged Michigan undergraduates in the course Rednecks, Queers, and Country Music. A 2007 course, Uses of Trash, afforded me the special pleasure and opportunity of coteaching with my sister Jolene Hubbs. From Jolene and her work on poor whites in twentieth-century American literature and in dialogue with our students, I gained grounding and orientation that helped put this project firmly on the rails. I am deeply grateful to Valerie Traub, who as my department chair suggested both courses to me, allowed me to make them part of my teaching load, and hired Jolene, then a PhD candidate at Stanford, as my coteacher. Certain graduate and undergraduate students at Michigan contributed to this project virtually as colleagues, and I particularly thank Aaron Boalick, Grace Goudiss, Rostom Mesli, Brandon Biswas Phillips, and Emily Youatt for their input and readings.

A number of friends and colleagues spurred me on with good advice, encouragement, and sources, and I am therefore grateful to Tammy Chalogianis, Dorothy Sue Cobble, Liz Cole, Suzanne Cusick, Joe Dubiel, Lynn Eckert, LeAnn Fields, Marion Guck, Nancy Guy, Lucas Hilderbrand, Heather Love, Brenda K. Marshall, Andy Mead, Sridevi Nair, Esther Newton, Gayle Rubin, Bev Skeggs, Pavitra Sundar, Valerie Traub, and Aimee VonBokel. I am indebted, too, to colleagues and editorial readers who read parts of the manuscript at various stages and offered indispensable feedback: Sarah Banet-Weiser, Ayse Erginer, Scott Herring, Andy Mead, Karl Hagstrom Miller, Susan Siegfried, Travis Stimeling, Jessi Streib, Daniel Thomas Davis, and anonymous readers for *Southern Cultures* and University of California Press. I can hardly find words to express my heartfelt appreciation to those colleagues, brilliant readers all, who generously read the entire manuscript and offered expert perspective and critique: Maxime Foerster, David Halperin, Jolene Hubbs, Barry Shank, Sidonie Smith, and Valerie Traub. Liz Roberts read, edited, and provided invaluable commentary on the manuscript, the blurb, and nearly all aspects of the project. This book is better for her thoughtful attentions and astute input, and it has benefited richly from the contributions of everyone just named.

For love and sustenance in difficult, and deadlined, times, I am in awe and in the debt of P. Gabrielle Foreman, Juliet Guzzetta, Jack Hubbs Jr., Jolene Hubbs, Nancy Z. Hubbs, Holly Hughes, Maren Klawiter, Susan E. Watts, and some new friends arriving toward the end of this process, Erik and Max Mueggler, Rachel Neis, Matt Leslie Santana, Daphna Stroumsa, and Mariah Zeisberg. Special thanks go to Carla McKenzie for sharing her unfaltering wisdom and enormous heart and to Andy Mead and Amy Hamburg for opening their hearts and home to me time and again over more than a quarter century of friendship.

Finally, I thank my family members to whom this book is dedicated. My mother, Jerrie, a lover of Dolly Parton and Johnny Cash, among others, provided my earliest, most formative introduction to country music. My Aunt Jan and Uncle Mike, through their tavern the J&M Club and its beloved jukebox, offered an evolving array of country music throughout my childhood and adolescence, and an ideal atmosphere for absorbing it in the cornfields of the Great Black Swamp. My father, Jack, would have liked this book. I thought of him as I wrote these pages, and of all these four who delighted in being together when they found respite from daily labors and struggles, often accompanied by sounds of country music.

Intro

White working folk in the American hinterlands are rednecks. And rednecks are bigots and homophobes. This is common knowledge and reliable terrain for launching any number of stories, jokes, and armchair analyses. So the alternative rock band Foo Fighters stood on solid ground when, in late summer 2011, they posted online a jokey music video marrying two incongruous types, the redneck and the queer. The video featured an original song track titled "Keep It Clean (Hot Buns)" and four band members in hillbilly and trucker getup depicting long-haul drivers rendezvousing at a truck stop. Complete with wailing pedal steel and a drawling vocal, the song presented faux honky-tonk style—but with a twist. Its first verse opens with the couplet "Drivin' all night, got a hankerin' for somethin' / Think I'm in the mood for some hot man muffins." And the rest of the lyrics carry on in the same vein—of an adolescent gay joke in which redneck and queer worlds collide. Foo Fighters' country music send-up parodied the redneck and the queer by uniting them in a single, unfathomable figure: the queer redneck trucker. These truckers show a taste for blue-collar duds, diner grub, and low-key country on the jukebox but also—as revealed when the quartet enter a steamy truck stop shower—brazen disco, homoerotic water play, and posterior penetration (wearing nothing but a crazed grin, frontman Dave Grohl lowers himself onto a shampoo bottle).[1]

With its sly play on charged stereotypes, Foo Fighters' music video attracted mild notice and some YouTube hits.[2] But when the band released a new, live version of "Keep It Clean (Hot Buns)" unleashing the same redneck queer imagery in front of apparent real-life redneck homophobes, *that* video went viral. Foo Fighters performed their song across from a street protest by the notorious Kansas antigay Westboro Baptist Church (WBC) and posted online video of the event. Immediately *Huffington Post*, the

Washington Post, Advocate.com, and dozens of other news and media out-lets proclaimed the band gay champions and political heroes. View counts for both "Keep It Clean (Hot Buns)" videos skyrocketed.

Foo Fighters' gay-redneck-joke-as-country-song and its euphoric media reception highlight certain tenets of conventional wisdom on sexuality, politics, and provincial white working people that are central to *Rednecks, Queers, and Country Music.* The instance points to changes over recent decades in American attitudes toward sexuality and their significance, par-ticularly as an index of class status. Foo Fighters' lionization as gay freedom fighters owed to their sonic and visual parody of rustic white working-class "rednecks." When this parody was performed across from a homophobic group of white Christians from Topeka, metropolitan media profession-als—members of what I call the narrating class—rendered it a triumph of Good, progressive, middle-class whites over Bad, bigoted, working-class whites. A familiar association was thus confirmed, between the provincial white working class and homophobia. Common knowledge holds that this group, often known as rednecks, has long been a prime source—if not *the* source—of America's homophobia problem.

But the associations illustrated in this episode—that tolerance of gay, les-bian, and queer people is middle class and good and aversion to them working class and bad—have become established only recently, by historical stand-ards. We glimpse a very different picture, for example, in the U.S. Navy's investigations of sexual activity at a training station in Newport, Rhode Island, circa 1920. Some young enlisted men signed on for a mission to flush out local men who were soliciting navy personnel for sex. The sailors knew when they volunteered that the work would involve accepting sexual favors from other males, men known as *queers.* But their experience in working-class milieus led them to fear no threat to their own masculinity or social standing, so long as they took the insertive, "man's" role in such encounters. The recruits were surprised, then, when they came under sexual suspicion in the trial that ensued. As chronicled by the historian George Chauncey, this benchmark instance shows a collision between an early-twentieth-century white middle-class world in which any sex act between males placed them in the distinct, morally condemned category of *pervert* and a white working-class world in which male-male sex overlapped with mainstream social life, was often widely tolerated, and did not necessarily mark one as deviant.[3]

Earlier twentieth-century perspectives in this realm are very different from those that prevail today. For much of the twentieth century, accept-ance of gay, lesbian, and queer people was bad and working class and aver-sion to them good and middle class. The current view, emergent since the

1970s, reverses the values that attached for decades to queer acceptance (formerly bad, now good) and queer aversion (formerly good, now bad)—or what we nowadays call homophobia. But one thing remains notably constant: the valuations of middle-class and working-class positions.

"I'LL LISTEN TO ANYTHING BUT COUNTRY"

We can see the same class valuations mirrored in other areas of American culture, including musical taste. Though often viewed as highly personal and subjective, taste is a crucial marker and determinant of one's place in society. Its importance in this regard was famously shown by the French sociologist and theorist Pierre Bourdieu in his magnum opus, *Distinction*. Using data collected in the 1960s, Bourdieu mapped the correlations of different tastes in music, art, food, entertainment, and other realms to particular social class positions.[4] A study by the sociologist Bethany Bryson in the 1990s inverted the usual perspective on taste and social position by focusing on the relations between musical *dislikes* and social class. She found that contemporary high-status, middle-class Americans distinguished themselves not by cultural exclusiveness—for example, listening only to classical music (as in Bourdieu's 1960s)—but rather by cultivating broad, inclusive, often global musical knowledge and tastes. Their inclusiveness, however, had limits: these powerful individuals expressly excluded musical styles associated with the least-educated audiences, including heavy metal, gospel, and country.[5] Bryson's study affords insight into the role of country and other styles of music in contemporary U.S. class formation—that is, in shifting, ongoing processes of economic and cultural differentiation of capitalist society into class and status groups.

Distance from country music can help to define one as a middle-class *individual*, which is precisely a matter of distinguishing oneself from the tastes, characteristics, and people of the working-class *masses*.[6] Conversely, embracing country, with its emphasis on working-class themes and its significantly working-class constituency, can help to define one as working class. Film, TV, and other media sound tracks make frequent use of the cultural associations between country music and a working-classness often inflected as rural or southern, or both. Even just a few banjo or fiddle notes can suffice to convey qualities including rusticity, southernness, stupidity or lack of sophistication, and violent bigotry, especially racism and homophobia. The same associations operate off screen, in real life, and help to explain recent years' spread of the phrase "Anything but country" as a declaration of one's musical tastes.[7]

This book contextualizes the declaration "Anything but country," and it challenges both the conventional wisdom that renders the white working class America's perpetual bigot class and the presentism—the static framing and historical forgetting—on which it depends. I examine working-class cultural repertoires, with particular focus on gender and sexuality, from a dual perspective drawing on published empirical research (on-the-ground observations and interviews) and on history and critical analysis of American country music. Through these inquiries, I historicize the contemporary construction of the white working class as severe and intolerant in the realms of gender and sexuality. That is, I argue that the working-class homophobe is a construct with a specific history, and I date its rise from the 1970s to the present.

THINKING REDNECKS AND QUEERS THROUGH COUNTRY

Rednecks, Queers, and Country Music investigates rednecks and queers by listening to country music. This title announces the three main topics that are brought together here and occupy the inquiries and arguments ahead. In the contemporary United States, these topics are not typically thought together. Or more precisely, two of them, rednecks and country music, are very often thought together, even to the point of merging, but neither is typically imagined in combination with the remaining one, queers. In fact, the two topics that refer to social identities—rednecks and queers—are so remote from each other in the American cultural imaginary that putting them together is perceived not as a combination but as a juxtaposition. When the redneck and the queer are found together, therefore, it is often a cause of surprise, irony, or humor. This book takes up several cultural instances illustrating this point, on the one hand, and illustrating, on the other hand, the ease with which sounds and symbols of country music serve as proxy for "redneck," a notion that itself readily morphs into nearby constructs like "hillbilly" and "poor white trash."

My scare quotes around this last set of terms hint at another aspect of the combination, or juxtaposition, of the topics at hand, an aspect that amplifies the charge of surprise, irony, or humor thus created. That is, rednecks and queers and, unquestionably, country music are tender, potentially volatile, subjects. Each term represents something that is sacred in the eye of certain beholders and profane for certain others, and these beholders are frequently seen as occupying very different positions on the social and ideological spectrum. My point in bringing rednecks and queers together in the presence of country music is to question the implicit assumptions and explicit claims that assert vast and meaningful distances between them and to contest the skewed, ill-fitting cultural perspectives on the white working class that these claims and assumptions often rely on. Such perspectives sometimes reveal less about the group in question than the group articulating them. But they nevertheless mold public perceptions in ways that preserve middle-class cultural supremacy—even as its terms shift, often dramatically, over time.

Rednecks, Queers, and Country Music is a cultural studies project that analyzes country songs in musical, textual, and visual dimensions and draws on an interdisciplinary range of sources—including country music scholarship and criticism; cultural commentary and analysis; U.S. history; lesbian, gay, bisexual, transgender, and queer (LGBTQ) scholarship; social research; and social theory. In it, I aim to spotlight the inscriptions and erasures that frame the white working class as a discrete bigot class responsible for America's social and political ills. And I argue for the need to include working-class perspectives in American cultural discourses.

Part I, "Rednecks and Country Music," deals substantively with class and country music largely apart from the queer—that is, from questions of nonnormative, or "deviant," gender and sexuality. It traces the unchecked bias whereby white working-class people and worlds are judged according to the values and assumptions of the dominant middle class and thus found lacking, appalling, and blameworthy. I analyze cultural instances that use country music as proxy for the provincial white working class—a label meant to invoke the white working class located outside the coastal metropolises. Mainstream representations of "redneck" bigotry, which often feature country music, perform the conservative work of erasing privileged whites and institutions from prevailing images of racial and sexual bigotry past and present.

Part I also investigates the actual relations of country music to the white working class. I confirm country's links to this demographic group and to its values and cultural repertoires, using country music scholarship, available empirical research, and my analyses of selected country tracks. Drawing on a body of prior social and linguistic empirical research, I flesh out a set of working-class repertoires and values and analyze their manifestations in selected country songs. The discussion highlights ways in which my culturally engaged analyses differ from, and often contradict, standard country commentary and critique in media and academic sources. My treatment of country music here seeks to instigate an informed critical discourse on working-class music and broader culture.

Part II, "Rednecks, Country Music, and the Queer," builds on the class and culture arguments and frameworks elaborated in part I to examine dominant notions of how gender and sexuality work in country music and in the white working class—gender and sexuality being, along with race, areas in which the white working class is viewed as a prime agent of bigotry. My critical reading of Gretchen Wilson's 2004 breakout hit, "Redneck Woman," uses the track to explore gender and class and their crucial intersections. I examine "Redneck Woman" in light of the Virile Female construct that surfaced in the American media in 1990 and articulated the middle-class framework in which heterosexual, provincial, white working-class women are viewed as gender deviant. Ultimately my analysis underscores the point that modern gender forms are class-specific (and started out that way).

Dominant-culture images of working-class gender and sexual bigotry stress the implausibility of queer life among the white working class in America's so-called fly-over country. This is illustrated most emphatically by several legendary murders of gay and trans people: Matthew Shepard in Wyoming (1998); Scott Amedure in Michigan, a.k.a. the *Jenny Jones Show* murder (1995); Brandon Teena in Nebraska (1993), remade in the Hollywood film *Boys Don't Cry* (1999); and a nameless gay man in Wyoming and possibly, depending on one's interpretation, Jack Twist (Jake Gyllenhaal) in Texas in the fictional plot of *Brokeback Mountain* (2005). This book's culminating argument interrupts a forgetting of history and rewriting of cultural narratives now under way, which asserts that gender and sexual freedoms are new social advances in American society representing a middle-class victory over long-standing working-class bigotry. I challenge this version of events with an alternative reading that views sex-gender deviance as recently moving out of a century-long period of primary residence in the realm of the working class, where the two disreputable groups shared conceptual and, often, physical space while enduring abjection from middle-class moralism, social norms, and institutions (including psychiatry, medicine, government and law, and the media).[8] Official medical and legal conceptions of gender and sexual deviance, from late-nineteenth-century sexology up to Alfred Kinsey's research circa 1948, stressed its rampancy among the working class.[9] What happened in postwar America to transform the working class from queer hotbed to queer deathbed?

I argue that the decades since the 1950s, and especially since the 1970s, have witnessed a gradual *middle-classing of the queer*, in which sexual and gender deviance—now conceptually disarticulated—has been recast, in various ways domesticated, and moved upmarket, brought from working-class disrepute into the respectable realm of the middle class (the "homonormativity" targeted in recent queer left critique is a symptom of such middle-classing, or embourgoisement).[10] This social-cultural transformation represents most significantly a victory over *middle-class* prejudices and exclusions by middle-class strategies of queer activism. At the heart of these strategies is the respectability by which the middle class distinguishes itself from both upper- and lower-class (alleged) excesses. Tracing the origins of respectability, the British sociologist and theorist Beverley Skeggs notes that "a significant move in the definitional history of class was made by the bourgeoisie who, in order to morally legitimate themselves, drew distance from the figures of the decadent aristocrats above (again sexed and gendered: usually represented by the lascivious woman or the feminized man) and the unruly hordes below."[11] Skeggs's account of respectability emphasizes its interlocked workings with sexuality, gender, and race, in addition to class.

Middle-class postwar homosexual activists demanded that the boundaries of respectability be extended to include otherwise respectable, gender-normative individuals whose romantic and sexual partners were simply of the same rather than the opposite sex, relative to their own. Surely the history of queer activism and resistance includes certain moments when working-class actions have attracted great attention—none more than the unplanned, police-provoked, violent midsummer 1969 protest, with queens and butches arguably prominent, known as the Stonewall Riots.[12] But current queer politics and cultural standing bear more obviously the imprint of the 1950s and 1960s homophile movement, whose tactics of respectability were exemplified by members' orderly demonstrating against institutional policies while dressed in gender-normative professional business attire. Such activism grew over the years to enlist well-leveraged academic arguments; middle-class rhetorical and communicative strategies; a politics of recognition erected on middle-class distinguished individualism; and eventual appropriation and refiguring of working-class queer practices of femme and butch lesbianism, drag performance and perspective, and refusal of the homo/hetero paradigm and its official authority.[13]

This book shines a light on the fast-fading history of queer–working-class alliance through the remarkable prism of the hard country icon and ex-convict David Allan Coe's 1978 underground track "Fuck Aneta Briant" [sic]. I hear the record as an artifact of disreputable working-class deviance and irreverent, noneuphemistic resistance. It exemplifies a lost strain of antihomophobic rebellion that is simultaneously, inextricably antibourgeois. "Fuck Aneta Briant" sounds a working-class voice and position that remain illegitimate by dominant-culture standards. That its salient political dimensions are unrecognized and unreadable by those same standards raises questions about class and the politics of what counts as political, and about what narratives of the past and present emerge from the middle-classing of the queer.

Several key issues and concepts are used throughout these pages and require definition from the outset. They include country music and the music industry, class, and class culture, as well as issues of who likes and dislikes country and by what standard (if any) this music, and the contexts in which it resonates, can be called working-class culture.

SITUATING COUNTRY

Country music was born around 1923 in acts of recording, marketing, and dissemination of popular American sounds through records and over the radio airwaves. Modern country, briefly known as folk or old-time and then, for decades, as hillbilly music, was from the start commercial and a product of eclectic and shifting musical, cultural, and regional influences. Scholars agree that there is no original, pure, or authentic form of country music of which commercial country represents a variant, dilution, or corruption. Many a tirade on country music owes its existence to a lack of recognition that the music is and always has been a hybridized, commercial cultural and media form.[14] Thus, if the latest country record sounds a lot like roadhouse blues, a 1970s rock power ballad, bubblegum teen pop, or early 2000s R&B, some listeners and critics complain that it has betrayed its tradition. In a very real sense, however, such music upholds the core traditions of country music, which was founded on and has been carried forward by stylistic mixture and constant change in response to shifting market demands—that is, what people will pay for. Indeed, much of the music now regarded as classic, or as exemplary "real" country, was criticized in its own time as being outside country tradition—tracks, for example, recorded by Ferlin Husky, Jim Reeves, Patsy Cline, Dottie West, and others using the Nashville sound production style and countrypolitan records by artists like George Jones, Lynn Anderson, Charley Pride, and Glen Campbell.

When the Nashville sound hit the scene in the late 1950s, it displaced honky-tonk as the hot country style of the day. Where honky-tonk had pedal steel guitar and solo fiddles, the Nashville sound had jazzy six-string guitar, violin sections, and tinkly piano. Where honky-tonk singers were nasal and wailing, the Nashville sound featured close-miked crooning and lush backup vocals in four-part harmony. By the mid-1960s, the Nashville sound was itself overtaken by the Bakersfield sound, which replaced smooth strings and cool restraint with a driving backbeat beneath soaring pedal steel and twangy Fender Telecaster guitars, the "freight train" sound print

FIGURE 1.   Buck Owens (r.) and his musical soul mate, Buckaroos lead guitarist, fiddler, and tenor harmony singer Don Rich, on stage in 1968. The hard country Bakersfield sound they created with their twin Telecasters remains legendary, beloved by listeners and influential among country and rock musicians. Courtesy of Country Music Hall of Fame® and Museum.

of Bakersfield stars Buck Owens and the Buckaroos and Merle Haggard and the Strangers (figure 1). By the late sixties, this style in turn was challenged by countrypolitan, which matched the Nashville sound's string arrangement and raised it a horn section, while upping the emotional ante with a little more urgency in the vocals—less crooning, more tearful catch-in-the-throat inflections—and lyrics sometimes tinged with contemporary psychological consciousness. Examples include Tammy Wynette's "I Don't Wanna Play House" (#1 1967), in which a little girl's avoidance of a favorite children's game telegraphs the anxieties of her romantically abandoned mother, and George Jones's "Grand Tour" (#1 1974), whose narrator's spiel as he leads a sideshow tour of his now-empty house suggests a kind of split consciousness, whereby his words describe the symptoms of a loss that his mind cannot grasp.[15]

The stylistic pendulum swings captured in the preceding two-decade snapshot, circa mid-fifties to mid-seventies, illustrate the alternations of a hard/soft duality that the sociologist and country music scholar Richard A. Peterson identifies as a perennial dialectic in commercial country. Its roots trace back to an earlier male, public, instrumental performance practice centered in the barn dance and a female, domestic, vocal performance practice centered in the parlor.[16] Modern hard and soft country concepts align with gendered meanings of masculine and feminine and, further, with "rough" country and smooth pop-crossover sounds, with working-class and middle-class or aspirational cultural styles, and with critics' attributions of authenticity and inauthenticity, respectively. These hard versus soft country associations circulate throughout the zigzagging postwar style shifts just glossed and in country music produced up to today.

This book cites over one hundred songs. I analyze or describe most of them in connection with my arguments concerning class, politics, and sexuality. The country music under discussion here is not the hip and cool kind, whether that might be classic country or alt-country. Rather, it is what the poet and indie musician David Berman, invoking obvious uncool resonances, has called Walmart country.[17] Of the hip alternatives, the latter, alt-country music—comprising artists like Ryan Adams, Gillian Welch, and Uncle Tupelo and the *O Brother, Where Art Thou?* sound track—is fairly remote from Nashville country in its production, preoccupations, and audience (and so it is unfortunate that "alt-country" is the designation that so often sticks to this music rather than one of its other labels like Americana or No Depression). Classic country includes music by the handful of country and crossover artists listed in *Rolling Stone* magazine's "100 Greatest Singers of All Time": Johnny Cash (#21), Hank Williams (#27), George Jones (#43), Patsy Cline (#46), Dolly Parton (#73), Merle Haggard (#77), and Willie Nelson (#88).[18] Classic country surely also includes a few other artists apt to be claimed as forebears by rock-affiliated "roots" musicians, from Bob Dylan to Lucinda Williams, who would not be caught dead listening to current Nashville fare (hipsters "hate modern country music," writes the critic Chuck Klosterman, "because it speaks to normal people in a rational, tangible fashion"). Bluegrass, too, is highly regarded by roots rockers, among others, and carries intellectual capital as an "authentic" folk form (it is actually a postwar commercial invention, albeit with folk music ties).[19] In this respect, bluegrass contrasts with mainstream country, with which it overlaps only occasionally in production, preoccupation, and audience, and so lies outside my musical purview.

Although this book cites certain songs from the classic country canon, the music under consideration, with one notable exception, is mainstream Top 40 country (the principal exception being "Fuck Aneta Briant," an underground release by Coe, a well-known, chart-topping singer-songwriter). In examining contemporary images of the white working class in

relation to gender, sexuality, politics, and dominant ideology, *Rednecks,
Queers, and Country Music* focuses on American culture in the decades
since the civil rights struggles and social transformations of the 1960s. Its
main musical focus is likewise on country songs of the mid-1960s to the
present—though earlier examples figure in the discussion at some points.

Country music is closely associated with notions of place and region.
Some scholars argue that significant country artists have come mainly from
the South, others counter that California and the Southwest have been crucial, and we might note that the Midwest has also yielded a number of
important artists.[20] Reception research shows that commercial country was
initially a music of rural more than southern audiences; that by the 1970s its
audiences were not distinctly rural or regional but preponderantly midlife,
working- and lower-middle-class whites; and that in the 1980s and 1990s
country made significant inroads into suburbia.[21] Other indicators suggest
that in some regions of the United States country music is less a distinct
cultural object than something woven through the fabric of everyday life.
For example, in certain areas of the South and the West, country records are
integrated in pop Top 40 radio rotation, and country audiences often include
members of the middle and even the upper classes, like the Texans and self-
proclaimed country fans George H.W. and George W. Bush.[22]

I bring to this discussion of country music a perspective shaped by lifelong residence in the Great Lakes region, specifically the Detroit-Toledo
orbit. My industrial Midwest neck of the woods boasts significant country
music engagements past and present. In fact, U.S. Census data show a
higher rate of affinity for country music among white residents of the
Midwest (52.7 percent) than in any other region nationally, with the South
coming in next (49.5 percent), followed closely by the West (49.0 percent),
and the Northeast trailing at some distance but still registering a "like" rate
of almost two-fifths of the white adult population (38.1 percent).[23] As these
numbers indicate, country music is not just a southern thing. But there are
good reasons for the customary association of country music with the
South, including country's early history in rural southern song collecting
and record industry talent scouting, and the persistence of southern themes
in song lyrics, band names, and other aspects of country music culture.

That said, this book does not treat country music as a southern phenomenon per se. The musicians whose work I discuss most extensively, Gretchen
Wilson and David Allan Coe, are both natives of the Great Lakes Midwest
(Illinois and Ohio, respectively). My choices here are not meant to advance
any particular regionalist claim, though admittedly they may amplify the
midwestern slant already present in my authorial perspective. In general,

however, this book is more concerned with the identities of country *audiences* than artists and producers—except to the extent that these might link to audience engagements. Indeed, a crucial assumption behind virtually every country music inquiry and assertion pursued here concerns a two-way relation between country and its listeners. This assumption, which is supported by empirical research, is that popular music both influences and reflects the cultural values of its audience.[24] The cultural values of particular interest to me in this book are those connected with differing class positions in American society—shared group values that hold up, in certain ways, across boundaries of region, race, and locale (e.g., urban vs. rural).

THE CLASS OF COUNTRY

By broad agreement of the American public and country music experts alike, country is a music of working people. Referring to the postwar country scene, country music's preeminent historian, Bill C. Malone, portrays country's creators, audience, and songs in working-class terms. He notes that country songwriters in this period "have been part of the audience for whom they write," an audience that has been "basically working class with middle-class aspirations." Country song lyrics, on Malone's account, are "realistic in that they concern themselves with the petty details of human existence" and "describe life as it is, not as one might wish it to be"—and we might note, these lyrics convey stories that are central to the listening experience and (unlike many rock lyrics) are meant to be heard and understood. In *Real Country*, a study of a local community of working-class country devotees, the ethnomusicologist and linguistic anthropologist Aaron A. Fox argues that "country music is deeply embedded in the textures of working-class life" and that it is "the cultural and intellectual property of working-class people and not only of the Nashville-based industry or the stars" who are the subject of much country music coverage.[25]

Contemporary country music is focused on the values, concerns, and perspectives of the white, and sometimes broader, working class. Country's songs, videos, artists, and publicity material traffic in themes, language, and musical idioms linking to identities characteristically working class (though Americans rarely identify themselves as such, often claiming middle-class status even when positioned above or below it), and it links to identities southern, midwestern, southwestern, and provincial; white; Christian; and heterosexual. Country music trains an intent focus on these social identities and is arguably the most widely circulating discourse on white working-class (not to mention southern and provincial) life and identity in

American culture. Also arguable is whether its representations are accurate. The answer surely varies according to the instance, but it is important to note that country, like other popular music, is both a commercial product and an artistic medium. It directs its appeals to fantasy and imagination as well as selected perceptions of reality.

Country is a rarity on the American media landscape inasmuch as it addresses working people and their lives, and not for laughs or in an objectifying frame. As a cultural symbol, country music not only sonically evokes a certain type of social persona—usually figured as working-class, white, and provincial—but often stands as proxy for that persona. Thus sounds of country in a television or film sound track can telegraph the presence of this persona even when it is not visible on screen. In another symbolic process, exclusion of country from middle-class listeners' musical tastes serves, according to sociological research, as a symbolic exclusion of the lower-status persona associated with it.[26] Country music in turn is filled with resistance to the dominant middle-class culture, its privileges and values and its judgments of those deemed less-than.[27] Of course, country is not written, created, or consumed exclusively by white working-class people—or for that matter, southern, rural, Protestant, or heterosexual ones. Characterizations of country music as speaking for or to a narrow constituency defined along such lines are at odds with (among other things) the long presence in country music of African Americans in the South and Mexican Americans in the Southwest and the diaspora, the middle-class suburbanization of "new country" audiences in the 1980s and after, and the music's pivotal role in lesbian and gay two-step bars and International Gay Rodeo Association (IGRA) events.[28]

Whatever the demographics of country audiences, they are distinguished by their receptivity to a music heard and frequently stigmatized in terms of working-class, provincial, and southern themes and, very often, implicitly white identities. Country listeners' receptivity is notable in light of the hostility and contempt that have been directed at the music as backward and, since about 1970, menacing—a turn crystalized in the reception of Merle Haggard and the Strangers' "Okie from Muskogee" (#1 1969). Haggard's characterization of antihippie, antiprotest sentiments provoked fervent positive and negative responses both and exposed ideological divisions in American society that would figure in the coming decades' culture wars. Bryson's much-cited 1996 study identifies middle-class dislike of country music as class based and as a means of separating oneself, through the medium of taste, from the less educated social group associated with country (a 2005 quantitative study also confirms middle-class listeners' lesser affinity for country music).[29] This research suggests that the dominant culture's responses to country music are responses to the working-class, white, provincial people it stands for—in stereotypical terms, rednecks.

Traditionally, *redneck* is a pejorative term referring to a white, working-class, provincial, often boorish, sometimes (but not always) southern male. The word has long been used accusatively, but since the 1970s *redneck* has also been reclaimed as a defiant antibourgeois self-designation—signaling, among other things, a rejection of the euphemistic rhetoric of the middle class (if euphemism is "the neutralization and distancing which bourgeois discourse about the social world requires and performs," it is also a frequent object of working-class perceptions of middle-class hypocrisy, duplicity, and condescension).[30] Wilson's use of *redneck* in "Redneck Woman" renders the term gender-inclusive and builds on its use as a "redneck pride" self-identification to create a statement of cross-gender working-class consciousness and solidarity. *Redneck* is a marker of white working-class identity, freighted with history and with multiple complex and contradictory connotations. Its use in my title and throughout this book invokes the word's accusatory, othering sense, with its frequent imputations of bigotry, as well as the self-identificatory sense arising with the advent of self-ironic redneck pride in the 1970s.

Both the redneck persona and the country that is heard as its theme music arouse scorn in the dominant middle-class culture. Both are shunned by members of the middle class as uneducated and are further perceived as racist and homophobic.[31] A 2005 analysis of U.S. Census data indicates that country listeners indeed have lower levels of formal education than rock listeners and lower income levels, too, and research conducted around 1970 found comparably that country radio audiences reported fewer years of education than other radio audiences, were overrepresented in low-prestige occupations, and (in that time of strong labor unions and working-class prosperity) were "moderately affluent." These data support the widespread notion that white country audiences are significantly working class, and have been throughout the period in question. Research further indicates that country music and its listeners display different values and styles of self from those of rock and its listeners and that these country and rock values and selves prevail in the working and middle classes, respectively.[32]

In short, historians, ethnographers, and quantitative researchers present evidence that country music is a working-class cultural form, created largely by working-class artists, addressing working-class values and notions of self, and engaging significantly working-class audiences. Whether or not the point is obvious, it is important to acknowledge that not all white working-class people like or listen to country music and that even those who do may well be engaged with and influenced by other kinds of popular music as well. Conversely, country attracts non-working-class listeners, too, including middle-class listeners, and it attracts nonwhite listeners. We might note in this connection that quantitative and other research can miss crucial facts beyond people's present social identities, including their *identifications*—which are shaped by unseen personal and family histories, fantasies and yearnings, denials and disaffiliations.

CLASS AND CULTURE

Class analysis is not only the province of scholars or demographers. Socioeconomic class is what teenagers invoke when they refer to a high school classmate as a member of the "preppy" clique or the "burnouts." It is what adults invoke, too, when they refer to "Barbie and Ken people" or "people of Walmart."[33] And it is what pundits and commentators invoke when they refer to "Upper Easties" or "NASCAR fans." Registering this point, Bourdieu stresses that the social actors who are "objectively" observed and classified by researchers are observers and classifiers in their own right— from whom researchers even cop terminology: "Many of the words which sociology uses to designate the classes it constructs are borrowed from ordinary usage, where they serve to express the (generally polemical) view that one group has for another. . . . Sociologists . . . forget that the 'objects' they classify produce not only objectively classifiable practices but also classifying operations that are no less objective and are themselves classifiable."[34]

Bourdieu speaks of the modern capitalist arena in which such classification takes place—or gets fought out—as "the social space." It is a space where money, property, influence, and other resources are unevenly distributed. The players here, referred to by scholars as "agents" or "subjects," are not only objectively seen and classified differently according to their differing positions; they subjectively *see* the game and playing field differently according to them. They "have points of view on this objective space," in Bourdieu's words, "which depend on their position within it and in which their will to transform or conserve it is often expressed."[35]

Recognizing that there is more than one way to get ahead, or to fall behind, in the game that is played out in the social space, Bourdieu identifies several forms of capital, extending beyond the original, economic sense of the word:

Economic capital: wealth, property

Cultural (also "educational") capital: having the "right" knowledge, tastes, expression, in food, music, speech, possessions

Social capital: knowing people, having useful connections

Symbolic capital: prestige, honor, recognition, pedigree, legitimation[36]

Bourdieu's multiple categories of capital acknowledge the exchange value that may reside in intangible assets. A defining feature of social, cultural, and symbolic capital is that all, under certain, specific conditions, can be converted to economic capital—and vice versa.[37] Identifying the various asset types is especially useful for elucidating the workings and origins of social and economic power.

For example, everyone knows that economic capital can be inherited and thus give certain people a strong start in life. But we may seldom think about how some people also benefit from family transmission of cultural capital—privileged forms of knowledge and taste that confer confidence and entitlement—and how valuable that legacy might be. Of course, to "seldom think about" any of these things often means that one has not had to think about it by virtue of having been dealt a good hand, or that one does not wish to think about it and thus question notions of merit and self-made success. An important concept for Bourdieu is that of *misrecognition*, which (in one crucial manifestation) misattributes intrinsic superiority to the privileged and powerful. It works by a process of systematic forgetting, in which one acquires prized knowledge and skills through cultural inheritance, family expenditures and elite education, or exploitation of others, but the gains are subsequently recognized—that is, misrecognized—as individual achievements and innate distinction. Erasing the intensive processes and resources that endowed one with exceptional knowledge and capacities, society credits the individual with personal accomplishments and inborn talents. Misrecognition serves to justify and naturalize, and thus to conserve and compound, the privilege of individuals who already possess the capital to acquire elite knowledge and "gifts."[38]

Another important function of Bourdieu's forms of capital lies in marking and forming an individual's patterns of heart and mind and imparting a particular "'feel' for the game," a "practical sense for what is to be done in a given situation." Bourdieu views the types of capital as congealing in one's body early in life and shaping the persona over a lifetime. The result is an embodied set of propensities to certain everyday postures and attitudes, ways of speaking and interacting, preferences in food, socializing, media, and so on, which he calls *habitus*.[39] So, for example, insiders often draw distinctions between the ways of "new money" and "old money" people. Relatedly, when actor-comedians Roseanne Barr and Tom Arnold were a celebrity couple starring in the hit sitcom *Roseanne*, they quipped that they were "America's worst nightmare: white trash with money" (in 2006, the country superstar Toby Keith released an album under the title *White Trash with Money*). Both of these scenarios point to habitus, and they suggest that acquiring wealth does not miraculously transform humbler folk into members of the upper class. A mismatch between class habitus and economic capital was also the pivotal gag (regionally inflected) in the 1960s sitcom *The Beverly Hillbillies*, in which a family of dirt-poor Ozark mountaineers move to Beverly Hills after discovering an oil gusher on their land: sitting pretty in the world of perpetual sunshine, wealth, and glamour, they never lose their simple, trusting ways or their taste for moonshine and fresh-killed squirrel. But even people who take a class mobility journey involving acquisition of new cultural, social, and symbolic (more than economic) capital report feeling themselves caught between worlds—a state the journalist and author Alfred Lubrano explores in his book *Limbo*.[40]

The present book takes a Bourdieusian approach to class, using the work of Bourdieu and other scholars who build on, and sometimes modify or diverge from, his formulations, especially Skeggs and the American cultural anthropologist and theorist Sherry Ortner. Following Bourdieu, I understand class as something "not defined solely by a position in the relations of production [e.g., owner vs. worker, as in Marx], but by the class habitus which is 'normally' . . . associated with that position."[41] This view acknowledges the class-constituting role of social, cultural, and symbolic, as well as material, assets in late capitalist society. And it acknowledges the importance of one's position in relations of, not just producing, but consuming goods and services. Writing about the contemporary U.S. context, Ortner underscores consumption and symbolic relations when she sums up class as "almost entirely a matter of economic gradations of goods and privilege" and "embedded in narratives of snobbery and humiliation."[42]

If, according to another characterization, "class works by specifying the costs and opportunities facing different people," it does so through all of the material, social, and cultural dimensions I have been discussing.[43] This book focuses on the workings of class in its cultural aspect. It illumines how, on the one hand, country music functions in dominant-culture representations as a projected symbol, often antagonistic and derisive, of the white working class. And it details, on the other hand, how the music functions *within* the white working class in a two-way cultural relation, both reflecting and shaping the tastes and values of its working-class audience (which is not to imply that either the music or its audience possess class "purity"). In both instances, country music contributes to class formation and identity. For listeners whose occupation, education, income, and other factors position them as working class, identifying with country, its messages, and its constituency can help to produce class consciousness and formation. Conversely, excluding country from one's tastes can help individuals of middle-class positionality to establish the individual distinction that defines middle-class identity.

By examining middle-class aversion to country, I aim to anatomize an instance of the "aesthetic intolerance" in which Bourdieu locates a capacity for terrible violence and to register its disavowed social, ideological, and political thrusts.[44] My naming and analysis of working-class rhetoric, values, and culture in the themes and stylistics of contemporary country songs are intended to highlight the frequent errors and irrelevance of bourgeois-centric country commentary and the need for culturally attuned country criticism. However irrelevant the dominant culture's misreadings of country music may be as music criticism, they reverberate in broader dimensions, further discrediting an already discredited group and serving to justify its low status. In light of these mechanisms and stakes, I especially hope to stimulate dialogue on class cultures in relation to country music and other cultural forms—including other types of music, food, style, media, and more.

In deploying the notion of class culture, this project joins and extends prior discussions of class cultures in ethnographies and social practice theory by Ortner and Skeggs and in Barbara Ehrenreich's well-known study of middle-class culture, *Fear of Falling*. Malone and Fox are among the scholars who employ the concept of class culture in the study of country music. And certain LGBTQ histories use the notion of class culture in documenting working-class same-sex cultures on twentieth-century U.S. sites, including Chauncey's *Gay New York*; Elizabeth Kennedy and Madeline Davis's history of lesbian Buffalo, New York, *Boots of Leather, Slippers of Gold*; and Nan Boyd's history of lesbian and gay San Francisco, *Wide-Open Town*.[45] My final chapter engages these histories of class-specific gender and sexual cultures in order to question current perceptions of the working class vis-à-vis gender and sexual deviance. Read in conjunction with Coe's concrete antihomophobic instance in "Fuck Aneta Briant," these class-aware queer histories help me trace working-class cultural logics unfathomed in many contemporary discussions of (perceived) redneck bigotry.

OVERVIEW

Chapter 1, "Anything but Country," along with portions of chapter 2, examines the dynamics of country music dislike and the prevalence, since about 1970, of representations of both country music and the white working class in terms of political conservatism and racial and sexual bigotry. The chapter analyzes several contemporary cultural instances illustrating commonplace representations of a monolithic white working class driven by bigotry, which often use country music as proxy for the working-class bigot. I also highlight the professional middle class's role as the narrating class in America's knowledge economy, interpreting and narrating all levels of American life—including working-class existence—in academic, media, and other channels.

Chapter 2, "Sounding the Working-Class Subject," contests assumptions of a universal middle-class culture and argues the existence of a distinct working-class culture. A substantial portion of the chapter is devoted to fleshing out the particular character of working-class culture and the ways in which country music gives voice to it. I analyze selected country songs in connection with an account of contemporary white working-class culture and "subjectivity" (social selfhood) developed here from a body of empirical research. Of course, country music and working-class culture both contain complex tensions and contradictions, and neither displays uniform values and perspectives. But my song analyses identify values that recur frequently in country music, including "being country," walking the walk, implicit communication, and community-oriented individualism or "sociocentrism," and I identify parallels between these themes and working-class values and repertoires, as delineated by empirical research. Ultimately, I read country music's themes and values as unified by an ethos stressing substance over style and surface appearance.

The final two chapters examine gender and sexuality in white working-class contexts through a close reading of a particular country song. Chapter 3, "Gender Deviance and Class Rebellion in 'Redneck Woman,'" uses Wilson's blockbuster single to demonstrate some of the ways in which working-class subjectivity is modeled in country's music and lyrics while listening closely to intersections of class and gender and to the antibourgeois resistance that is sounded in much country music. Examining layered references in sounds, text, and video images, I read "Redneck Woman" as a gender and class manifesto that outsmarts the pitfalls and double binds attending its narrator's doubly devalued identity position and that calls attention to gender's contingency on class—particularly the dominant culture's exclusion of the working-class "Virile Female" from respectable femininity. In the case of "Redneck Woman," all this is accomplished in a musically compelling three-and-a-half-minute track.

Finally, chapter 4, "'Fuck Aneta Briant' and the Queer Politics of Being Political," builds on the preceding chapters' arguments on U.S. country music and on gender in the white working class to examine contemporary representations of homophobia past and present. In instances from the Newport naval trial of the World War I era, as chronicled by Chauncey, through the enforced adoption of the transgender concept, as documented by the anthropologist David Valentine in 1990s New York, the twentieth century saw grassroots cultures of sex and gender deviance come under correction from middle-class institutions—clergy, courts, public health organizations—that not only censured, but "rectified" poor and working-class communities' sex and gender self-designations and self-definitions.[46] The court and clergy reclassified men from "normal" to "homosexual" in the case of navy sailors who were "manly" (insertive) partners in same-sex acts, and public health agencies reclassified people who deemed themselves collectively "gay" into the bifurcated categories "transgender" and "gay," gender deviant versus sexually deviant, in the case of the poor queer community of color documented by Valentine.[47] In my reading, these and other instances tell a quite different story from one repeatedly asserted in contemporary public discourse and media culture, in which a menacing working class is the face of homophobia.

The twenty-first-century strangeness of Coe's simultaneously irreverent, vulgar, antibourgeois, and antihomophobic standpoint—as he defends "all them faggots" against the antihomosexual crusader Anita Bryant—serves as provocation for my final chapter's exploration of the relations between twentieth-century class cultures and (what we now call) sexual and gender queerness. Ultimately, my conclusions in chapter 4 indict, not the middle-classing of the queer, but that cultural logic whereby the associations now forged between the queer and the middle class necessitate demonizing the white working class as homophobic and erasing and depoliticizing their deep historical relations to queer culture.

The brief conclusion is titled "Outro," borrowing a popular-music industry term for a tag or coda. It considers treatments of LGBTQ themes in recent country songs and their relations to rural, as well as working-class, social codes. Current research on rural sociality describes it in terms resembling those of working-class sociality and resonating, too, with messages that recur frequently in country music. All of this points to practices of social and sexual tolerance different from, but no less valid than, middle-class recognition politics. My closing underscores the intellectual, moral, and political stakes of recognizing perspectives, values, and tastes beyond those of the dominant middle class.

PART I

Rednecks and Country Music

1. Anything but Country

> Any judgement of the working class as negative (waste, excess, vulgar, unmodern, authentic, etc.) is an attempt by the middle-class to accrue value. That is what the representations of the working-class should be seen to be about; they have absolutely nothing to do with the working-class themselves, but are about the middle-class creating value for themselves in a myriad of ways, through distance, denigration and disgust as well as appropriation and affect of attribution.
>
> BEVERLEY SKEGGS, *Class, Self, Culture*

There is a phrase I have heard on the first day of classes for the past decade, ever since—for ice breaking as much as informational purposes—I began asking my undergraduates, "What do you listen to?" Now, every semester, it issues from students of various sorts, a line so familiar as to be recognized by all, even when mumbled hurriedly by the shy and self-conscious: "Anything but country."

In discussions of popular music on campuses throughout the Midwest and in the Northeast, mid-South, and Deep South, college students have told me that this phrase prevails (it is *the* standard answer, one Alabama undergraduate attested) in response to questions about listening preferences—questions, as the students well know, that get at who one is and wants to be. The same "ABC" formula circulates off campus, too, among adults out in the world, when they are asked to declare their musical tastes. Indeed, across generational groups, country stands out as a music that Americans are often at pains to exclude in these culture-focused moments of social self-construction.

This chapter asks what is going on in such instances. Why is "Anything but country" such a common refrain? Who invokes it? What does it mean? And is it really about the music? My approach to these questions begins with an investigation of the meanings of country music—meanings not from inside the songs (the subject of chapter 2) but from outside. That is, I begin by examining the meanings that attach to country music as a cultural category and brand.

COUNTRY MUSIC AND THE PHANTOM HILLBILLY

Long heard as an affront by those targeted with it, the word *hillbilly* marks one as being from the country, originally, from Appalachia, and it bears

23

connotations of ignorance and lack of sophistication. Notably, "hillbilly" was also for thirty years the standard industry label for the music now known as country. The music's name change to "country and western" in the 1950s recognized *hillbilly's* derogatory status, but it was not a complete image makeover. Country audiences are still associated with white working-class, provincial, and southern identities, as well as ignorance and, in recent decades, bigotry.[1]

Bryson's 1996 empirical study yields perspective on the social meaning and function of country music in late capitalist U.S. society. The study confirms previous research finding that high-status individuals no longer brandish cultural capital by the means that reigned throughout most of the twentieth century—that is, narrow, exclusive involvement with classical music and "high" culture forms uncontaminated by mass culture. George Jones and Tammy Wynette's couplet "Our Bach and Tch'ikowsky / Is Haggard and Husky" stands as a relic of that defunct cultural order, serving in "(We're Not) the Jet Set" (#15 1974) as one musical metric among others—of geography, transport, food, society—that gauged the distance between the exclusive "jet set" and the less distinguished regular folk. By contrast, in the current cultural system (solidified since the 1980s), entitled middle-class subjects wield *multi*cultural capital through knowledge and engagement in a broad range of global musics—deploying them as "potential ingredients in a singular and singularly distinctive cultural mix ... [that] signals a high level of educational attainment, untrammeled access to cultural goods, and command over the time and resources necessary to master a variety of social and aesthetic codes."[2] As I mentioned above, the new system of distinction-by-inclusion depends on crucial exclusions. The "cultural omnivores" in Bryson's study expressly excluded the categories of music associated with the least educated audiences, including country (published research identified country audiences as lacking in education and occupational status as early as 1975).[3] In the light of her findings, a taste declaration like "Anything but country" appears first and foremost as a gesture of *social* exclusion. Musical exclusion is secondary, a vehicle and symptom.

And so, a half-century after shedding the "hillbilly" designation, country music continues to trail a phantom hillbilly. Country's cultural meaning remains tethered to the image of a certain kind of social subject. It is a figure stigmatized by ignorance and constitutive—by its exclusion—of middle-class status and entitlement. The racial and class (and sometimes geographic) designation "hillbilly" is one sign under which this figure is known. There are others, as we shall see.

"UNAFRAID TO GET POLITICAL":
FOO FIGHTERS IN JED-FACE

In the waning days of summer 2011, Foo Fighters, a celebrated, long-established alternative rock band fronted by Nirvana veteran Dave Grohl, released a video to promote and kick off a North American tour. Their tour promotion video "Keep It Clean (Hot Buns)" consists of two main scenes, both set in a truck stop. The first scene takes place in the truck stop diner, where the band's "faux country" song "Keep It Clean" plays on the P.A. system.[4] The song is a broad parody of country music, sung in a voice as close to bass-baritone as Grohl can manage—with a phony drawl, references to "Mama" and "Daddy," steel guitar flourishes, and other musical and linguistic markers that signal country, southern, redneck, and hillbilly tropes in popular culture.

"Keep It Clean (Hot Buns)" weds sonic and visual parody to a mash-up of hillbilly, cowboy, and redneck identity. The video features band members costumed as "redneck truckers," according to the gay news site the *Advocate*. Alternately, they are "hillbilly cowboys," by *Huffington Post's* account. Using still another term to describe the costuming, the music magazine *Spin* invoked the slur *white trash*.[5] In fact, it is impossible to untangle redneck, trucker, poor white, hillbilly, cowboy, and country music images in the video. And that is consistent with the way these images circulate in American culture, in a muddled blur of stereotypes that also at times includes fundamentalist Christian, racist, and homophobic elements as markers of provincial white working-class identity. My own label for the band's performance practice here borrows the name of Jed Clampett from *The Beverly Hillbillies*, combines it with the concept of blackface minstrelsy, and designates Foo Fighters' production as an instance of Jed-face (figure 2).

Scene 2 of the video takes place in the men's shower room of the truck stop. Leading into this is a transition from the diner scene that pivots on a sight gag. The group is sitting at the counter over plates of disgusting food, irritating the waitress and jiggling a bowl of urine-colored Jell-O, when one guy's shower reservation number is called. At this—and here is the gag—all four stand up and set out for the shower, in orderly single file and without a word. On their way in, they pass a self-service hot dog stand with a compartment labeled "Hot Buns." The camera lingers meaningfully, drawing out the question hereby implied: are these hillbilly truckers kinky or simply accustomed to shared bathwater?

In its dramatic change of look and sound, the shower room immediately suggests an answer. Several techniques conspire to create a cheesy porn

FIGURE 2.   Jed Clampett (Buddy Ebsen), *The Beverly Hillbillies.*

effect. Camera work consists mainly of close-ups and slow motion, speaking voices have vanished, and the music now originates from outside the scene of action (i.e., is extradiegetic). Stylistically, faux country has given way to quasi-disco. The song is "Body Language" by Queen, and the white-tiled shower room recalls the setting of that song's polymorphously steamy 1982 video.[6] Onscreen action here, by contrast, consists of "kinky" erotics played for laughs, with another splash of potty humor. Foo Fighters, drenched and naked, are still wearing their hillbilly drag, trucker caps, and cowboy boots (figure 3). It is a goofy, stagey "gay" enactment that works to reassure you that its enactors are anything but. This is a gay shower scene that might have been written by junior high school boys, and it seems telling that, on YouTube, the censored, underage audience video registered nearly double the viewings of the uncensored version that is off-limits to many younger viewers.[7]

A couple of weeks after the release of their video, Foo Fighters were scheduled to play Kansas City, and Fred Phelps and his Westboro Baptist Church from nearby Topeka announced plans to picket the concert venue. The congregation is infamous for picketing the funeral of Matthew Shepard, among other events, while carrying signs with messages like "God Hates Fags." In recent years they began picketing military funerals, wielding antigay and anti-U.S. slogans, including "Thank God for IEDs," referring to the improvised explosive devices that caused thousands of American military casualties in Iraq and Afghanistan. Critics see Phelps and the WBC as attention seekers

FIGURE 3.   Foo Fighters in Jed-face: "Keep It Clean (Hot Buns)" shower scene.

who are better ignored than counterprotested. Foo Fighters, however, saw the opportunity to get back into their hillbilly-trucker getup and play "Keep It Clean."[8] This was an excellent move for purposes of their own attention seeking—the reason for their video in the first place.

The day after Foo Fighters' performance on the streets of Kansas City, they posted a video of it, and the new video went viral. Widespread online media coverage from *Huffington Post* to the *Washington Post* and from *Spin* to the *Advocate* greatly expanded publicity for the band's tour. Surprisingly, it also depicted Foo Fighters as the newest champions of "tolerance" and as artists "unafraid to get political."[9] The *Advocate* observed that the WBC picketers "at first seemed unaware the band was making fun of them." But the *Advocate*, billed as the oldest continuous LGBT publication in the United States, seemed in turn unaware that the band was making fun of *them*. As I discussed above, the whole song, and the video, is an extended gay joke. So how could a gay magazine and dozens of other media sources miss this fact in depicting Foo Fighters as righteous heroes of gay solidarity?

One answer is Jed-face. A tired and by now dicey (in public) gay joke is given new life, and its homophobia refigured as political progressivism, thanks to a hillbilly/trucker/country music joke. Foo Fighters' Jed-face in this song and video taps the stereotype of the oversexed and perverse poor white/hillbilly that surfaces in *Tobacco Road*, *Deliverance*, and other cultural instances, which one scholar has dubbed the "priapic [i.e., always erect] hillbilly."[10] The band's hillbilly/country/trucker persona allowed them to act out homosexual and scatological fantasies with impunity in the comic guise of a depraved other. In the process, they even won praise in the liberal and gay media for their "tolerance" and political courage.

Some observers identified with the rural working class were less enthusiastic. YouTube comments underscore the offensiveness of Foo Fighters' Kansas City hillbilly-drag performance. A viewer who signs as truckdawg43 wrote, "The one thing I hate more then WBC is some assclowns coming in acting like they are rural and gonna tell us poor simple folk how to live. . . . They could have done it just the way they are without the drag on rural folk and shined their asses at em and then I would have given em a big hell yeah [sic]."[11] Here, to hate the Westboro Baptist Church is to hate being lumped together with them in Foo Fighters' broad-brush travesty that, as the commenter attests, destroys prospects for progressive political solidarity.

What cultural logic is at work in Foo Fighters' performances and their celebratory receptions? It is a logic that links "hillbilly" and "pervert," the result of which is caricatured here for laughs (in *Deliverance*, the same hillbilly pervert figure carries a menacing charge). At the same time, it is a logic in which "gay" and "country" figure as opposites—and so their collision also plays for laughs (on stage in Kansas City, Grohl underscored the gag, juxtaposing gay icon Lady Gaga with country trio Lady Antebellum to illustrate his assertion that "it takes all kinds"). It is a logic of Good Whites versus Bad Whites, in which Foo Fighters score points for the good, enlightened, metropolitan whites by comically impersonating and facing off with bad, benighted, backwater whites. And it is a logic of fighting hillbilly with hillbilly, in which WBC's fundamentalist hillbilly is bested by Foo Fighters' hypersexual hillbilly and in which mockery of poor and working-class people is simultaneously a mockery of gay people but can be read as a victory for tolerance, because it reaffirms that the real bigots and homophobes are redneck/hillbilly/country music lovers.[12]

THE USE OF COUNTRY MUSIC IN
QUEERS *V.* BOONE *V.* QUEERS

Another summoning of country music to signify homophobia surfaces in a mass communication from a national LGBT advocacy organization to its constituency. Occupying center stage in this story is the unlikely figure of Pat Boone. The singer ascended to fame at the dawn of the rock 'n' roll era with his wholesome act and vanilla renditions of R&B songs, including Little Richard Penniman's "Tutti Frutti" in 1955 and "Long Tall Sally," which Penniman cowrote the following year in the express hope that Boone would not sing it. In Boone's hands, hot songs were cooled and hip songs squared. Rhythms lost their syncopation, vocals dropped blue notes and inflection, clever double entendre lyrics were reworked into bland twaddle. But Boone, a white artist, often sold more records with his insipid crooner covers than the African American musicians who originated the songs, and his record sales during the late fifties were second only to Elvis Presley's.[13] Like Presley, he starred in Hollywood films (a dozen of them) and, later, television shows. In the seventies, Boone turned to southern gospel and was eventually inducted into the Gospel Music Hall of Fame (2003). In 1997, at the age of sixty-three, the outspoken conservative and born-again Pentecostal Christian even released an album of heavy metal covers performed in big band style, which he promoted with an appearance at the American Music Awards in leather fetish wear including a studded dog collar—all of which briefly put him back on the talk show circuit and the Billboard charts (albeit the far reaches) and got him temporarily fired from his Christian television gig. Clearly, there are lots of things you could call Pat Boone. "Country singer," however, is not one of them.[14]

Yet that is how he was identified by the Human Rights Campaign (HRC), a lobbying and advocacy group that describes itself as America's "largest national lesbian, gay, bisexual, and transgender civil rights organization."[15] "Country singer and right-wing pundit" served as the opening grab phrase of a December 2008 e-mail blast from HRC, an upmarket, establishment outfit by reputation, which, characteristically, solicited member donations by relaying news of a purportedly urgent threat to LGBT people and their rights. Here, the threat was inflammatory homophobic rhetoric from Boone, newly published on a right-wing blog.[16] In the wake of protests over California voters' passage of Proposition 8 banning same-sex marriage and, elsewhere, deadly terror attacks in Mumbai, Boone forged an outrageous equation between the peaceful protesters and the bloody terrorists. HRC, for its part, seized the opportunity for fund-raising. And in its effort to present Boone as the kind of figure LGBT rights supporters would want to oppose materially, the group called him a country singer.

Perhaps HRC knowingly took license, linking Boone to country music in hopes of pumping up donations, or perhaps the error was accidental. At the very least, HRC was guilty of unfounded assumptions and gross lack of fact checking. Even on the offending blog, Boone's blurb line clearly labeled him "a top-selling recording artist" during the "rock & roll era."[17] In any case, whether conscious or inadvertent, HRC's error is suggestive. If its misidentification was accidental, then the e-mail suggests that HRC assumed some special linkage between right-wing homophobia and country music, over against other musical styles; it suggests that the organization, in the absence of knowledge about Boone, presumed the sexually bigoted singer came from the country music world. Alternately, if HRC knowingly misidentified Boone, it might suggest that the group expected its membership to be more galvanized by an appeal against a right-wing country singer's homophobic rant than one by a right-wing rock 'n' roller.

Whether HRC assumed a false connection between homophobia and country music or knowingly imposed the connection, the instance points to a notion that underlies a variety of cultural representations: that LGBTQ people and culture are incommensurable with country music and its culture. Country music is conventionally associated with heterosexual white, provincial, working-class, southern, and midwestern identities and cultures, and with redneck personas.[18] LGBTQ identity is imagined especially in terms of gay men, who in turn are linked to metropolitan, bourgeois, coastal lifestyles. In the dominant middle-class perspective, rednecks and queers are thought to occupy opposite ends of various political, social, and cultural spectrums.[19] Further, as HRC's mass communiqué may suggest, country music has also become linked to homophobia. The "country music" entry at *glbtq*, an online encyclopedia of LGBTQ culture, notes queer objections to the music on the grounds that "country speaks to a straight, conservative, white society and that many fans of country music are homophobic and racist."[20] Country music and its constituents are coded in culture as not only conceptually opposite, but ideologically opposed to the queer.

THE STAKES OF REPRESENTATION

Why do representations like those of Foo Fighters and HRC matter? The reason is that such representations play a pivotal role in the making of social inequality. To investigate how this works, we must establish some cultural and historical context.

Since the early twentieth century, knowledge workers—the "intellectuals" in a broad sense of the word—have grown as a proportion of the American workforce. At the same time, the specialized, "objective" knowledge they possess has gained central importance in the culture—a shift that has accelerated since the 1990s with the rise of the Internet, the 24/7 news cycle, and a global explosion of media and communication technology.[21] By the end of the twentieth century, the United States was moving from an industrial economy to a knowledge economy. The prime commodity in the new economy is not agricultural or industrial goods but knowledge. One's socioeconomic status in a global landscape now depends on creating and controlling this commodity.[22]

In the years since World War II, America's knowledge class, the upper middle class, has grown from 2 to 3 percent of the population to a mass grouping expected to comprise about 33 percent of the population by 2020 and 40 percent by 2030.[23] Typified by professionals with a postgraduate education and managers with a bachelor's degree, the upper middle class is also labeled the professional-managerial class.[24] The white working class, meanwhile, which comprised the majority of the American population after World War II, has been shrinking in recent decades. Members of the working class have a high school education, maybe some college, and are employed in service jobs or manual labor.[25] The upper middle class, while growing, has also been consolidating—its members marrying partners with high levels of education like their own and living in affluent neighborhoods among people like themselves.

In fact, between 1970 and 2007 (thus even before the 2008 economic downturn), U.S. metropolitan areas showed a dramatic increase in residential income segregation at both ends of the income spectrum—though the affluent (including the upper middle class) are more segregated than the poor. The rise in residential income segregation paralleled the equally dramatic rise in income inequality in America, and it serves to exacerbate its effects: researchers note that income-segregated neighborhoods magnify social, economic, and physical advantages for high-income families and magnify disadvantages in the same realms for low-income families.[26] The cultural sociologist Michèle Lamont highlights another implication. She notes the increasing isolation of the upper middle class and hence the difficulty for the educated class "to see how distinctive their particular understandings of the world are."[27] Lamont worries, in other words, that having little acquaintance with people from different walks of life might allow the upper middle class to universalize its own worldview, falsely.[28]

Evidence suggests that there is indeed reason to worry about this. Undoubtedly we have cause to worry, too, about the particular implications of social isolation and distorted vision within this group. After all, as Barbara Ehrenreich notes, "ideas are simply part of the business" of the professional middle class (PMC), which includes the "journalists, academics, writers, and commentators" who "are paid to provide the 'spin,' the verbal wrap . . . that gives coherence to events or serves to justify [social and political] arrangements."[29] And how does the distinctive, perhaps even insular, perspective of middle-class news and entertainment media professionals affect white working-class people, the kind associated with country music? Judging by the annals of America's so-called culture wars, the answer is, very badly.

CULTURE WARS

For a generation we have been told that we live in a country polarized by culture wars—that Americans are bitterly divided by ideology, particularly in their stances on sexuality, morality, and religion. The term *culture wars* made a prominent appearance in 1991 as the title of a book by the sociologist and religious scholar James Davison Hunter, who mapped "new lines of cultural warfare" in terms of a polarizing "political and social hostility rooted in different systems of moral understanding," which he identified as "orthodox" versus "progressive."[30] Since then, countless politicians' and pundits' statements and media features have embroidered on the theme, and it has been advanced in several of the biggest political and pop sociological books of the period, including the 2000 best seller *Bobos in Paradise*, by the conservative pundit and current *New York Times* columnist David Brooks.[31] Culture wars chatter is still with us, though it may have peaked in the 2004 election year. That year we heard much about "latte liberals" and "NASCAR dads," red- or blue-state status was offered as the explanation for every tendency and taste imaginable, and some pivotal new culture wars volumes appeared.

Possibly the most famous and influential of these was left-leaning author and journalist Thomas Frank's *What's the Matter with Kansas?* (2004). Frank argued that the white working-class had been led over the previous twenty years into "backlash" voting against their own health, safety, and economic interests by a Republican Party that persuaded them to place "cultural issues" like minority rights, gun control, abortion, and gay marriage (all of which, by this account, they fervently oppose) ahead of their own economic interest and material well-being. Frank's argument still surfaces daily as an explanation for the supposedly irrational political and civic actions of America's white working class generally, who spoil things for themselves and the rest of us (his book was marketed internationally as *What's the Matter with America?*).

Three examples, arising within a few weeks of each other in late 2011, illustrate characteristic ways in which the *Kansas* thesis continues to surface in public discourse, years after the appearance of Frank's best-selling book. These examples come from the *New York Times*, long regarded as the national newspaper of record, and today the U.S. newspaper with the highest on-line readership. The *Times* is particularly useful for present purposes, because its website publishes readers' comments on certain columns and articles and tallies fellow readers' recommendations, yielding a readers' ranking of readers' comments. I selected the following examples by an admittedly unscientific method, flagging a trio of comments that seemed representative of recent summonings of the *Kansas* thesis as observed in my daily newspaper reading. It is striking that each of these *Kansas*-flavored comments climbed to near the top of the rankings in the hours and days following their initial publication. The examples suggest that *Times* readers are familiar with Frank's 2004 argument, are persuaded by it, and continue to apply it not only as an explanation for the problems of the U.S. white working class—who, by Frank's account, have been hoist with their own petard—but also as an explanation for the economic and social problems of the nation at large (I encountered similar comments on other online media boards, but they did not provide rankings and are omitted here).

The first example is a comment on an unsigned *Times* editorial titled "The New Resentment of the Poor," criticizing congressional Republicans' proposal to raise taxes on the poor and the working class at a time when the ranks of poor Americans were growing. The reader wrote:

> You have to wonder why these poor people in Kansas and others keep voting Republicans. They must think higher tax for themselves is a fair price for preventing gays from getting married or the evolution from being taught in the public schools. *[sic]*

Notably, the editorial inspiring this comment contained no mention of Kansas, gay marriage, or teaching evolution. It mentioned poor people, but sympathetically, as targets for unjust tax increases and not as voters, Republican or otherwise. The comment at first glance might therefore seem a non sequitur, and surely it would be incomprehensible to any reader unversed in what is clearly the backstory, Frank's *Kansas* thesis. But *Times* readers evidently grasped the comment's references, and they emphatically endorsed its message. It ranked in the top 3 percent of comments on this editorial, nineteenth out of 593. It is hard to miss the irony of such a result, which suggests a remarkable unanimity of resentment toward the lower classes among *Times* readers and the Republican legislators condemned by the editorial, which was very popular with those same readers.[32]

Three weeks later, the *New York Times* published an article titled "In Small Towns, Gossip Moves to the Web, and Turns Vicious." It was a report on small-town and rural social disruptions sparked by anonymous postings on Topix, a social media website that hosts local forums. One reader responded:

> The sad thing is that these are the people who vote Republican. . . .
> easily manipulated to vote against their own self-interest because they
> don't understand economics, don't read national or international news,
> and don't have educational opportunities. As the author said, "What IS
> the matter with Kansas?" Well . . . now we know. (Ellipses and emphasis
> in original.)

There is no mention of Kansas or of party politics in the *Times* article, which
examines the effects of anonymous online smears in communities where
anonymity is scarce (smears that could be coming from anywhere on the
Internet, as some commenters pointed out). Once again, the comment—and
its reference to "the author," meaning here not the *Times* reporter but
Frank—might seem to arise out of the blue. But clearly it did not seem that
way to *Times* readers. They ranked it in the top 1 percent of comments, third
out of 245.[33]

Less than three weeks after this instance, the *Times* op-ed columnist and
blogger and Princeton economist Paul Krugman published a piece titled
"Panic of the Plutocrats," discussing what he called the "hysteria" of economic elites and their apologists over the Occupy Wall Street protest
against economic injustice. A reader wrote:

> I can understand why the cosy CNBC crowd reacts with venom, but
> what I do not comprehend is how they manage to convince working
> class folks to join them in sustaining a rigged system that hurts
> ordinary working people. . . . . I guess there's always a chicken willing to
> vote for KFC. [sic] (Ellipses in original.)

The comment's opening picks up on a reference by Krugman to cable network CNBC's "talking heads" and their overreactions to the protest. This
tie-in serves to launch another mustering of false-consciousness charges
against the working class—which Krugman's column, displaying clear popular sympathies, in no way suggests (in fact, Krugman's *Times* column and
blog have often refuted the notions on which Frank's *Kansas* thesis rests).
The commenter here does not cite "moral voting" issues or Kansas but does
invoke as hard fact the image of a working class manipulated into opposing
its own material interests. Again *Times* readers piled on to recommend the
Kansas-style explanation of America's ills, placing this comment in the top
1 percent of its group, ninth out of 603.[34]

Though one would scarcely guess it from *New York Times* readers' comments, the *Kansas* thesis has been credibly debunked on multiple occasions,
starting as early as Morris P. Fiorina, Samuel J. Abrams, and Jeremy Pope's
Culture War? The Myth of a Polarized America (2004).[35] Fiorina, a Stanford
political scientist and Hoover Institution fellow, refuted the *Kansas* thesis

with polling data showing that the majority of American voters are actually moderate and tolerant, not ideological, and are concerned primarily with leadership and security, not moral values. Further refutation of Frank came from the Princeton political scientist Larry Bartels's 2006 review article, "What's the Matter with *What's the Matter with Kansas?*," and from Andrew Gelman's 2008 book, *Red State, Blue State, Rich State, Poor State: Why Americans Vote the Way They Do*. Bartels shows, among other things, that white working-class voters in 2004 were focused on economic more than cultural questions, no less than they were twenty years earlier (a 1984 study by Jerome Himmelstein and James McRae had already argued that "New Republicans" who switched parties to vote for Reagan in 1980 were not, in fact, disproportionately lower to middle class, socially conservative, more religious, or angrier at government).[36]

Gelman, a statistician and political scientist at Columbia University, pores over data showing that individual lower-income voters nowadays go for Democrats and individual rich voters for Republicans, just as they have for decades. For various reasons, rich versus poor voter patterning breaks down at the state level and indeed is already fuzzy at the county level—except in the places where national media outlets are located: metropolitan New York and Washington, DC; Los Angeles and San Francisco. In these areas, *upper*-income voters are unpredictable: so many of them vote Democratic that they create a new, reverse pattern whereby rich counties are more likely than poor counties to support Democrats. The phenomenon of rich counties displaying more liberal voting patterns is the essential basis for the stories told in *Bobos in Paradise, What's the Matter with Kansas?*, and other culture wars accounts by both liberal and conservative national journalists. Gelman shows, however, that this voting phenomenon is concentrated in the states where the journalists live.[37] Thus it seems that national commentators have mistaken their particular coastal, major metropolitan locales for the United States overall. Such foreshortened perspective is called *parochialism*—at least when the accusation falls on residents of small towns or so-called fly-over states. Not surprisingly, the media commentators' error has been resonant. After all, they are the people who interpret the nation and explain us to ourselves, with tremendous authority and influence.

Distortions like this one result from what cognitive scientists call *availability bias*, that is, generalizing on the basis of the nearest available information.[38] But the journalist and blogger Ezra Klein sees more going on here. He points out that this bias is also "quite convenient" from a career perspective. Rather than being punished for their neglect of fact checking, journalists, editors, and producers rise swiftly through the ranks for promoting the narratives already known and understood in the profession. Frank and other journalists have access to the same exit polls Gelman used and could have consulted them, but they reap career rewards for playing to a professional bias toward familiar, favored story lines.[39] Fiorina points to another, supremely powerful bias, the media appeal of controversy—here, spectacular headlines declaring "national polarity." Indeed, Frank's story of white working-class America going Republican offers what may be the most salable story form in the contemporary U.S. media marketplace: it turns conventional wisdom (poor voters support Democrats; rich voters, Republicans) on its ear.

We might further note that class bias facilitates each of the other biases and that the low power and status of the white working class relax the stakes of whether one's news stories about this group are watertight. This point may remind us that media consumers also play a role in determining which narratives come to the fore, by reading and viewing critically—or not. Significantly, the *New York Times* has published articles citing and sometimes written by Bartels, Fiorina, Gelman, and others who contest the *Kansas* thesis and related culture wars arguments. By all indications, reader response to these items has been muted. The arguments have not enjoyed an influence comparable to that of Frank's *Kansas* account, as gauged by rankings of articles most e-mailed and most blogged and by readers' comments.

Interestingly, the three data-driven rebuttals of Frank cited here share one finding in common. All three find that there is indeed a sector of American society that has since the 1980s become vehemently, ideologically intent on "cultural issues." It is not the white working class who have grown rigidly ideological but social and political "elites"—"better-educated white voters" and the political elites of both parties.[40] Why, then, would these middle- and upper-middle-class traits get pinned on the white working class? There can be no single simple answer to this question, but it hints at a related question, and at least a partial answer. When was the last time you saw or heard a working-class media commentator, editor, or producer?

In both entertainment and news media, representation of the white working class, when it is not scarce, is generally reductive, offering a simple, untextured, often stereotyped portrait. For example, media sources in 2004 reported on a constituency newly dubbed "NASCAR dads." Amid all the complexities and uncertainties of the election season, including various swing constituencies deemed unpredictable, audiences were assured that this group could be counted on to speak with one voice—indeed, they seemed to share a brain. Time and again we heard that George W. Bush had these white male NASCAR types securely in his pocket. And so when Bush made an appearance at the annual Daytona race, reams of mutually parroting coverage depicted a jubilant reception. Readers had to depart the beaten path of media chatter to find any perspective that contradicted or even complicated that story (figure 4). One account that did so was by a youthful African American journalism intern, Matt Thompson, who reported from the Daytona stands that NASCAR fans expressed a divergent range of views on the incumbent president. Thompson further reported, by dramatic contrast to the prevailing media chorus, that race fans heckled Bush's presidential motorcade and greeted it with a gesture sometimes referred to as the redneck salute. "One middle finger went up in the crowd, then another, and soon they were everywhere," Thompson wrote.[41]

The expanding ranks of media and academic commentators alike are members of the professional middle class, positioned to represent its interests and perspectives while also representing those of the upper class. In modern capitalism, managers and professionals serve as intermediaries between capital and labor. Their job is often to "conceptualize . . . what others must do" and, on behalf of the ruling-class owners, to command those who do the labor.[42] The professional-managerial class is thus situated antagonistically vis-à-vis the working class—a point registered clearly in many country songs. As outsiders to the working class, the professional-managerial class lacks knowledge of working-class worlds and lifeways, especially given that their own middle-class world dominates the culture at large, in which middle-class existence is "silently marked as normal and desirable."[43] Nevertheless, the professional middle class are the narrators of working-class life and reality, because they are the narrating class: the analysts and experts, the language, representation, and knowledge specialists for the whole society. Cultural representations of the working class therefore reflect the (purportedly neutral) viewpoint of the middle class—whose identity and privilege depend precisely on its distinction from the working class. In media, institutional, and professional contexts, members of the middle class speak of and for the working class, acting, officially and with authority, as interpreters of the class other. But why would middle-class commentators be charged with representing a group of which they are not members and on which they may have little perspective?

One reason is that middle-class professionals are sanctioned in their authority and expertise, and their observations and assessments bear the marks of legitimacy. Another is that class cultures are not acknowledged as such. As Fox observes, for Americans, class cultures are "not wholly other"

FIGURE 4.   October 2004: At a Bush campaign stop in Canton, Ohio, country fan Janice King stands for Kerry in an Alan Jackson T-shirt and a cross necklace. Polling data show that lower-income voters favor Democrats, but media representations assert the conservatism of the white working class. This wire service image offered a rare glimpse beyond the prevalent narrative and elicited bloggers' consternation ("Is she holding the wrong sign?") and snide derision (including references to her cigarette as a Marlboro, a brand associated with white working-class women: see chapter 3). AP photo/Laura Rauch.

and do not "exist in relative independence . . . in the same sense as 'other' cultures do."[44] The view described here contrasts with that of Bourdieu, who stresses that neighbors inhabiting different class realms may "be more remote than strangers." It contrasts, too, with the anthropologist and political theorist James C. Scott's vision of the classes as so segregated and mutually opaque as to warrant the term *class apartheid*.[45] Ironically, this very segregation and opacity allows middle-class people to presume that they understand the working class. After all, it takes a modicum of knowledge to recognize the extent of one's ignorance in any sphere. But there is a further notion at work here, an assumption of transparency in one's social inferiors. The British sociologist Stephanie Lawler points out (citing Gayatri Spivak) that working-class people, as the other, are assumed to be knowable by the middle class.[46] This situation may help to explain the resonance of a line made famous by Dwight Yoakam and Buck Owens in their Tejano-flavored duet, "Streets of Bakersfield" (#1 1988). The song opens with a pair of back-to-back verses, after which the instruments drop out for a full bar to frame the arrival of the chorus. Yoakam and Owens enter climactically in a cappella harmony, singing, "You don't know me, but you don't like me."

THE TROUBLE WITH COUNTRY

As a popular-media source of alternative, working-class perspectives, country music is a rarity. But country is frequently condemned as phony, disingenuous, and inauthentic by music critics and cultural commentators. The following pair of examples illustrate characteristic critiques from sources on both the right and the left of the political spectrum. The first example comes from an opinion column by the author and journalist Mark Judge for the high-profile conservative news website the *Daily Caller*:

> It's time to abolish country music. Just ban it outright. It has become a
> toxin in American culture, retarding the cerebellum of the body
> politic. . . . Modern country music is the phoniest music in the world. . . .
> What is most noticeable [in country] is the deep resentment.[47]

Judge pathologizes country music in terms of cultural toxicity and civic cerebral retardation. He levels a phoniness charge at country and rails against its "deep resentment"—which he depicts as real, not phony.

Comparable in many ways is this excerpt from a music column by the Los Angeles indie musician, underground music critic, and *Acid Logic* e-zine publisher Wil Forbis:

Like most decent Americans, I've never been a big fan of country music. It's always struck me as musically dull, lyrically trite, overly obsessed with its own themes and disingenuously traditional, as if writing songs about hopping trains in 2005 (or 1995 or 1985) is somehow relevant in some metaphorical way to the present human condition. Too many country artists . . . [reject] any appearance of modernity as if it were a mail pouch of poisoned chaw.[48]

This passage might be read as a personalized "Anything but country" declaration, inscribed with the author's particular country music pet peeves. But in fact Forbis's inventory of faults in country—"musically dull, lyrically trite, overly obsessed with its own themes and disingenuously traditional"—is quite typical of country critiques from nonfans. It overlaps with a litany launched by Judge at one point in his article, denouncing country's "adherence to formula, its resentment, its anger and its lack of innovation," though Judge alone cites anger and resentment among country's failings. Like Judge, Forbis accuses country music of phoniness, but he further specifies the target of his critique: it is the traditionalism of country lyrics that is "disingenuous." Forbis underscores this point with a hyperbolic flourish rendering "any appearance of modernity" as a "mail pouch of poisoned chaw" from country artists' perspective. But the real rhetorical kicker here is the opening clause, "Like most decent Americans," which invokes a view of country fandom as morally suspect. This is not an isolated view. The Arab American lesbian writer Joanna Kadi, a country music lover, observes that people who dislike country feel unusually entitled to share their negative feelings about the music, which are often coupled with anger or disbelief directed at country fans themselves. "Even when people don't like my choice of reggae, hard rock, or classical, they don't respond so viscerally and angrily," she writes.[49]

We have seen that listening to country can make you culturally, educationally, and socially suspect through its associations with the least educated members of society—here, the white working class. Now Forbis and Kadi raise another kind of suspicion that surrounds contemporary country fandom, a moral suspicion. The moral cloud hanging over country—in Forbis and in Judge's conjuring of toxicity and retardation (as his article later makes explicit)—is not simply a matter of identity politics, of country's guilt by association with the least educated listeners. For, as Forbis's critical language shows, the *aesthetic* dimension of country is very much in play in his moral assessment of the music. This points to the crucial role of culture, aesthetics, and taste in producing social distinctions—a subject that has been greatly illuminated by Bourdieu.[50]

Building on Bourdieu's work in *Distinction,* Lawler draws a clear link between the cultural construction of taste and that of moral value and highlights both constructs' production of social classes. Taste works in tandem with its other, disgust, as "part of a long-standing middle-class project to distinguish [middle-class individuals] as different" from the working-class masses. Lawler notes that the working class are frequently represented "as disgusting rather than merely 'common'" and sees this as indicating "the degree to which they must be 'pushed away'—expelled from a normative and normalized middle-classness." She explains, "Once an aesthetic is established as 'tasteful' those . . . endowed with this appreciation are able to legitimately claim a place as 'properly human,' while those . . . unable to appreciate what they *ought* to appreciate are rendered disgusting . . . [and] can be robbed of any moral worth." In this connection, we might recall Bourdieu's observation that "aesthetic intolerance can be terribly violent." And we might note Lawler's emphasis on the importance of challenging "an unmarked and unproblematized middle classness which claims a monopoly on 'true humanity.'"[51]

Forbis's "Anything but country"–like critique presents a kind of corollary to Lawler's formulation. Here, those who appreciate what they ought *not* appreciate, country music, are rendered disgusting, outside the realm of "decent Americans." A taste for country music is the failure of taste that flags a lack of moral value—indeed, a lack of humanity, along the lines just sketched. Lawler's explication bolsters the sociologist and minister-theologian Tex Sample's claim, in his book on country music, the church, and working people, that "elitist taste legitimates inequality."[52] We might further deduce from all this that a taste for country music serves as not only a symptom of low social status, but a cause of it.

Of course, tastes and their meanings are constantly shifting, as are the objects of middle-class disgust. Cultural changes since the 1970s have largely leveled the old hierarchy of high and low culture, and middle-class musical tastes are now broadly inclusive. Certain sounds once marked as exclusively country have been taken up in other styles. Timbres of banjo, mandolin, and, occasionally, fiddle circulate more widely, for example, through Americana roots music. Still, years on from the granting of connoisseurial status to formerly debased styles like jazz and rock, country music remains a taste apart. Indeed, over four decades of shifting style and taste, cultural meanings of the music once known as "hillbilly" have been remade in such a way as to perpetuate, if not redouble, its status as an object of disgust.

Fox locates the cause of country's contemporary cultural "badness" in racial ideology:

For many cosmopolitan Americans, especially, country is "bad" music precisely because it is widely understood to signify an explicit claim to *whiteness*, not as an unmarked, neutral condition of lacking (or trying to shed) race, but as a marked, foregrounded claim of cultural identity—a bad whiteness. As "white" music, unredeemed by ethnicity, folkloric authenticity, progressive politics, or the *noblesse oblige* of elite music culture, country frequently stands for the cultural badness of its adherents. Country is, in this sense, "contaminated" culture, . . . mere proximity to which entails ideological danger. (One example: while I have never seen a personal advertisement in a newspaper that lists a preference for any other musical genre among the disqualifications for potential romantic partners, the stipulation "no country music fans" is quite common in such ads.)[53]

I find Fox's analysis incisive and concur with his reading of country as marked by pronounced, hence tainted, whiteness. I would note, however, that our culture's ascription of badness to country music and its adherents invokes a broad-spectrum bigotry, encompassing not only racial bigotry, but other forms—including gender and, increasingly, sexual bigotry. The examples in this chapter illustrate that the moral suspicion attaching to country music is the moral suspicion attaching to the white working class as (purported) ground zero for America's most virulent social ills: racism, sexism, and homophobia. In Foo Fighters' video and its reception, in Frank's *Kansas* thesis and its uses, in Forbis's music criticism, and elsewhere, we encounter images of the white working class as America's bigot class. Such representations have become commonplace in the dominant culture. For obvious reasons, this is a problem for white working-class people. For less obvious reasons, it is a problem for everybody.

EVERYBODY'S PROBLEM

In 2011, DreamWorks Studios released *The Help* as a major motion picture, following on the success of Kathryn Stockett's 2009 best-selling novel of the same name. Set in the 1960s, *The Help* is a story about African American domestics in the service of genteel white families in the segregated Deep South. Shortly after the movie's release, the *New York Times* published a related opinion piece by Patricia Turner, a professor of African American studies in California. Turner reports a diversity of opinions in her professional and social circles concerning the film's depictions of southern blacks and whether its white author is capable of telling the black maids' story from their perspective, as she purports to do.

But Turner's main point concerns an aspect of the story that she finds problematic and even dangerous: its message that certain white housewives "are bad people, therefore they are racists." She notes, "To suggest that bad people were racist implies that good people were not." In fact, she argues, "Jim Crow segregation survived long into the 20th century because it was kept alive by white Southerners with value systems and personalities we would applaud." Turner elaborates with an example of another novel-turned-movie about the Jim Crow South, the most celebrated of the entire genre. "The fallacy of 'To Kill a Mockingbird,'" she writes, is "a troubling falsehood: the notion that well-educated Christian whites were somehow victimized by white trash and forced to live within a social system that exploited and denigrated its black citizens, and that the privileged white upper class was somehow held hostage to these struggling individuals." She concludes, "My parents, and the countless other black Americans [who endured the Jim Crow era], . . . would not have wanted us to whitewash that earlier world."[54]

The interpretation of southern politics and race relations given by Harper Lee in *To Kill a Mockingbird* has been widely disseminated for more than half a century, thanks to the extraordinary popularity of both the novel and movie versions of this American classic. But it was not invented there. The historian Joel Williamson finds U.S. southern white elites placing the blame for racial violence on poor whites as early as the turn of the twentieth century. He labels this persistent narrative the Grits Thesis.[55]

Turner's op-ed piece, titled "Dangerous White Stereotypes," identifies class-based stereotypes in the popular 2011 movie *The Help* and the 1962 classic *To Kill a Mockingbird* and locates danger in their whitewashing of the nature and origins of segregation and white racism. The stereotypes pertain to poor and working-class whites, people who come under the identity labels "redneck," "hillbilly," and "white trash" (among others). These identities and their functions are the focus of many years' study by the anthropologist John Hartigan. Like Turner, Hartigan sees the scapegoating of poor and working-class whites in standard accounts of U.S. racism as historically distorted and socially regressive and as instrumental in perpetuating racism. Writing on "rednecks," "hillbillies," and "white trash," he concludes:

> This imagery [performs a] critical function in the maintenance of whiteness, for these are the figures whites use to delimit an attention to the subject of racism. . . . After all, poor whites are not the bank officers who deny mortgages and other loans to African-Americans . . . at rates two to three times that of their white counterparts; poor whites are not among the landlords who refuse housing to [people of color], nor are they the human resources managers who are racially influenced in their

hiring and firing decisions. . . . To deconstruct whiteness [we must recognize] the important work these stereotypes perform in maintaining a prevailing image of whiteness as racially unmarked and removed from the blot of racism.[56]

Turner's and Hartigan's analyses highlight the role of stereotyped images of poor and working-class whites in producing and maintaining racial inequality in America. The stereotypes are shifting, to be sure, but not necessarily in a helpful direction. Lawler writes, for example, that, in "a racializing move which, one might say, 'hyper-whitens' them, there is, increasingly, an implicit coding of 'the working class' *as* white. Of course, working-class people are not exclusively white, but their emblematic whiteness might be necessary to a continued disparagement."[57] Lawler frames her comments in a British context, but they are also apt to the contemporary United States. The American working class has long been coded, however accurately, in terms of a whiteness that in recent years has become less a default status and more a marked condition. Whereas unmarked whiteness still wields tremendous power as privilege, marked whiteness is a growing burden, carrying racist and imperialist stigma. Disparagement of the working class is not new, but its coding as hyperwhite is a relatively recent development, and so is the central role of imputed whiteness in the group's "continued disparagement."

As both Turner and Hartigan demonstrate, class and race are mutually entangled in American social and cultural life, so pursuing one often entails confronting the other. Racial difference surfaces frequently in this book's analysis, not as a primary category of inquiry, but as a crucial element in the workings of class and of gender and sexuality in country music contexts. Racial sameness surfaces, too, undergirding many of the instances under analysis. These intraracial instances always involve conflict across class and status boundaries, unfolding at times exclusively within the category of whiteness, as defined under contemporary U.S. racial regimes.

Foo Fighters' "Keep It Clean (Hot Buns)" video serves up familiar images of poor and working-class whites as hillbilly-redneck country music lovers, conveying these visually through characterization and props and sonically through country music. The band's faux-country performance of "Keep It Clean" at a Westboro Baptist Church protest and its extensive media coverage in terms of a bold progressive gesture posit a scenario in which enlightened Good Whites isolate and fight homophobia *at its source* by mocking uneducated, provincial, country music–loving Bad Whites. This instance fits Hartigan's description of the "complex and emotionally charged contests over belonging and difference that engage whites intraracially."[58] In Hartigan's analysis as in Turner's, charged intraracial contests result in a distorting and dangerous story of the causes of U.S. racism, taking the spotlight off of upper- and middle-class white people and institutions and focusing it glaringly on poor and working-class whites.[59]

Charged intraracial contests play out similarly in "Keep It Clean (Hot Buns)" and its media treatment. Band members "Jed up" in stereotypical imitation of poor and working-class whites, and commentators frame the spectacle as a victory over the people thus caricatured, indicatively the backward, intolerant, guilty party in America's homophobia problem. This, too, is distorting and dangerous, for some of the same reasons identified by Turner and Hartigan. At the least, it reinforces a notion that homo- and transphobia are confined to certain groups of bad people rather than systemic throughout the culture, and it locates the problem in a low-status and relatively powerless segment of society while ignoring the institutions— including the law, medicine, education, and the media itself—possessing the greatest power to produce and maintain, or to eliminate, gender and sexual bigotry and its effects.

At a more fundamental level, Foo Fighters' performance and its reception show country *music* functioning as proxy for the *people* of the white working class, figured as ignorant and bigoted. This jibes with Bryson's data indicating that high-status cultural omnivores—modern middle-class subjects with broad, multicultural tastes—exclude country as a cultural form associated with certain people—specifically, audiences with the least education. Bryson theorizes that cultural omnivorism has limits, which serve purposes of social exclusion. Her study is important in suggesting that shared distaste may be as culturally significant as shared taste, the usual object of inquiry in studies by Bourdieu and many other researchers.

Bryson also underscores the interrelations of race and class in this realm. She emphasizes, *"cultural tolerance should not be conceptualized as an indiscriminate tendency to be nonexclusive, but as a reordering of group boundaries that trades race for class."* Bryson notes that "the correlation between race and class [i.e., the tying of class privilege to skin privilege] is an important feature of modern industrialized societies" and remarks that "the relationship creates substantial room for ideological confusion" (e.g., in widespread cultural notions presuming that whites automatically occupy higher class positions and people of color, lower class positions). In this sociocultural context, Bryson posits, "educated respondents resist racial integration only when it means class integration."[60] This principle finds illustration in her privileged research subjects' tendency to expand their tastes into diverse racialized styles like Latin music, jazz, and blues, thus enlarging their multicultural capital while drawing the line at styles associ-ated with the least educated—that is, lower-class—fans of whatever race or ethnicity, including gospel, rap, heavy metal, and country. The same pat-terning of symbolic exclusion is echoed in material acts recently docu-mented by Diane Reay. The British sociologist studied white middle-class parents in London who, out of a principled commitment to diversity (and against the grain of their class), chose to send their children to disadvan-taged urban schools. Reay found that these parents showed positive emo-tional responses to the "ethnic minority other" but more "wariness" toward the "class other."[61]

HRC traces familiar musicosocial boundaries in its Pat Boone–themed fund-raising letter, which also mines both the queer/country opposition that is a source of humor in "Keep It Clean (Hot Buns)" and the country-homophobia linkage that grounds Foo Fighters' lionization in the media as champions of gay tolerance. HRC's mass e-mail banks on its identification of former teen idol Boone as an outrageous and vocal homophobe while misidentifying him as a country artist. The missive skillfully crescendos in its account of Boone as an incendiary liar and fearmonger and a "mouth-piece of bigotry." Although these provocative descriptions appear to be apt and accurate with reference to Boone, HRC nevertheless uses them to launch its own fictions and fearmongering. The opening words of its e-mail, *country singer,* forge a link to Boone and hence to his queer hating that is, however tactically valuable for the group's fund-raising purposes, com-pletely false. In crafting its appeal to constituents, HRC deploys a narrative that is known and accepted among well-educated middle- and upper-middle-class Americans. Indeed, to judge by *New York Times* readers, it may be an article of faith. It is a narrative that locates sexual (and other) bigotry in the realm of country music, which is understood as a realm of white working-class people.

Everyday representations of this group in advertising and entertainment media gain support and legitimation from intellectual media like *What's the Matter with Kansas?* and the civic dialogues that engage such produc-tions, online and elsewhere. Frank's influential and best-selling argument holds that members of the American white working class are so bent on ideology—opposition to gays, abortion, minorities, gun control—that they act, irrationally, against their own material interests. More education, *New York Times* readers frequently attest, would surely improve the situation. Yet *Times* readers themselves are demonstrably well educated and still dis-play remarkable ideological attachments through their unshakable faith in the *Kansas* thesis, notwithstanding several well-researched, cogent studies refuting its most fundamental claims—including the notions that lower-income voters have turned Republican, that white working-class voters are focused on cultural over economic issues, and that the white working class (rather than cultural elites) have become rigidly ideological.[62] Indeed, such a fervent embrace of Frank's story may suggest that his real accomplishment in *Kansas* was less about formulating a new explanation of recent GOP gains than about articulating, with colorful characters, engaging narratives, and a compelling case-study framework, an explanation that many readers were already inclined to accept.

What would incline Frank's readers, many of whom evidently are also *Times* readers, to believe, and to believe in, his *Kansas* thesis, a story of "how conservatives won the heart of America" (to quote the book's subtitle), evoking the nation's heartland and its common folk? Perhaps the prime factor in receptivity to the *Kansas* thesis would be nonmembership in the white working class. After all, Frank's argument seems unlikely to find devotees among the people he dissects and explains via the damning notion of false consciousness. A factor that could well predispose one to the *Kansas* thesis is membership in a class adjacent to the one under scrutiny, since anxious policing of a class boundary is inspired by proximity to it (hence Ehrenreich's title *Fear of Falling*).[63] The middle class is positioned adjacently and, indeed, antagonistically to the working class. So could it be that *Kansas*-thesis adherents from the American middle class—a group defined above all in terms of distinguished individualism and conscious, deliberate agency—are simply acting their scripted part, are realizing, in their reproof of the working class, the inevitable implications of a hierarchic and competitive class structure?

ANYTHING BUT WORKING CLASS (CONCLUSION)

Mutual aversion between the middle class and the working class is a structural given, the most predictable result of a socioeconomic system that positions groups unequally in relation to economic power, social prestige, and vocational and cultural authority. Nevertheless, to characterize middle-class champions of the *Kansas* thesis as simply realizing the implications of the class structure would be misleading. Rather, their actions are among those that *produce* the class structure, the system of socially and economically ordered groups recognized as such from within and without. The class structure is dynamically created and re-created on a continuous basis, in forms that have shifted and continue to shift over time. As discussed in this chapter, for example, the upper middle class has become a larger, more influential, and more insular segment of U.S. society in recent decades, whereas the white working class has become smaller, and the shift to a knowledge economy affects the two groups very differently.

The cultural instances examined here also provide a glimpse into a tendency, increasing since about 1970, toward representation of the white working class in reductive terms foregrounding social conservatism and bigotry.[64] The rise in such representations has been concurrent with the rise of neoliberal subjectivity—which emphasizes privatized, individual agency and commodified identities—and with the rise of (what Bryson dubs) "multicultural capital" and of the stigmatization of bigotry. Thus over four decades that have witnessed tremendous growth in the importance of presenting a cosmopolitan and tolerant self, we have increasingly seen the attribution of present-day and historical racism, sexism, and homophobia moving from privileged whites to less powerful social groups. These include the poor and working-class whites who are associated with, conjured by, and often mocked through images of country music. In our present moment, language and perspectives on race, gender, and sexuality powerfully mark class and status positions and figure in the production of social hierarchies. Representing a group as bigoted carries high stakes.

Relatedly, this chapter has questioned the capacity of professional middle-class commentators to act as informed and unbiased narrators vis-à-vis the white working class. Gelman's research uncovers an evident parochialism underlying coastal metropolitan media professionals' dominant narrative of the 2004 presidential election year—which painted an ideologically entrenched, values-voting white working class eager to cut off its nose to spite its gun-loving, gay-, minority-, and abortion-hating face. Though its accuracy has been credibly questioned on virtually all counts, the *Kansas*-style culture wars narrative maintains a powerful hold on the dominant cultural imagination—as *New York Times* readers (among others) demonstrate daily. The "middle-class stereotype" of a bigoted working class, described by Ehrenreich in 1989 as "too durable to be affected by the facts," has found renewed durability in Frank's twenty-first-century retread.[65]

If there is cause for optimism in this scenario, it may lie in the research findings of Fiorina, Bartels, Gelman, and others showing that so-called latte liberals and their lower-income compatriots share political interests to a far greater extent than prevailing wisdom would suggest. Gelman's identification of cross-class, Democratic voting among many upper-income residents of major metropolitan areas suggests possibilities for political alliance between the well-connected, influential upper middle class and the working-class whites indicted by the *Kansas* thesis. Fostering such alliances calls for more contact between increasingly segregated sectors of American society. It calls for higher standards of media production and consumption, including better-quality messages and more critical reception of sensational, skewed, and formulaic messages in news, entertainment, and new media. And, most important, it calls for political will.

Finally, then, is the declaration "Anything but country" really about the music? This chapter has examined it as a boundary marker loaded with meanings that exceed the musical, an expression of social, aesthetic, and other differences, and distances, between class cultures. Thus "Anything but country" is not only and not simply about the music. But neither is this charged exclusionary gesture or its considerable cultural baggage removed from the music. Country music is a flashpoint. Within and around it, class tensions that are elsewhere quiet hum, crackle, and emerge audible. Country songs take part in cultural dialogues that both produce and push against class and status, gender and sexuality, race and ethnicity, and other formations. The songs do their cultural work by means of sounds wedded to lyrics and images, which both reflect and produce various cultural notions. Country music is thus for some hearers the sound of working people, small-town America, and an idealized simpler time, while for others it is the sound of closed-mindedness, racism, sexism, and homophobia.

The examples above demonstrating disidentification with country music attest that country, an object of delight and devotion for some listeners, is an object of alienation and revulsion for others. To regard this as merely a matter of taste and thus ultimately mysterious relegates the question to individual and purely aesthetic realms. But the phrase "Anything but country" resonates in realms of the social and political—and aesthetics, of course, are rarely pure. Country as a social symbol and cultural brand is harmonious with certain—namely, working-class—subject positions and is therefore dissonant with other—namely, middle-class—subject positions.

Indeed, the middle class is defined by distinction from all that is working class. As Lawler puts it, "Working class-ness forms the constitutive outside to middle-class existence." Representations of the working class in the dominant culture—several of which this chapter has examined in both country music and political media contexts—work as a foil to "produce *middle-classed* identities that rely on *not* being the repellent and disgusting 'other.'"[66] Country music's potency as a creator of classed taste and identity is evident in the derision and anxiety it arouses in the dominant culture. And it is evident in middle-class cultural omnivores' exclusion of country and other styles associated with the least educated listeners—education being one of the standard markers, along with income and occupation, of class status (and considered by many researchers the most reliable). Of course, people like the Bushes, patricians far removed from middle-class/working-class border skirmishes, can afford all manner of cultural and faux-populist indulgence—though it may not protect them from middle-finger-flipping stock car racing fans. Bourdieu observes that "social identity lies in difference, and difference is asserted against what is closest, which represents the greatest threat."[67] This principle is key in explaining the ferocity of boundary-making activity between the working and middle classes.

Even apart from country's brand aura, its audible musical effect—of delight or disgust or something in between—depends on a perceiver's social position. Such is the nature of taste, which, although regarded as conferring individuality, is collective and class-based.[68] Indeed, country music's message, relevance, and value vary dramatically when perceived through the lenses of middle-class and working-class culture and subjectivity, respectively. The middle-class ear, so to speak, is ill attuned to country music and is often as deaf to its virtues as to its genuine flaws. To hear country on its own terms, we must seek out the particular values and devalued culture of the working class. Only then can we assess country music's qualities and messages, including its messages concerning gender and sexuality.

2. Sounding the Working-Class Subject

> Working-class culture is not point zero of culture; rather, it has a
> different value system, one not recognized by the dominant
> symbolic economy.
>
> BEVERLEY SKEGGS, *Class, Self, Culture*

> There is something about the freedoms of working class culture that is
> the opposite of the melancholy and [life traps often associated with it].
>
> PAUL WILLIS, in HENK KLEIJER and GER TILLEKENS,
> "Twenty-Five Years of *Learning to Labour*"

Chapter 1 examined the declaration "Anything but country" and other instances of country music exclusion as acts that help to produce the American middle class, a process of distinguishing oneself from the working class, which since the 1970s has been increasingly figured in terms of conservatism, whiteness, and bigotry. The present chapter takes a 180-degree turn, to examine engagement with country music as an act that helps to produce the working class, the white working class in particular. The epigraphs above suggest two principles guiding this inquiry: that working-class culture is a culture in its own right, embodying a value system distinct from that of the dominant middle-class culture; and that there are particular qualities that animate working-class culture.

The present investigation of country's working-class productions moves among three sites of inquiry: country music, working-class culture, and working-class subjectivity—a notion encompassing both the interior "self" and the "person" as recognized in the outside world.[1] Empirical research on contemporary American social life identifies different forms of subjectivity connecting to different class locations. One representative study finds that middle-class subjects seek to express their (purportedly) unique inner qualities and thereby change the world, while working-class subjects strive to withstand the world's pressures without *themselves* changing to compromise their integrity.[2] These characterizations concur with the wide range of resources engaged in the following pages: popular country songs, country music criticism, and an array of scholarship on topics including class worlds and aesthetics, working-class representation in the media, U.S. working-class and middle-class history, the history and segregation of American popular music, classed language and rhetoric, classed child-rearing practices, and theology and humanism in country music. Engaging these discourses and others, this chapter composes a portrait of working-class subjectivity and culture that attempts to flesh out both of these with some detail and texture (not to say exhaustively). The chapter thus points to the need to include working-class perspectives in American cultural discourses and traces some routes along which such inclusion might proceed.

COUNTRY AUTHENTICITY AND THE WORKING CLASS

Two commentaries quoted in the previous chapter register a criticism of country music that arises frequently outside fan circles—that country lacks authenticity. The conservative commentator Mark Judge calls contemporary country "the phoniest music in the world," and the indie rocker and critic Wil Forbis charges that country is "disingenuously traditional." Forbis scoffs at the notion that "writing songs about hopping trains in 2005 . . . is somehow relevant in some metaphorical way to the present human condition."[3] And here, despite the phrase "in some metaphorical way," Forbis seems intent on literalism. How else to explain the imaginative failure of a critic who is also a singer-songwriter but can find no contemporary "relevance" in train hopping—say, as a figure for a romantic American ideal of freedom? Perhaps Forbis would also question the relevance of roping and riding as subjects in the most-played country song of the 1990s, Toby Keith's "Should've Been a Cowboy" (#1 1993), whose narrator pictures himself among the cowboys of classic Hollywood westerns and legendary figures of the Wild West.[4]

Country is not the only music that trades on images of an American past. The hip roots music known as alternative country or Americana (among other labels) depends on such images. Underscoring this point, Berman describes alt-country as "a fetishization of Depression-era country life," and *Rolling Stone*'s "100 Best Albums of the 2000s" admiringly sums up an album by the alt-country artist Gillian Welch as "what rock & roll would have sounded like had it been invented in the 1930s Dust Bowl." Indeed, alt-country's inaugural opus is the 1990 Uncle Tupelo album, *No Depression*, whose title track is a cover of the Carter Family's "No Depression in Heaven" from 1936.[5] Berman continues, "If authenticity is the issue, then there's something more authentic to me about Wal-Mart country, which speaks to the real needs or lives of the people who listen [to it,] more than talking about grain whiskey stills."[6]

Here, again, the subject of country's authenticity rears its head. Authenticity in country music has inspired a literature of its own and will not receive substantive treatment in this book.[7] But the fact that the question is so often raised—by Judge, Forbis, Berman, and others—demands attention. Commonplace charges of country inauthenticity often treat the music as some sort of direct, unmediated, and literal representation of life. They deny the possibility that country music might involve the kinds of conventions characteristic of other artistic forms and genres. The classical pastoral, for example, can engage urban artists and listeners without raising questions about authenticity. These literalizing views of country, coming from the vantage points of dominant middle-class culture, belie the usual association of naive and literalistic approaches to cultural representation with rural, lower-class, and racialized audiences. The media historian Lisa Gitelman notes that "in the fictions of Dickens and Twain it is the uncultured bumpkin who takes theatrical production literally, and many 'true' anecdotes circulated during the nineteenth century" of audience members answering back to characters on stage or voices from the gramophone. Such anecdotes "present and assert culture as an exclusive activity for those who have it and 'get it,'" and the cultural associations they illustrate persist into the twenty-first century.[8] But it is middle-class critics—connoisseurs and expert commentators—who have been led into naive, unsophisticated readings of country music and its culture by their *projection* of literalism onto country music and its audiences.

Literal-minded perspectives on country music are at the heart of the literary and cultural critic Barbara Ching's critique in *Wrong's What I Do Best*. The book focuses on postwar hard country—music by Hank Williams Sr. and Jr., George Jones, Merle Haggard, and David Allan Coe and other Outlaw Country artists, among others—which Ching analyzes as a "burlesque abjection" of culturally low, ineffectual white masculinity. Enlisting Peter Stearns's "American Cool" concept, she argues that hard country deliberately produces an uncool—economically and emotionally uncontrolled—abject masculinity and frames it with irony that goes mostly unrecognized in the cultural mainstream. Ching contends that critics fail to hear the self-consciousness in hard country's pathos and emotionalism and that in missing this pivotal element of the style they misread hard country.

Ching also registers the important point that the rural in this music is not a merely literal matter of geography. Rather, rusticity—being "country"—is counterposed to urbanity in hard country songs, and the two serve as proxies for low and high social-class positions, respectively.[9] These symbolic meanings attach to the urban/rustic binary in all kinds of country music and in working-class speech—and yet, discovery of urban affiliations on the part of a country artist (or fan) is often taken as damning evidence of country's phoniness. Singers' diction comes under similar scrutiny. Some, though not all, country singers perform with southern accents, which may draw criticism for either their perceived realness or their perceived fakeness (in a striking example, Robert Christgau, the self-proclaimed "Dean of Rock Critics," wrote in a *Village Voice* review of Louisianan Tim McGraw's 1994 breakout album that McGraw "draws his phony drawl so tight he sounds like a singing penis").[10] The notion that country-musical diction might follow performance conventions is unheard of—though audiences unquestioningly accept the use of American, often African American, diction by white British rockers from the Rolling Stones to Coldplay and working-class British diction by American punk rockers (of whatever class background) from the Ramones to Green Day.

Country artists are also judged disingenuous for treating working-class themes after having achieved fame and fortune in the music industry. The judgment bespeaks, among other things, a fundamental lack of understanding of class and its workings. For, as Bourdieu's habitus concept recognizes (and experience has long shown), an individual's class upbringing profoundly imprints body and psyche in ways that are not simply erased by a later change in circumstances.[11] Indeed, it may be the truth of this fact and its profound, life-shaping significance—rather than the naïveté of country fans, or their susceptibility to marketing hype—that explains country's persistent appetite for declarations like one that featured in a recent review of a Loretta Lynn concert. "Even in sequins and chiffon," it attested, "the pride of Butcher Holler, Ky., will always be the coal miner's daughter next door" (figure 5).[12] One interpretation of this statement renders it equivalent to the phrase, heard frequently in country music culture, "She never forgot where she came from." It expresses admiration for an individual whose life has surpassed its humble beginnings but who maintains love and respect for humble people, places, and ways of life, and so retains the values instilled by such beginnings.

Besides the conceptual flaws in tropes constructing country as phony and disingenuous, we should note that other styles of music are not held to the same reductive and literalistic standard: it does not apply to alt-country, for example, and certainly not to rock. Rap is indeed subject to comparable scrutiny of its authenticity and to expectations of hardscrabble bona fides among its artists. So why would country and rap be subject to a more literal, essentializing standard of performance (and sometimes, audience) authenticity than rock and its offshoots like alt-country?

Bryson's and others' research affirms rock's cultural status as the standard of middle-class musical taste.[13] Rock represents a music for all purposes,

FIGURE 5. "Even in sequins and chiffon": Loretta Lynn, ca. 2004. Courtesy of Country Music Hall of Fame® and Museum.

and the range of its styles and affects—like the range of subjectivities associated with it—is understood as broad and open-ended. By contrast, country, like rap, is marked by race and class and associated with particular, rather than neutral or universal, subjectivities (though country's suburbanization since the 1980s and rap's mainstreaming since the late 1990s complicate the picture). That is, both country and rap are marked as class others by association with poor and working-class constituencies. Rap is further marked as an African American art form and hence racially other, while country is *marked by* whiteness: it appears white not as a "neutral condition of lacking (or trying to shed) race, but as a marked, foregrounded claim of cultural identity."[14] Indeed, country's glaring racialization is a foregone conclusion in a recent scholarly article titled "Why Does Country

Music Sound White?"[15] Thus we can trace the constraints on country and rap authenticity to the *social identities* of each music's perceived core constituency. These authenticity constraints reflect the tendency toward reductive, literalizing portrayals of the cultural other and the fixity—the narrow typecasting—that is imposed on lower-status social identities in the dominant culture.[16]

RESENTMENT AND ITS DISCONTENTS

If country is plagued by restrictive notions of authenticity, perhaps it is its own fault. After all, the music continually flags its difference, its specificity in countryness. This is, in fact, Judge's chief complaint. Song after song touts the country values and virtues of its narrator or some community with which he or she claims affiliation, whether a town, region (the South, the heartland), the country crowd, or the U.S.A. In addition to, and sometimes in tandem with, its affirmations of country pride, the music expresses anger and resentment. Judge is surely right in hearing angry and resentful affect in country—although he is wrong in characterizing this as a recent development. And he is absurd (not to say unprecedented) in his further, completely unsubstantiated claims that contemporary country music "valorizes ignorance, crude behavior, poor hygiene and illiteracy" and, more specifically, that a 2011 CD by Justin Moore "bitterly criticize[s] people who live in clean houses, have manners, and are articulate."[17]

The anger, resentment, and self-referential country pride that Judge rails against in recent country music have been mainstays for decades. Indeed, Judge's country idols Merle Haggard, Johnny Cash, Loretta Lynn, and George Jones helped make these themes what they are today. Haggard is baldly cantankerous in "Fightin' Side of Me" (#1 1970) and his resentment unabashed when he sings of Mama's "Hungry Eyes" (#1 1969), recalling his hardworking Okie parents' fruitless attempts to achieve a better life and to be regarded with dignity by "another class of people." Cash's "San Quentin" (1969) was a vehicle for angry catharsis among inmates at the same California prison where a young Haggard first heard the singer perform and was inspired to follow him into a country music career. In "Oney" (#2 1972), Cash gives voice to long-smoldering resentment and fantasies of retribution through the character of a laborer on the eve of retirement from twenty-nine years of toil under the thumb of an autocratic, overbearing foreman. These songs and others, including Lynn's "Coal Miner's Daughter" (#1 1970) and "You're Lookin' at Country" (#5 1971) and Jones's "(I Was Country) When Country Wasn't Cool" (with Barbara Mandrell, #1 1981), influenced subsequent expressions of class resentment and working-class "country" pride.

Next-generation examples include Garth Brooks's "Friends in Low Places" (#1 1990). A country classic and one of Brooks's signature songs, "Friends in Low Places" combines an irresistible, highly inflected country vocal with a good-time, hierarchy-flipping vignette in which the lowborn narrator plants a faux pas squarely and deliberately in his ex-lover's shining hour and thus achieves sweet, high-spirited revenge that resonates on class-status levels beyond the particular situation. The song's lyric affirms that it is better, and lots more fun, to get high on whiskey and beer with low-placed friends than to succeed in belonging among the champagne-sipping fancy people. Its impeccably landed climax comes at the close of the third verse, with the narrator's promise to his ex that he will finally leave her black-tie affair—where he is an uninvited and unwelcome guest—and rejoin his friends at the bar: "Just wait till I finish this glass / Then, sweet little lady, . . . you can kiss my ass." A crescendo ushers in the final entrance (and repeat) of the chorus, now sung—in slightly sloppy but joyful fashion—by a vocal assemblage of regular folk conjuring the Oasis, the oft-invoked bar to which the song's Odysseus-in-boots has made his triumphant return.

A less cheerful note of resentment surfaces in other songs. Eric Church's "How 'Bout You" (#14 2006) quietly simmers in its declaration of pride in "know[ing] where I come from" and unflinching follow-up question, "How 'bout you?" The song's tone in the verses, intent and almost menacing, derives not only from the lyric, but from stark instrumentation (a bare, twangy banjo riff opens the track and continues throughout) and Church's no-nonsense vocal—low ranging to the point of growling and scarcely ornamented. The narrator professes to have no use for hipster fashion accouterments and "blueblood trust fund[s]" but affirms the value of personal integrity, self-reliance, hard work, and respect for one's parents and country. Tone, register, and instrumentation break out and offer more allure in the hard-rocking chorus. Here the lyric also adds the line "I think we're the chosen few" and thus effects the same values reversal heard in "Friends in Low Places" and many other country songs: human, moral value trumps economic value, so working people come out on top (Lamont observed the same move in her working-class ethnography: see chapter 3). Other post-1980s country expressions of working-class resentment and pride are Reba McEntire's "Fancy" (#8 1991), Aaron Tippin's "Working Man's Ph.D." (#7 1993), Gretchen Wilson's "Redneck Woman" (#1 2004), and Montgomery Gentry's "What Do Ya Think About That" (#3 2007), all discussed below.

But what is wrong, anyway, with expressing class resentment? Whether or not members of more privileged classes relish hearing it, it should come as no surprise that working-class cultural expression, including much country music, gives voice to complaints about the relatively high costs and meager rewards of life in the lower strata of American society. Judge fingers the resentment in country with little explanation, however, as if its illegitimacy and repellency are self-evident. He does elaborate that country in its anger, resentment, and unoriginality is "not much different from gangsta rap" and hence concludes that country must be included "the next time a conservative commentator deplores the latest pop-culture offense against style, intelligence and good morals."[18]

A few months after publication of Judge's article, class resentment as a self-evident moral—and now, political—offense surfaced elsewhere, in accusations of "class warfare" directed against the Obama administration by Republican legislators and fall 2011 presidential primary hopefuls. The pivotal assumption behind conservative dismissals of class resentment is that American society is a meritocracy granting citizens equal opportunity to pursue wealth, power, and happiness: those who lack the gumption, intelligence, or willingness to take risks or do the hard work that success requires have only themselves to blame. In early 2012, GOP primary candidate Mitt Romney staged an attack on class resentment and placed it at the center of his campaign, characterizing President Barack Obama as a threat to "free enterprise" and an agent of divisiveness through "the bitter politics of envy." At that moment, U.S. inequality as measured by income stood at its highest levels since the 1920s and was even greater when measured by wealth.[19] But inequality was not the object of Romney's moral indignation. The object of moral indignation, for the candidate Romney as for the commentator Judge, was the *resentment* of inequality.

Liberals and progressives often register indignation over inequality, and they sometimes express skepticism about the degree to which American society is really a meritocracy. But middle-class liberals and progressives as a group are no more receptive to country music's class resentment than the conservative critic Judge. Middle-class "cultural omnivores" distance themselves from country music and its constituency, and middle-class liberal media professionals portray these as backward and intolerant (illustrated in the reception of Foo Fighters' "Keep It Clean (Hot Buns)" video and performance). More broadly, even apart from country music, the middle-class Left regards the white working class as gripped by racial and sexual bigotry, as recurrent appeals to Frank's *Kansas* thesis in *New York Times* readers' forums demonstrate. This perception of bigotry is important, for it serves to justify further the Left's lack of interest in the white working class and its resentment—especially when such resentment is itself cast as resentment of women, racial others, and sexual minorities. Justification here connects in the first place to a more widespread notion that socioeconomic disadvantage among whites is their own fault, the result of laziness, stupidity, or lack of self-control. A 2003 study by the cultural anthropologist Kirby Moss found this cultural script uniformly in place across a diverse group of research subjects already by the teen years: the high school students he interviewed, rich and poor, white and of color, attested that failure to prosper in America is justifiable only under conditions of racial minority status.[20]

Resentment as it arises in country music narratives—which it does, frequently—is conventionally framed in interpersonal terms, and not only in love-gone-wrong songs. Jeannie C. Riley scored a big hit with "Harper Valley P.T.A." (#1 1968), a paradigmatic country song of resentment whose protagonist calls out her small-town accusers, the targets of her anger, by name. The song tells the story of a widowed single mother, Mrs. Johnson, whose teenage daughter comes home from school one day with a note. It is a message from the Parent-Teacher Association (P.T.A.), which accuses the mother of unfitness, citing her manner of dress and social comportment— going out and drinking with men of the town. Like many country songs invoking resentment or social indignity, "Harper Valley P.T.A." finds moral justice by song's end, and it transforms private shame into vindication on a higher plane. Here, the higher plane is social and public, but in some songs—for example, Martina McBride's classic "Independence Day" (#12 1994), with its stunning dramatic coupling of wrenching tragedy with a soaring, ecstatic chorus—vindication (for suffering and shame) resonates on a cosmic and transcendent plane.

"Harper Valley P.T.A." benefits from a well-crafted vignette by the songwriter Tom T. Hall, one of country music's most celebrated storytellers. But the song's dramatic impact also owes much to the way the music inflects the narrative and shapes its emotional arc. The musical setting in "Harper Valley P.T.A." recalls the pop-country artist Bobbie Gentry's self-penned No. 1 pop classic and multichart crossover hit of the previous year, "Ode to Billy Joe" (#17 1967). In both songs, lyrics gain declamatory emphasis from a spare accompaniment and unchanging chords. Like Gentry's "Ode," "Harper Valley P.T.A." uses strophic form, unfolding the drama ceaselessly, verse upon verse, without the interruption or textual repetition of a chorus. In "Ode to Billy Joe," static tonality—a scarcely progressing chord progression—paints the "sleepy, dusty Delta day" of Gentry's southern gothic lyrics and sharpens the juxtaposition of an adolescent's suicide in rural Mississippi to his neighbor's response to the news: "Pass the biscuits, please." Indeed, tonal stasis is key to making "Ode to Billy Joe" a masterpiece of pop-musical atmosphere and mystique whose possible meanings still inspire speculation among listeners.

By contrast, "Harper Valley P.T.A." delivers a pointed message with unmistakable clarity and amplifies its effect through the use of *shifting* tonality. Each verse is presented over a set of twelve-bar blues changes (the chord progression heard in countless blues, country, and rock 'n' roll songs, including "Johnny B. Goode," "Hound Dog," and "Wipe Out"). Verses 1 and 2 stage the song's dramatic exposition over two statements of blues in A. Then a step-up key change to B-flat heightens tension in the dramatic conflict of verses 3 and 4, where Mrs. Johnson at the P.T.A. meeting reveals the sordid transgressions of her accusers, all small-town aristocracy and paragons of respectability. One more step-up key change to B ushers in the dramatic resolution of verse 5 plus a brief coda and leaves Mrs. Johnson's climactic line, "You're all Harper Valley hypocrites," sounding, literally, on a high note. The song opens at a low point tonally and emotionally, with the protagonist being called out by social superiors for the way she wears her clothes and her sexuality, enjoys herself in off-hours, and raises her child— a scenario offering ample ingredients for resentment. Having summoned listeners' vicarious engagement, "Harper Valley P.T.A." then leads them step by step from degradation to cathartic triumph, as the denouement audibly rises above the condemnation of a society that morally sanctions those with rank and presumes to judge those without.

The protagonist's victory consists in defeating others' power to brand and thus debase her. Mrs. Johnson brings down a group of high-handed hypocrites and restores her social status, fighting off an attack that threatened to push her over the social boundary labeled "trash" and into the realm of abjection. The story exemplifies a potent and popular fantasy in country music, and its variants play out in countless songs. It is potent in that it addresses a vast, ongoing source of resentment in working-class life, the dominant class's power to classify and name, represent, and adjudicate working-class persons, lives, and realities. It is a fantasy inasmuch as the protagonist succeeds in wresting this power from her middle-class accusers and turning it back on them.

For the middle class is the knowledge class and the adjudicating class, possessing the power not only to classify and label the social other but also to declare which acts and utterances count as political and which are mere whining or venting of that illegitimate affect, resentment. Country music has given voice to resentment at least since Hank Williams (ca. 1950), and for just as long has made a self-referential theme of social lowness. Emblems of lowness in country songs have varied over time but include poverty, provincialism, hillbilly and redneck identity, the working person, and "being country." Sounding some recurrent criticisms of country music, Forbis and Judge charge that country is phony and "obsessed with its own themes," chief among them the "country-centric" theme. In these accounts, country's self-referential themes and its thematic obsessions, like its resentment, are regarded as patently damning, evidence of country music's "offense against style, intelligence and good morals."[21] In this discourse of judgment and censure, we encounter no hint of inquiry or curiosity. Thus, the question is not asked, What might an obsession with "being country" mean here?

THE IMPORTANCE OF BEING COUNTRY

Country music is preoccupied with the theme of being country to an extent that can indeed be characterized as an obsession. Scholars and listeners recognize this country-pride theme, in both country music and working-class speech, as a statement of working-class identification and middle-class resistance. For working-class–identified listeners, the gesture contained in the "being country" theme is most powerfully one of naming oneself as country, redneck, or hillbilly before the dominant culture confers the same title. It points not to self-fascination or self-loathing, or any hope of magically transforming the cultural meaning of the category. Rather, the reward offered by the "being country" theme lies in naming oneself, thus rebuking the continual affront of middle-class interpellation; and in sourcing the epithet from an alternative space of knowledge and social existence, thus invoking a true, positive meaning of working-class identity, as known to insiders, and refuting the false, negative one, ignorant and yet authoritative, of the dominant culture.

Country music's preoccupation with being country attests to the urgency and continuity of the needs this theme addresses. Ethnographic research reveals that working-class life frequently entails a daily struggle for self-worth, played out against the devaluations of the dominant culture.[22] The British epidemiologist Michael Marmot has shown that in rich countries like the United States, having low social rank and little control over one's life leads to chronic stress and greatly affects health and longevity, and these status-linked processes begin early in life.[23] It is difficult to find a cultural zone free from devaluations of the working class. Television, for instance, is a popular means of escapism, but as the media scholar Richard Butsch shows, it is hardly an escape from demeaning images of the working class.

In an article titled "Ralph, Fred, Archie and Homer," Butsch analyzes network family sitcoms over a forty-five-year postwar period, finding middle-class and affluent characters persistently overrepresented and working-class, especially blue-collar, characters grossly underrepresented. In 1970, for example, when 45 percent of American families were headed by a blue-collar worker, blue-collar families constituted only 4 percent of families in prime-time series. Surveying media studies more broadly, Butsch summarizes, "Studies of 50 years of comic strips, radio serials, television drama, movies and popular fiction reveal a very persistent pattern, an underrepresentation of working-class occupations and an overrepresentation of professional and managerial occupations among characters." In television, matters may only worsen when working-class people *are* represented. Butsch cites *The Honeymooners'* Ralph Kramden, Fred Flintstone, Archie Bunker of *All in the Family,* and Homer Simpson as examples of a character that television continually re-creates, the "white male working-class buffoon" who serves as the husband "in almost every sitcom depicting a blue-collar (white) male head of house."[24]

One effect of these media representations is, as Butsch notes, to "justify class relations of modern capitalism" and maintain the class status quo. So the ineptness and irresponsibility of the white male working-class buffoon character affirm the notion that blue-collar workers require supervision from professional-managerial workers—typically represented in family series as sensible, wise, and mature.[25] In similar ways, media representations serve to justify social hierarchy and inequalities. And the working class's underrepresentation and demeaning representations in the media surely have further, affective fallout for working-class people, in realms of alienation and demoralization.

But country music may offer an antidote. Pointedly acknowledging the media's hunger for images of white working people as rednecks and "trash"—replete with dirty kids, clothes on the line, and cars up on blocks—allows Tracy Byrd's "Lifestyles of the Not So Rich and Famous" (#4 1994) and comparable songs to transform alienation and private shame into class camaraderie and humor, a shared laugh in a "counterpublic" sphere.[26] By contrast to television and other entertainment and news media, country music provides frequent, sympathetic working-class representations. Indeed, it offers an inverse perspective relative to other media, to the extent that it normalizes working-class lives and values and often criticizes middle-class values and practices. In this light, it is easy to understand the importance of country music in the lives of many fans with working-class affiliations.[27] It also seems entirely logical that commentators representing middle-class perspectives should find country perverse—as Judge and Forbis, and others, do.[28]

THE POLITICIZING MOMENT

In the noir early days of the Watergate scandal, Richard Goldstein, a young, left-leaning New York journalist, published one of the first statements of a view of country music that has proved remarkably durable, of country as an ominous force of social menace. A frequent writer on rock and longtime contributor to the *Village Voice*, Goldstein would come out as a gay man later in the seventies and add HIV/AIDS and gay issues to his reportorial focus. His 1973 article "My Country Music Problem—and Yours" heralds a "dangerous" and "sinister" development in American culture. It is the adoption of country music by suburban youth, by even Goldstein's fellow New Yorkers, and by the Nixon administration, which pursued country affiliations in conjunction with its populist crusade and Southern strategy. The piece darkly warned New York trend-chasers against cozying up to country, a music imbued with a "very specific set of values, which include . . . political conservatism, strongly differentiated male and female roles, a heavily punitive morality, [and] racism."[29]

Goldstein was right in sensing a reshuffling of alliances. Hindsight reveals this moment as a turning point in American politics, in the economy and relative positioning of the classes, and in the dominant image and meaning of country music. The British Marxist historian Eric Hobsbawm has called 1973 the end of the postwar "Golden Age" and beginning of the "Crisis Decades," and the cultural and political writer Ellen Willis flags it as the year when "the economy contracted amid the first conspicuous domestic symptoms of what would come to be called globalization." Surveying the period and its epidemic of labor strikes—the largest in some twenty-five years—the U.S. historian Jefferson Cowie observes that labor unrest "peaked in 1974, before rapidly subsiding into history with little trace," in a subsequent erosion of the New Deal landscape, and he thus pronounces the 1970s "the last days of the working class." The film and cultural scholar Derek Nystrom locates in the decade's economic transformations the origins of "the current lopsided balance of power between a triumphant, mobile capital and a weakened working class, along with the disproportionate growth and concomitant strength of the professional middle class."

Nystrom's book *Hard Hats, Rednecks, and Macho Men* views the 1970s eruption of "class identity as a central feature" of American cinematic characters, and particularly the movies' fascination with white working-class masculinity in that decade (e.g., in *Easy Rider, Walking Tall,* and *Saturday Night Fever*), as a staging of middle-class anxieties about the period's upheavals and of fantasies (notably, often violent) of their resolution.[30]

It was also "in the late sixties and early seventies" that, according to Malone, "for the first time in its history, country music began to be identified with a specific political position, gaining a reputation for being a jingoistic and nativistic music." Peterson dates the birth of America's redneck pride vogue to 1973, tied in part to the release of several redneck-themed country songs. Recounting this era of redneck, trucker, CB radio, and country music fads, the historian Bruce Schulman chronicles the rise of "demi-rednecks" and notes that "genuine rednecks could not account for the sales" of so many redneck-themed country records. Goldstein in the original moment had flagged the same slumming trend. His misgivings about country find illustration in the figure of a middle-class teenager, someone who "dotes on underground comics and progressive politics," donning boots and a western shirt and embracing country music on the naive assumption that one can "experience [country's] way of life without subscribing to its values . . . [of] Wasp supremacy."[31]

The tone of Goldstein's essay, one of suspicion bordering on paranoia, would have been difficult to imagine in mainline media commentary on country music a few years earlier. True, the archetype of the monstrous down-home demagogue was there for the conjuring, as Elia Kazan had done in *A Face in the Crowd* (1957), with Andy Griffith as folk-country singer and snaky charmer Larry "Lonesome" Rhodes. Also true, country music had exploded in popularity and presence in the 1960s, especially at the end of the decade: the number of full-time AM country radio stations grew from 81 in 1961 to 650 in 1970, and country's share of total U.S. record sales nearly doubled between 1967 and 1970. These statistics alone could rouse anxiety in anyone who, like Goldstein, feels "a strange chill" when he encounters a truck driver playing country music on the radio and a "murderousness" when he encounters a white southerner— "as though . . . his ethnic history predisposes him" to racial violence. Goldstein almost certainly would have known his *Village Voice* colleague Christgau's 1969 comments on country music and similarly essentialist characterization of it as "naturally conservative."[32] In any event, the sounding of such a tone as Goldstein's in a 1973 *Mademoiselle* article is part of a broader cultural turn, which was crystallized in Merle Haggard and the Strangers' blockbuster "Okie from Muskogee" and its phenomenal reception.

The song may have been conceived as a joke (as Malone reports), and the opening line, "We don't smoke marijuana in Muskogee," penned by Haggard and drummer Eddie Burris as their tour bus passed near Muskogee, Oklahoma, may have itself emerged in a haze of smoke (as legend has it).[33] Whatever the case, the circumstances and intentions of the song's spontaneous origins were overtaken by its instant embrace among millions of listeners who took up its pro-establishment, antiprotest message unironically and made it their anthem. In late 1969, "Okie from Muskogee" spent four weeks at the top of the country charts and nearly broke the pop Top 40, climbing to #41. Haggard's ex-con, outlaw image and sensitive evocations of life on the social margins had given him cachet among liberals and hippies. Now, "Okie" appealed to socially and politically conservative audiences and earned the singer-songwriter a 1973 White House invitation from Nixon, who became keen on country when his "Silent Majority" target constituency rallied around the song. "Okie from Muskogee" unloosed a windfall by discovering this audience. Other listeners, meanwhile, especially those familiar with Haggard's oeuvre, heard clues suggesting the song was, at the least, tongue-in-cheek.

Nothing from his previous output—best known in songs about train hopping, prison, and life on the lam—would have suggested that Haggard was concerned with the question of whether "the kids here still respect the college dean." Nor, it might be noted, had this deft and supple musician ever before produced a song so musically square and simplistic. Indeed, in connection with the cliché melody, two-chord harmony, and foursquare groove and formal scheme in "Okie," its climactic chorus can sound like a punch line—"Muskogee / A place where even squares can have a ball." In interviews, Haggard went so far as to say the song's narrator was a persona. Surely to distance himself any further from the lyrics' message would have insulted his "Okie"-loving audience sector, with possibly disastrous career results. But Haggard's next move after this unexpected success would effectively dampen any intrigue surrounding "Okie from Muskogee" and its ambiguities. Over a rehashed "Okie" groove and chord progression, he immediately wrote and recorded a follow-up, "Fightin' Side of Me," that targeted his newfound audience with flatly earnest and ornery antiprotest sloganeering and went to No. 1 just a few months after the success of "Okie" (figure 6).[34] Haggard attests that Capitol Records squelched his initial idea for a follow-up single, the self-penned "Irma Jackson," whose narrator sings of his love since childhood and "till I die" of a woman forbidden to him because she is black (the song was eventually released in 1972 but only as an album track).[35]

FIGURE 6. Merle Haggard in the "Okie from Muskogee" era. Courtesy of Country Music Hall of Fame® and Museum.

In recent years, Haggard has dedicated live performances of "Fightin' Side of Me" to members of the military, revealing that the pugilistic song, like Toby Keith's controversial "Courtesy of the Red, White and Blue (The Angry American)" (#1 2002, #25 Pop), finds its most plausible niche in troop morale boosting. Ultimately, Haggard's various songs and actions still thwart attempts at conscription under any partisan political banner. More recent headlines have highlighted his thrill on meeting former President Bill Clinton and his defense of another Democratic president, Barack Obama, against detractors (during the 2007 primaries he had backed Obama's rival Hillary Clinton and performed his song "Hillary" on tour). Recalling his 1980s appearance at a GOP fund-raiser for President Reagan—the person who, as California governor, had granted the ex-felon a much-desired full pardon—Haggard wrote in his autobiography, "I don't judge a man by his politics, any more than I judge him by his color."[36]

In Malone's even-handed summary of country music in the Vietnam era, "Okie from Muskogee" figures as the best known of a rash of antiprotest songs that appeared, along with a smattering of antiwar songs, between

1965 and the early 1970s, when U.S. involvement in Vietnam ended. But "the obsession with politics had been out of character," he writes, and after 1973 country music resumed "a more comfortable, and traditional, absorption with the world of the working class."[37] Recent work by the U.S. historian Daniel Geary goes further in arguing that "while many New Right politicians sought to capitalize on the popularity of country music, the genre was not inherently conservative." Geary points to the 1971 syndicated news column by Kevin Phillips, an architect of Nixon's Southern strategy, "claim[ing] country music for conservatism" and for the "Silent Majority," and he recounts similar efforts by George Wallace and Ronald Reagan to solicit support from country artists and fans. But Geary emphasizes that "the most popular country records of the late 1960s *challenged* backlash politics."[38] Focusing on Johnny Cash's live prison recordings, *At Folsom Prison* (1968) and *At San Quentin* (1969), he notes that both reached #1 on the country charts and enjoyed crossover success. In fact, Cash's prison albums, with 6.5 million sales in 1969, made him "the best-selling musical artist in the world, eclipsing even the Beatles," while conveying a "left-oriented Southern politics" and a "politics of empathy" that was antiauthoritarian and sympathetic to the prison inmates, the American working class, and the counterculture.[39]

If country music, like the culture at large, returned to less political preoccupations following Vietnam, in the national imagination its politicized image endured and included—as it had in Goldstein's 1973 litany—a reputation for racial and sexual bigotry, conservatism, and moralism. By 1978, an essay by the geographer and country music scholar Charles Gritzner opened with a list of the ways in which country was viewed by its critics, including "right-wing, ... redneck, ignorant, and *probably* racist."[40] Two notable cultural shifts, also glimpsed in Goldstein's complaint, contributed to this change in the image and meaning of country music, and of the white working class.

One was the demi-redneck phenomenon. Country music found favor with and began sometimes to cater to a new, upscale, politicized audience segment with a taste for socially and politically conservative messages. "Okie from Muskogee" marked the beginning of an era in which, as Schulman explains, country music was embraced

> by millions of migrants to the South's cities and suburbs, refugees from the rural South and the urban North. Most were not rednecks by birth, fewer still rednecks by social position. But they adopted the term *redneck* as a badge of honor, a fashion statement, a gesture of resistance against high taxes, liberals, racial integration, women's liberation, and

hippies. . . . Millions of middle-class and upper-class Americans became "half a redneck." Along with boots and trucks, these demi-rednecks also brandished a set of shared political attitudes: they resented government interference, . . . disliked bureaucrats, pointy-headed intellectuals, and "welfare Cadillacs." . . . Demi-rednecks formed the foundation for conservative populism, the tax revolt, and the Reaganite assault on the welfare state. The ascendant Sunbelt [was] a new political force.[41]

In the 1970s, country music became a cultural space where middle- and upper-class conservatives and the white working class shared common ground. Since then, "country music lover" has served as a rubric under which these two socially, economically, and politically divergent groups have been conflated and sometimes rendered indistinguishable to outside observers.

A second relevant shift in this period was a culture-focused backlash against the *actual* working class. Willis reminds us that the "renewed class warfare" of the 1970s "was presented as a *cultural* offensive." The experts in this moment determined that American workers were spoiled and had an attitude problem. As Cowie chronicles, "elite opinion makers" lectured that "working people simply made too much money, were too protected from the discipline of the market, and were so demanding as to destabilize the entire economy." Politicians, economists, commentators, and "corporate spokespeople" on both the left and the right, Willis notes, "justified lower wages, layoffs, and assaults on public goods and social welfare programs as moral correctives to Americans' hedonism, profligacy, and excessive expectations." The writer Tom Wolfe, a leading voice in the rebuke of the working class, coined the phrase "Me Decade," and it stuck. At the end of that decade, President Jimmy Carter called on Americans to turn down the thermostat and put on a sweater. The Reaganites proffered a vision of freedom—as the ability to pursue wealth without limits—and enjoyed a longer reign.[42]

THE MIDDLE-CLASS ORIGINS OF COUNTRY MUSIC'S WHITENESS

Since the late 1960s–early 1970s appearance of politicized country song topics, demi-rednecks, and cultural backlash against the working class, country music has been subject to certain recurrent strains of criticism. One strain disparages country's authenticity and sincerity. This criticism sometimes has to do with perceptions of demi-rednecks among country's audience. But it also connects to what may be the oldest form of critique surrounding country (and blues) music, according to which the music at hand can never be barefoot enough, toothless enough, or "pure" enough to satisfy certain arbiters of authenticity. Another, historically linked strain of contemporary criticism focuses on the presence of the white working class in country music and thus holds country and its constituency in cultural contempt for the values of racism, gender repression, and sexual bigotry that have been increasingly imputed to this demographic group since the 1970s. Not uncommonly, observers even take country's apparent whiteness as proof of its racism. This view flourishes under widespread ignorance of the early-twentieth-century history of the music broadcasting and record-ing industries and their alliance with authoritative pseudoscientific knowl-edge of the day.

The authenticity critique of country music was pioneered by folk song collectors who traveled into Appalachian locales and constructed an "authen-tic" mountain music repertory by arbitrarily omitting songs they deemed insufficiently English or insufficiently hillbilly. They assumed, as many arbiters of musical authenticity have assumed after them, that authentic country music had to be distinct from music of nonsoutherners (and some-times, urbanites) and likewise from music of southern blacks. Because the music of these groups in fact shared considerable ground, the folk song col-lectors had to omit numerous songs to realize their vision.[43] The racial and class ideology that held great institutional and scientific sway in the early twentieth century regarded poor whites and poor blacks as biologically and culturally distinct groups and regarded both groups as fundamentally dis-tinct from middle- and upper-class whites. Musical categories and knowl-edge were established in accordance with these expert perspectives.

Born in this Jim Crow era, the American record industry segregated southern popular musical practice in the 1920s to create a pair of racially distinct marketing categories, dubbed "race" and "hillbilly." In his book *Segregating Sound*, the historian Karl Hagstrom Miller shows that these categories were quasi-anthropological, having been conceived under the influence of the new science of folklore, and were kept separate from record companies' general catalogs. By now, the arbitrary marketing scheme devised by early record industry executives has been institutionalized, and the two categories of music, known today under the labels "R&B" and "country" are reified not only in imaginings of country's (true, deep) whiteness, but in ways that are woven throughout American cultural and social life.

In Miller's account, the arrival of the phonograph and the radio created a new standard of musical authenticity, demanding correspondence between an artist's racial identity and musical style. In this way, the twentieth-century music industry played a part in the invention of the color line.

Industry professionals imposed racialized boundaries on the products of musicians' drive, respecting no boundaries, to devour and reproduce music by trading licks, absorbing influence, and copping ideas wherever they might hear them. The music industry thus extended concepts of blackness and whiteness across audible dimensions.[44] Miller recovers stories of black hillbilly bands, white blues artists, and southern performers of Broadway and Tin Pan Alley music who were rejected by record company talent scouts and turned into walking oxymorons, and thus historically obliterated.[45] But the shared roots of R&B and country have continued to push up, stubbornly, through artists from Jimmie Rodgers to Tina Turner and Ray Charles to Wynonna Judd (figure 7). And today the black string band tradition is being revived by the Ebony Hillbillies and Carolina Chocolate Drops.

The term *blue-eyed soul* designates R&B music made by white musicians, but there is no comparable term for country music by African American musicians. Still, African American artists, many southern born and best known under R&B or jazz classifications, have continued to create and perform country music even after the industry's imposition of segregated style formats. The list here includes Louis Armstrong, Ella Fitzgerald, Ray Charles, Tina Turner, Aaron Neville, Donna Summer, Alice Randall, and Lionel Richie, in addition to those African American artists who are best known under a country rubric, like DeFord Bailey, Charley Pride, Linda Martell, Stoney Edwards, O.B. McClinton, Big Al Downing, Cowboy Troy, and Darius Rucker. The degree of musical exchange and shared musical culture between poor white and black southerners in the twentieth century is further demonstrated by the important influences of African American musicians on commercial country music through some of its most towering figures. For example, Lesley Riddle had a major impact through the Carter Family, teaching Maybelle Carter the "Carter scratch" guitar technique that would become a country music standard, working alongside A.P. Carter on his song collecting trips, and teaching the trio some of the songs they performed. And blues street musician Rufus "Tee-Tot" Payne was a musical mentor to Hank Williams who helped Williams get over his shyness and may have taught him his driving style of rhythm guitar playing.[46]

Authenticity seekers today reject modern commercial country and its market-driven anything-goes stylistic idiom, idealizing past artists and purist notions of a genuine folk idiom (sometimes imagined in terms hewing closer to bluegrass). Country music scholars agree, however, that country has always been a commercial music—Malone dates its birth to the first commercially produced and marketed "old-time" records, in 1923—and

FIGURE 7.   Born in an era of eugenics and Jim Crow, the American music
industry divided the music of poor southerners from middle-class fare and further
segregated it by race. But shared musical origins have continued to bear fruit in
the industry's race (now, R&B) and hillbilly (now, country) categories. R&B
superstar and Tennessee native Tina Turner's 1974 debut solo LP was a country
album featuring songs written by Dolly Parton and Hank Snow, among others.
Courtesy of Country Music Hall of Fame® and Museum.

history records market forces' shaping of European music from J.S. Bach's
time and earlier.[47] Moreover, Miller emphasizes that nineteenth- and twentieth-century southern musicians, black and white performers plying their
craft before the advent of the music industry, proudly cultivated broad,
eclectic repertories so as to be employable for a wide range of dances, events,
and audiences. His historical evidence illustrates in one fell swoop that both
commercialism and stylistic eclecticism, primary targets of detractors' disdain, have been present in country music from the start, and even before

the American music industry's invention of country (i.e., folk or hillbilly) music as a distinct category.

When the market shifted in the 1920s, black and white musicians had to change their acts to remain relevant. That meant trimming down to narrow repertories of the music that was expected of them within the new, racialized style divisions, and it often meant, too, dressing down and, for white musicians, "Jedding up" in hillbilly garb, in line with folkloric notions of cultural distinctness. From Miller's evidence we see that stereotypes were granted scientific and academic authority, and popular music became an important tool in folklore's project of demonstrating the natural remoteness of the folk from the civilized classes and the (putatively) inevitable distance between black and white folk cultures.[48] In the process was forged the rustic, poverty-ennobled image of country music that arbiters of authenticity still hold up as the ideal of country purity. And it was forged precisely according to the demands of the market.

COUNTRY THEOLOGY

God and Country: Grossman's Critique

Decades after the invention of hillbilly and race music circa 1923 and after America's class-focused cultural offensive circa 1973, invoking country music's racism, sex-gender repression, and conservatism is an automatic gesture in much cultural commentary. Indeed, in popular mainstream contexts, mere mention of country music can call up conservatism and racial, sex, and gender repression in a sweep, eliminating the need to name each one. In scholarly writing, however, professional standards dictate that authors question suppositions and present careful evidence. Still, scholarly arguments may revert to conventional wisdom—sometimes despite their own evidence. In 2002, the religious scholar Maxine Grossman published an article in the top journal in her field, the *Journal of the American Academy of Religion*. Titled "Jesus, Mama, and the Constraints on Salvific Love in Contemporary Country Music," her study surveyed recent country songs and found no evidence of homophobia, racism, or intolerance. Such a finding might seem like proof against the ideological status quo. But astonishingly, Grossman's interpretation renders it just the opposite: proof that the situation in country music is even worse than usually imagined. She concludes that country betrays no intolerance of sexual, racial, or religious difference because it *erases* any possibility of difference in these realms.

The aim of Grossman's essay is to investigate the dynamics of Christian salvation in country song lyrics.[49] Her analysis views contemporary country as a secular music rich in themes of (implicitly) Christian salvation. Grossman's conclusion, however, underscores what she identifies as two operative *constraints* on religious expression within country music norms, namely, that the messages in country lyrics must not be too explicitly Christian and that they must not refer directly to non-Christian religions, racial and ethnic minorities, or lesbian and gay issues, any of which would stray outside what, she contends, constitutes "the true" of country discourse.

Leading up to these conclusions, Grossman surveys country greatest hits collections of singles from the 1980s and 1990s, discovering that "easily one-third to one-half" and sometimes up to 80 percent of the tracks are "completely ambiguous with regard to gender and could just as easily be 'inhabited' by a gay or lesbian listener" as one with heterosexual identifications. In the absence of expressly gendered pronouns or situations, she acknowledges, the "'universalizing' tendencies" of country lyrics dealing with "passion, jealousy, joy, or sorrow . . . leave them open to personal interpretation." Grossman further acknowledges that same-sex love is a frequent country topic, particularly in parent-child relationships, and that "heterosexuality, when it is explicit" in country, "is not always pretty."[50]

This last description certainly applies to much country music since the rise of honky-tonk in the 1940s, and it may be an understatement in relation to earlier gothic murder ballads and many country songs, from the 1950s to the present, that examine from a woman's perspective the imbalances, unfairness, and abuses in heterosexual relationships and in heterosexuality as a social institution—albeit usually through individual stories, in accordance with country conventions. Examples range from songs protesting society's sexual double standard, like Kitty Wells's "It Wasn't God Who Made Honky-Tonk Angels" (#1 1952), Dolly Parton's "Just Because I'm a Woman" (#17 1968), and Loretta Lynn's "The Pill" (#1 1975), to the operatic tragedy of McBride's "Independence Day," in which a woman escapes her socially sanctioned predicament of domestic violence only by burning down the house that contains her and her abusive husband, leaving their young daughter orphaned.[51] McBride's record, like Lynn's and Wells's before it, was deemed controversial and banned by many radio stations, the conservative gatekeepers of the country music world.[52] But with time's passing, these once-jolting tracks ceased to shock—a process exhibited in any number of pop-cultural instances, and not only in country music—and "Honky-Tonk Angels" and "Independence Day," especially, became beloved classics.

Having observed that country songs are often intimately homosocial, are sometimes critical of heterosexuality, and are "open to a remarkable range" of both hetero- and homosexual interpretations, Grossman goes in search of explicit gay and lesbian references in country lyrics—and finds little.[53] She cites Garth Brooks's "We Shall Be Free" (#12 1992) as a call for justice whose controversial status owed to its perceived message on sexual orientation. Stanza 4 presents the lines "When we're free to love anyone we choose / When this world's big enough for all different views / When we all can worship from our own kind of pew," leading up to the refrain "Then we shall be free." Same-sex thematic interpretation is encouraged by apparently gay-affirmative moments in the song's video: footage of a pair of men embracing and jumping for joy following the line "Everyone has the right to be happy," spoken by Reba McEntire, and cameos by LGBTQ celebrities Martina Navratilova and Lily Tomlin. Grossman comments that the lyric "fails to mention homosexuality explicitly" and that Brooks, discussing the song in an interview, "argues for 'tolerance,'" asserting "not that 'gay is good' but, rather, that people should be allowed to be whatever they are."[54] Grossman is right in noting that the lyric in "We Shall Be Free" does not mention homosexuality by name, and she is persuasive in her argument that the line about being "free to love" contributed more than any other single line to the record's politicization. But her analysis falters at a few key points.

First, in homing in on sexuality as "the subject of the controversy over the song," Grossman neglects to take into account either the song's rhetorical effects or the particular pop-cultural context in which it appeared—both important factors.[55] "We Shall Be Free" imported a phenomenally successful 1980s pop-rock innovation into country music: the celebrity-studded, gospel-style, current events–invoking plea for social justice. But by comparison to the classic example of the genre, the 1985 benefit track for African famine relief "We Are the World," "We Shall Be Free" is much more explicit and thus tempts the limits of preachiness in this already preachy genre. Where "We Are the World" songwriters Michael Jackson and Lionel Richie wisely relied on poetic vagueness, themes of empowerment, and images of children, Brooks and his cowriter, Stephanie Davis, present a laundry list of social problems—hunger, political oppression, poverty, racism, environmental destruction, ideological and religious intolerance, graft, and inequality—in fairly specific terms. Moreover, they implicate listeners not as fellow sufferers and saviors of humanity, as Jackson and Richie did, but as wayward travelers who might still find their way. The result of this comparatively clumsy song craft is a do-good anthem—abandoning country's favored storytelling format—whose most off-putting element for many listeners may be, not its reference to affectional or other freedoms, but its heavy-handedness. "We Shall Be Free" risks violating a central value in country music to the extent that it might be heard as passing judgment on listeners and telling them what to think. Listeners with low social and workplace status have ample experience in being judged harshly and dictated to, and for such listeners (and others), condescending treatment of a subject can stir controversy just as much as, or more than, the subject itself.

Second, Grossman quotes only three words from the flagged line, "When we're *free to love*," omitting the pivotal words "anyone we choose." This formulation, as LGBTQ activists know, raises the most inflammatory proposition in sexual-affectional politics. By suggesting that sexuality is a choice, the line renders homosexuality much more controversial and less acceptable to Americans of various stripes than when it is viewed as an inborn, immutable condition.[56] Thus the lyric conveys a crucially different and more politically charged message than that suggested by Grossman's gloss, "people should be allowed to be whatever they are." In presuming individuals' given essence ("whatever they are"), her reading actually reverses the song's original implications of erotic-affectional open-endedness and free choice.[57]

Grossman's analysis raises further contextual questions. One pertains to the fact that, while her argument readily suggests there is something especially problematic in country's (non)treatment of themes of racial, sexual, and religious tolerance, it provides no context with regard to their treatment in comparable musical styles. Does 1980s–1990s Top 40 pop, rock, R&B, rap, or adult contemporary music address these issues, and if so, does it address them in a more progressive way? Finally, as I have suggested, Grossman's essay neglects to illumine how country's silences on racial, sexual, and religious difference signify within what is, by her own reckoning, the relevant frame of reference: the working-class world. Indeed, her discussion, like so many others, assumes that the operative codes and values of country music are transparent to, and identical to the codes and values of, the dominant middle-class culture. Country songs and empirical research, however, suggest otherwise.

Liberation, not Salvation: Country Theology according to Fillingim

David Fillingim was a professor and scholar of religion and philosophy when he published *Redneck Liberation* (2003), a book further informed by his prior experience ministering to working-class congregants as a pastor in a Carolina mill town.[58] *Redneck Liberation* analyzes country music as the "theological self-expression" of a constituency who (in Hank Williams's words) "some call the common people" and who are known elsewhere in terms of "the hillbilly or redneck."[59] Fillingim views country music as theology on the grounds that it "embodies certain basic beliefs about reality" or about "matters of ultimate concern." He identifies the essential premise of country's "redneck theology," or what he labels more specifically as "hillbilly humanism," in relation to Hank Williams and his music. It is the premise that all people are equal before God.

Fillingim's analysis differs in important ways from Grossman's account of Christian salvation in country. Whereas Grossman hears Christianity as implicit in country music, lurking even in secular song narratives, Fillingim hears the reverse: he reckons that country songs are "usually theistic," demonstrating belief in God, but they "deconstruct narrowly Christian structures of meaning and assert other experiences as ultimate."[60] In other words, where Grossman posits the presence of Christianity behind country's secular humanism, Fillingim posits the presence of secular humanism behind country's Christianity: he hears country breaking down Christian doctrine into more abstract, underlying universal humanist values. Grossman also perceives country music as concerned with Christian salvation, while Fillingim hears the opposite, a *rejection* in country of "the otherworldly solace that Christian tradition . . . espouses as the answer to the lived contradiction between human dignity and socio-economic marginalization."[61] Fillingim is right: country does not hold to the southern gospel ethos of patiently enduring injustice in this world and awaiting one's reward in heaven. His point implicitly contradicts the false-consciousness charge so often lodged against the working class via the Marxian quote "Religion is the opiate of the people."

Concerning Williams's "hillbilly humanism," Fillingim writes that it "starts from a Christian-based affirmation of the equal dignity of all persons." He continues, "In songs like 'Men with Broken Hearts' and 'Pictures from Life's Other Side,' Hank specifically urges compassion for those who are down and out."[62] Williams's songs reproach those who would judge the shamed and hopeless. "You have no right to be the judge / . . . Just think— but for the grace of God / It would be you instead of him," he declaims in "Men with Broken Hearts" (figure 8). This plea for compassion and against judgment surfaces in many instances throughout country music, whose artists, Fillingim notes, derive their humanist beliefs from a blend of sources including not only Christian theology but American populism and country music tradition as well.[63] Bobbie Gentry's self-penned "Fancy" (#26 1970, #31 Pop) provides another, later example. "Fancy" conveys the same human-

FIGURE 8. Hank Williams in his short-lived country music prime, ca. early 1950s. Courtesy of Country Music Hall of Fame® and Museum.

ist message as "Men with Broken Hearts" but through a specifically feminine-gendered and sexually stigmatized scenario of poverty and shame.

Many listeners know the song and its story from Reba McEntire's Top 10 country cover released some two decades after Gentry's arty, atmospheric pop original. As in "Ode to Billy Joe," Gentry presents a southern gothic tale. Here, a desperately poor mother spends her last cent on a red satin and velvet dancing dress for her teenage daughter Fancy and sends the girl "uptown" with the instructions that offer her best shot at survival: "Just be nice to the gentlemen, Fancy, / They'll be nice to you." As the song's now-grown, worldly, and wealthy narrator, Fancy recounts her unorthodox rags-to-riches story, saving her final verse for those who would judge: "Now, in this world there's a lot of self-righteous hypocrites / That would call me bad / And criticize Mama for turning me out / No matter how little we had." Both "Fancy" and "Men with Broken Hearts" invoke "the Lord" and "God" explicitly in their lyrics and thus establish a Christian ethical context. But within that context, the songs refuse to place a courtesan, her anguished mother, or hard-living, hard-drinking men beneath the respectable people who would condemn them.

The operative rationale is stated by Williams to close his track: "For the God that made you / Made them, too, / These men with broken hearts." Fillingim notes that Loretta Lynn and other female country artists' "rejection of sexual double standards ... [is also] often grounded, like Hank's hillbilly humanism, in a Christian-based understanding that all people are equal before God." Indeed, Lynn proclaims in her autobiography, "I don't believe in double standards, where men can get away with things that women can't. In God's eyes, there's no double standard. That's one of the things I've been trying to say in my songs."[64] With a statement of the "hillbilly humanist" creed neatly tailored to the instance ("In God's eyes, there's no double standard"), Lynn articulates her opposition to the gender-based inequality of social-sexual dignity and freedom—despite its institutionalization in the Christian traditions with which country music was, and still is, closely associated. In Lynn's argument, the humanist ethos of the equal dignity of all persons overrules any doctrine erected on discrimination and hierarchy, no matter whether it is religious or other doctrine, and no matter whether dignity is denied on gendered, sexual, or other grounds.

One recent study identifies the same moral counter-ideology as the basis for support of George W. Bush in 2004 among some white working-class voters, despite their disagreement with his policies. They doubted John Kerry's ability to represent their interests because they saw him, unlike Bush, as unable to perceive "the true human worth of everyone."[65] This was not the explanation of that year's "moral values" voters that pundits offered—which centered on abortion and same-sex marriage—nor does it support Frank's *Kansas* thesis of a hoodwinked proletariat. The discrepancies among these accounts of working-class voters and their reasoning underscore the need for attention to working-class cultural logic on its own terms.

Hillbilly humanism is still strong in country music and turns up in far more songs than can be mentioned here. Montgomery Gentry's 2007 hit single, "What Do Ya Think About That?," invokes the hillbilly humanist ethos in the line, "Don't judge me and I won't judge you / 'Cause we all get judged in the end." The theme links here to a growling dismissal of bourgeois censure and disdain, represented in neighbors' disapproval of old car parts in the narrator's front yard, his rough work clothes, beer drinking, and pool shooting. The song's response is one of defiance, heard in the chorus clincher: "I don't give a damn what other people think / What do ya think about that?" Elsewhere, the hillbilly humanism theme takes on other flavors and moods. Lorrie Morgan's "Rocks" (2004) updates Hank Williams's theme with explicit antihomophobic, antiracist, and religious tolerance messages. Its chorus closes with a scriptural reference linking to the song's title: "Ye without sin cast the first stone."

IMPLICIT COMMUNICATION IN WORKING-CLASS CULTURE AND IN COUNTRY SONGS

Concrete Rhetoric

Beyond issues of Christian salvation and humanism in country music, Grossman raises questions about country's silence on racial, sexual, and religious difference. Does neglect of such themes really mean that country "erases" difference in these realms, as she contends? Her claim rests on assumptions about the meanings of country songs' silence—or rather, relative silence, given that songs by Garth Brooks and other artists had included LGBTQ references before Grossman's 2002 publication date, and further references have appeared since then.[66] Her argument presumes that the values and signifying codes in country are those of, or at least transparent to, the dominant middle-class culture. Research on working-class culture and communication suggests, however, that working-class codes and values—the stuff of country songs—are different from, and sometimes at odds with, the codes and values of the middle class.

An example of such research is the communication scholar Dale Cyphert's 2007 study "Rhetoric on the Concrete Pour." It presents the author's description and analysis of rhetorical practices in an Omaha concrete crew, which she observed by shadowing and videotaping one crew member on the job for forty hours over the course of a month. Illumining operative logics and values in working-class communication and culture, the study's findings offer knowledge notably lacking in Grossman's and most other commentaries on country music. In the work method of the concrete crew, Cyphert documents "an implicit form of communal decision making that is grounded in the actions rather than the words of a public." Like other organizations working in complex and risky physical conditions, the group optimizes its cognitive power by relying on group thought processes and implicit, nonverbal exchange. The crew's decision-making process is "a dance that requires physical attentiveness to the surroundings and to others" to accommodate shifting circumstances and chance. Cyphert shows that this physical, nonverbal method is "not an abdication of rhetorical processes" but rather a rhetorical process in its own right that "protects and encourages autonomous decision making."[67]

When the crew must react to a midwestern thunderstorm unpredictably unfolding in real time and reckon with its potential effects on a fresh concrete pour, their decision-making process is radically collective and dynamic. Group deliberation proceeds by means of "implicit communication techniques" grounded in physical action and *avoiding* talk. Relevant knowledge is distributed among all members of the group. "Rather than wait for the articulated problem solving of a few eloquent leaders," Cyphert writes, "the work group maintains rapid, consistent, and mutually comprehensible interactions to produce an immediately reliable group response to environmental demands." In what she calls "the rhetoric of distributed decision making," each person "maintains responsibility for a sphere of expertise even as specific functions are shifted in response to environmental change." For example, highly skilled workers may perform low-skill tasks, as circumstances demand, to take full advantage of the crew's pooled talent.[68]

The efficient, embodied working-class rhetoric described here depends not on executives, stars, or top-down decision making but on shared knowledge and responsibility. Cyphert explains:

> Much of each man's autonomy on the job flows from presumptions that every man's unique store of information is vital. . . . There is no scripted role that an anonymous, decontextualized "individual" can play. Instead a solution evolves as unique, authentic people disappear or return to the [job site's] public sphere. Each man's contribution is an integral part of the solution—not in a socially polite attempt to validate each [other's] self-esteem, but with the authenticity of a problem-solving process that will be materially different when different people are present.[69]

Cyphert had originally set out in her field research to document "rhetorically 'significant' events" among the members of the concrete work crew, which she envisaged as "political talk, assertive attempts at persuasion, or problem-solving discussions." Once on site, however, she found that such events rarely occurred. The workers "dismissed such talk, typically a management activity, as a silly waste of time and energy. A group of 'real men' who had a problem to solve would not be sitting in an office discussing possible solutions; they'd be outside dealing with the situation." Accordingly, Cyphert notes that "the work group's communication does not conform well to the Western model of rhetoric, which puts a premium on agonistic displays to identify the 'best' solution."[70]

The crew's success depends on its members' ability to respond to cues from each other and from the environment. Thus, "rather than making proactive attempts to 'solve' problems and create a better world," which is a central ethos in the middle class, "these workers accept the environment as a given." Cyphert notes that so-called working-class fatalism ("Whatever will be, will be," to quote an old pop song lyric) is viewed "as a dysfunctional failure to conform to the assertive, goal-oriented rhetorical norms of the dominant culture." But in practice, the highly effective workings of the concrete crew "illustrate the advantages of accommodating a dynamic and potentially dangerous environment." Equally crucial is the preservation of communal function and feeling. In the crew's embodied deliberative process, "all perceptions are deemed inherently valuable, and information is held by the group for as long as possible" before further contingencies eliminate certain solutions. Cyphert observed abundant "linguistic conventions" that importantly solicit coworkers' further engagement in decision making and "protect an individual from any hint that his decisions are not valued." Crew members are "asked whether a certain action is a good idea, never told to take it." Sentences might begin with, "Why don't you" or end with "Right?"[71]

Perhaps the most striking aspect of the workers' method, by contrast to middle-class norms, is its avoidance of talk. Here, the need to articulate a command or an explanation is perceived as a sign of dysfunction, occurring when workers are untrained or incompetent with respect to the needs or expectations of the group. The result of what Cyphert calls the "dance" of nonverbal communication among the concrete crew is "a public sphere in which verbal communication is a signal that something has gone wrong with the community's preferred rhetorical dynamic." Crew members resort to verbal communication when someone "has missed a cue or bungled a step." A need to talk to each other is therefore "the visible evidence of a problem."[72]

Discussing further manifestations of these rhetorical practices, Cyphert raises some implications relevant to class cultures. She underscores a crew member's expression for describing his work as satisfactory, "No one can say anything to me," which affirms the notion that talk signals a problem. In light of her study, Cyphert observes too that "the working class's well-documented resistance to promotion to supervisory roles can be framed as a rejection of some key middle–upper class presumptions" about the public sphere as a realm of "explicit, analytical thought," by contrast to the working-class public sphere exemplified here, a realm of "common decision making" among autonomous individuals. Notably, Cyphert concludes that the workers she observed "not only devalue the use of language to make decisions, they find the highly articulated rhetoric of the dominant political/social world to be an unpleasant, even indecent way of being."[73]

Cyphert's analysis bears implications for working-class subjectivities molded by experiences of knowing and valuing collective accomplishment and its sustaining conditions, by nonverbal techniques for communication and consensus, and by autonomous action in the service of group effort. The work process she describes exhibits not merely an absence of middle-class distinguished individualism, but the presence of a different sort of individualism, operating within a richly social paradigm. Members of the concrete crew "pay attention to movements, gestures, moods, and meanings," Cyphert notes, "even as they avoid explicit comments on any of them"—and thus avoid what might make a "highly articulated" rhetoric "indecent": judging, labeling, or presuming to represent another person.[74] Cyphert's findings about talk and silence on this working-class site clearly challenge Grossman's assertions about country-musical ideology. That is, Cyphert highlights rhetorical-cultural tendencies to avoid talk and view it as a communicative method of last resort, to implement rhetorical conventions aimed at preserving communal feeling, and to shun ethically and viscerally the middle class's "highly articulated" social and political rhetoric and the mode of existence that comes with it. Accounting for such group-sustaining tendencies might be one means of approaching country music on its own terms. And then one could not easily arrive at Grossman's conclusion that country's silence on religious, sexual, and racial difference marks an erasure of any possibility of these differences.

Although Grossman views country music as a working-class cultural form, neither she nor any of the other country critics examined thus far comes to country with any demonstrated knowledge of working-class rhetoric. What is more—to invoke the terms of Grossman's own critique of country music—she and the other critics are blind to any possibility of difference in this regard. Cyphert argues that gaining recognition for the existence of working-class rhetoric is not difficult—after all, "any community will devise its own ways of reaching public decisions and acting collectively." She suggests that such recognition merely requires acceptance of "diversity" (however patronizing the construct), but she also acknowledges that the concept of cultural diversity has not been extended to the poor and working classes per se. An even greater difficulty, as Cyphert sees it, lies in gaining understanding for the nature of a rhetorical process that exists outside elite rhetorical norms. A Western "literary elite maintains its own social, political, and academic power by constructing alternative social practices as immature, immoral, uneducated, and criminal," she writes, "absent any evidence that middle-class intellectual values are inherently superior to the more socially oriented values of the working class."[75]

Working-Class Values in Country Themes

Cyphert affords invaluable perspective on implicit communication in the working class, but scholarly literature on class cultures is not the only source of discussion on this topic. Implicit communication is also treated, appreciatively, in country music. The theme is rendered a slogan in "A Little Less Talk and a Lot More Action," recorded in 1992 by Hank Williams Jr. and again the following year by Toby Keith, who included the track on his debut album and took it to #2 on the charts (1994). Bucky Covington's "A Father's Love (the Only Way He Knew How)" (#23 2010) provides another example of the implicit communication theme. The soft, mostly acoustic track presents a vignette in which a grown son gradually comes to hear the unspoken message of love in mundane acts bestowed by his seemingly gruff, tool-handy father. Not given to speeches, the father marks significant moments in the family's life by looking after repair and maintenance needs, like tuning up the son's car when he leaves the family nest and installing door locks on the house where he and his new wife are starting a life together. Narrated from the son's perspective, the lyric recounts these events and, finally, the father's sixty-fifth birthday in successive verses, each one clinched and interpreted by the refrain, "I didn't hear it then, but I hear it now / He was saying, 'I love you,' / The only way he knew how." The song's intensive focus on same-sex love and intimacy attaches to a parent-child relationship and thus enacts a characteristic theme in country songs, old and new, that is no less noteworthy for that.

A classic song on the theme of implicit communication is "When You Say Nothing at All," a Top 10 country hit for two different artists. Keith Whitley made a No. 1 record of it in 1988, shortly before his tragic death at age thirty-four. Alison Krauss and Union Station later cut "When You Say Nothing at All" (#3 1995) for a Whitley tribute album, and their track captured the Best Single award from the Country Music Association. The band's less-is-more arrangement foregrounds impeccable acoustic instrumental timbres and Krauss's exquisite, soft-focused soprano, creating the perfect vehicle for this song about lovers tuned in to communication beyond words. The lyric attests to the inadequacy and barriers of language for expressing the feelings and qualities that join two hearts. Love, longing, and devotion are best conveyed substantively, away from the noise of the world, by a meaningful smile, the truth in a lover's eye, a touch of the hand. The take-away message is given in the chorus closer: "You say it best when you say nothing at all." A corollary to the celebration of nonverbal exchange in country is the wary warning against language, often set in the context of romantic love, as in Marty Robbins's "Pretty Words" (#12 1954)—which, the narrator laments, "make a fool out of me."

Closely related and sometimes interwoven with the implicit communication theme is that of "walk the walk" values. Arising frequently in country songs, this theme rehearses the notion that "walking the walk" and not merely "talking the talk"—action, not lip service to one's accomplishments or intentions—is the social and moral measure of a person. Empirical research has identified this principle as a salient value in working-class social worlds. Comparing patterns and expectations in working- and middle-class male and female friendships, the sociologist Karen Walker locates (what I am calling) "walk the walk" values centrally in working-class friendship, which tends toward reciprocity and interdependence with regard to material goods and services.[76] In *The Moral Significance of Class*, the British sociologist and self-styled "postdisciplinary" scholar Andrew Sayer clarifies the significance of this value in a working-class context. He observes that "recognition through deeds can speak louder than verbal recognition. I may *say* things that indicate recognition of you but if everything I *do* indicates insensitivity to your needs and disrespect of your intelligence and worth my words will be worthless."[77]

A walk-the-walk, actions-over-deeds model of working-class friendship is illustrated in Tracy Lawrence's No. 1 single "Find Out Who Your Friends Are" (2007). Built, like various other modern country songs, around a popular saying, the easy-riffing, mid-tempo song extols the true friends who are revealed when the chips are down, those who "show on up" with big hearts and lend material support—a ride, a couch, a loan—when you are "in a ditch" or "in a bind." By contrast to this model, middle-class friendships in Walker's study show no such patterns of material exchange and reciprocity. Instead, these relationships focus on shared interests and leisure and serve to enhance the individuality of those involved—through travel, for example, or as connoisseurs of music, food, or film.[78]

Analogous working-class values apply in the occupational sphere, where the worth of a job depends on its "usefulness," and there is contempt for those whose usefulness falls short of their prestige. In a Canadian study titled "'Too Much Money off Other People's Backs,'" the sociologist Michèle Ollivier interviews both working-class and professional middle-class subjects and compares their outlooks on various occupations. She finds, on the one hand, that electricians, members of the working class, value skilled trades and professions and deem them useful by contrast to managerial and white-collar occupations, which they acknowledge to be prestigious but sometimes characterize as "overblown" or "overpaid." On the other hand, assessments of occupations by professors, members of the professional middle class, accord with the status and pay each profession conventionally garners and typically invoke no usefulness standard.[79] This is exactly the sentiment expressed in Aaron Tippin's "Working Man's Ph.D." (#7 1993), an affirmation of the "pride, honor, and dignity" of those who do honest labor each day without benefit of trophies or titles, concluding with the observation that "a lot more people should be pulling their weight." Comparably, the concrete workers in Cyphert's study scorned the management activity of talk and valued coworkers who contributed materially, and nonverbally, to problem solving on the job site.

CLASSED STYLES OF INDIVIDUALISM

As much as the patterns and ideals of group behavior define different class cultures, so do the forms of individual selfhood, or subjectivity. With subjectivity as with collective culture, however, the middle-class version serves as the visible, normal, and "right" version in the culture at large. The cultural anthropologist Adrie Kusserow points out that a bourgeois-centric perspective prevails even in the observation-grounded field of ethnography, where theories of "the Western self" are often built on "a generic individualism based on the American upper-middle-class." This skewed, middle-class- and U.S.-centered concept of self also links to a skewed concept of individualism.

Kusserow notes that qualities like self-reliance, self-promotion, assertiveness, and "an inner sense of owning opinions" are lumped together under a notion of individualism that is treated as universal, ignoring group particularities in different classes, subcultures, and local worlds. At the same time, and also problematic, an established theoretical perspective in empirical scholarship views middle-class subjects as individualistic or "self-directed" and working-class subjects as socially oriented, "relational," or "conformist." Recognizing the group stereotypes that are produced and perpetuated by such formulations, Kusserow emphasizes that *both* individualism and group orientation, or "sociocentrism," coexist across all class communities. She therefore proposes a subtly different model of American individualism that is attentive to the different proportions and styles of individualism and sociocentrism in different communities. In her effort to tease apart and "de-homogenize" varieties of American individualism, Kusserow conducted ethnographic research on three socioeconomically distinct sites in the New York metropolitan area, focusing on the culturally revealing practices of child socialization.[80] It is important to recognize that, while we may observe working-class cultural practices among concrete crew members on the job site, classed subjects become acculturated as such long before they begin adult work lives. Indeed, as the British historian Carolyn Kay Steedman powerfully illustrates in *Landscape for a Good Woman*, class consciousness is "a structure of feeling that can be learned in childhood, . . . an understanding of the world that can be conveyed to children."[81] And it is no less central in women's lives than in those of the male, mostly white, laborers who have been the focus of so many discussions of the working class.

Before reviewing the details of Kusserow's findings, I would note one important way in which they are identical to those of countless other studies. Research on child socialization in all classes and communities shows that parents strive to instill the knowledge, skills, and behaviors that they believe will best allow their children to lead happy, successful, and worthwhile lives. Of course, if the beliefs guiding adults' child-rearing approaches were identical across all communities, there would be little need for Kusserow's, or similar, research. But in fact, parents' beliefs vary significantly, according to their experiences and locations in society. For example, middle-class parents and teachers may impress upon children the paramount importance of a high-quality education that extends well beyond high school, while working-class parents' most emphatic lessons may focus elsewhere and may even contradict this view. In both cases, the adults' perspectives and advice are informed by what has worked and what has failed for them and the people known to them in their lifeworlds.

Given the dominance of middle-class culture, the devaluation of working-class culture, and the increasing social and geographic segregation of classes in the United States, we should not be surprised that working-class cultural practices are not only invisible but fictive outside the working class. This is brought home to me when well-educated middle- and upper-class university students I work with daily and meet on my travels insist that surely all parents, *if they love their children*, want them to pursue as much education as they can get. The ethnocentrism of young adults unable to fathom genuinely loving, caring parents with priorities different from those of middle- and upper-class parents bespeaks no special perversity or failing on their part. Their ethnocentrism is the ethnocentrism of the dominant culture overall.

In fact, the benefits of formal education for the middle and upper classes do not extend in the same way to the working class. The sociologists Richard Sennett and Jonathan Cobb's classic 1972 study, *The Hidden Injuries of Class*, shows that interactions with professors and other students indeed allow privileged, culturally capitalized students to gain knowledge and confidence at college. But the same interactions instruct other students in their own inadequacy and unworthiness, "subjecting them to an unfamiliar set of rules in a game where respect is the prize."[82] Whether such students complete a degree or drop out, the results are at best a mixed bag. In the world of higher education, they learn to regard the lives, selves, and families they know with shame and embarrassment, thus experiencing what Bourdieu and coauthor Jean-Claude Passeron call "symbolic violence" in evaluating themselves by authoritative, universalized middle-class standards.[83]

Many Americans see formal education as giving people "the tools for achieving freedom—by permitting [them] to control situations" rather than obey orders and by furnishing them "with access to a greater set of roles in life." But Sennett and Cobb conclude, "What needs to be understood is how the class structure in America is organized so that *the tools of freedom become sources of indignity.*" Indeed, the signal contribution of their book may be its revelation of the extent to which the efforts and toils of working people are directed toward, not just material gains, but the pursuit of dignity.[84] Speaking from the realm of work rather than education, on the basis of his research in various cultures throughout the world, Scott reached similar conclusions: "Even in the case of the contemporary working class, it appears that slights to one's dignity and close surveillance and control of one's work loom at least as large in accounts of oppression as do narrower concerns of work and compensation."[85] Hence, the quest for dignity is one that working people cannot ignore and, as Fillingim shows, cannot be put off until the afterlife.

Kusserow's research on styles of individualism focused on white parents' socialization of preschool children in one upper- and upper-middle-class community in Manhattan and two working-class communities in Queens, one of which was upper working class and aspiring to upward class mobility and the other lower working class and "staying put."[86] Kusserow's accounts of child socialization in these three differently classed New York communities mirror those of a number of other studies. Her theoretical perspective, however, treating individualism and sociocentrism as elements in *both* upper- to upper-middle-class and working-class settings, provides a more accurate picture than the either/or lens sometimes applied elsewhere. By contrast to analyses that characterize only middle- and upper-class subjectivities in terms of individualism, Kusserow's study speaks of differing styles of "American individualism" across the class spectrum. Besides offering greater nuance, this model is consistent with contemporary individualistic notions of self.

Interviewing diversely classed subjects in and around Manchester, England, the British sociologist Mike Savage and his coauthors found contemporary self-understandings to be cast in individual terms and thus at odds with any self-identification in terms of social class—which would represent a category error. The researchers characterize the logic they encountered: "classes are 'out there,' part of the social fabric, whereas people themselves are 'individuals,' who by definition cannot be parts of classes."[87]

Under the heading of individualism, Kusserow divides the styles of child socialization she observed into "hard" and "soft" types, corresponding to her study's working-class and upper- to upper-middle class communities, respectively. Socialization styles were "hard" in the former case to prepare children for the challenges of a tough world and "soft" in the latter case to gently unfold children's unique potentials. The soft individualism practiced by upper-middle- and upper-class parents (here, primarily mothers) of preschoolers is meant to assist the child in gently, delicately unfolding a unique self, thoughts, and feelings. These parents believe that realizing their authentic desires and preferences will allow children to be happy and self-actualized and to go forward "in a competitive society." Their socialization style involves great emphasis on the use of words to express feelings and desires. It encourages the child's perceived need for psychological privacy and so seeks to save face and to avoid humiliating the child. It also grants the child a sense of empowerment and control through discipline by suggestion and explanation, not command, and by qualifying discipline with apology. The approach attempts to put children on "equal footing" with adults, eliminating any adult-child power differential—something that upper- and upper-middle-class mothers and teachers, but not their working-class counterparts, view as damaging.

In the soft style, "self-confidence and expression of the child's unique feelings [are] paramount." Here, "talk of autonomy, uniqueness, individuality, and self-confidence" intertwines with "talk of the importance and rights of the psychological self (emotions, feelings, desires, tastes, personality) to emerge and be the best it can be." Children are allowed to express qualities including stubbornness and strong will, and parents are pleased to see such expressions—which would be out of line for children in other communities. These upper-middle- and upper-class parents regard societal constraints as a threat to children's budding individualism. Too much structure might inhibit children's expression of their unique selves and feelings. Group-oriented, or sociocentric, practices are seen as a threat to the child's individuality—indeed, even treating children as part of a social group (e.g., girls, boys, children) is seen here as demeaning.[88]

Lower-working-class parents practicing hard individualism speak of hardening the self to prepare children for survival in a harsh world. This notion is familiar in country music, too, where the classic example is Johnny Cash's "Boy Named Sue" (#1 1969). This comic song contains one poignant moment: the climactic revelation that the feminine name the narrator's father bestowed just before abandoning him was meant to help him grow up tough. Valuing toughness, the lower-working-class community in Kusserow's study exhibited the only parenting style in which mothers made little effort to save children's face. These mothers did not shield children, for fear of damaging their self-esteem, from the evidence of the adults' annoyance, boredom, or disinterest. The British psychologists Valerie Walkerdine and Helen Lucey discuss the same tendencies among working-class mothers and further note that the mothers speak openly with their preschool children about money and financial pressures (with the result that working-class children are far more knowledgeable and less naive about the workings of money than their middle-class peers).[89] Kusserow's lower-working-class mothers stressed not coddling children lest they become too soft, and not praising them too much lest they grow full of themselves. She notes that overconfidence can lead the child into hazards (and I would add that seeming cocky or arrogant can itself be a liability in working-class worlds).

In this view, children need strong values—family, structure, consistency, and hard work—to form a sturdy foundation they can "fall back on in hard times." Lower-working-class mothers and teachers instill a protective, defensive, independent, self-reliant style of individualism. Children will not always get what they want, so they need to learn hard truths and how to toughen up. Techniques for teaching necessary toughness and boundaries include humor and teasing at school and at home—for developing a thicker skin, as it were (something rarely practiced on the upper- and upper-middle-class site)—and a "get over it" attitude. Mothers do not always respond to whining and pleas, and preschoolers are praised for doing things on their own and for fighting their own fights and defending themselves in dealing with others.[90]

In the adjacent parenting style of the upper working class, mothers also speak of hardening the self, but with another aim: to allow children to ascend the class ladder—hence, more for self-determination and achievement than self-defense and survival.[91] In both of the working-class styles, parents use sociocentric discipline—encouraging the child to identify with the group and their social role (sister, brother, daughter, student) and encouraging "cooperation, empathy, conformity, and knowing one's place in a hierarchy"—without evident concern about damaging a child's self-esteem or building the child back up afterward, as the "soft"-style mothers and teachers do following a perceived possible injury. Both working-class "hard" styles use sociocentric and individualistic practices simultaneously and nonchalantly. Adults here seem to assume that children possess greater resilience and hardiness than soft-style adults do in their treatment of children as delicate beings.[92]

In her widely acclaimed book *Unequal Childhoods*, the sociologist Annette Lareau found comparable differences between middle-class and poor and working-class parenting practices by studying black and white families of nine- and ten-year-olds at both class levels (classed patterns of parenting were similar regardless of race). Lareau observed a middle-class parenting style that she labels "concerted cultivation," characterized by hectic extracurricular schedules meant to discover and develop children's interests and talents. She also observed a poor and working-class parenting style, which she terms the "accomplishment of natural growth," in which children have more autonomy, unstructured playtime, and daily interaction with siblings and relatives and are expected to resolve social conflicts among peers without adult arbitration.[93]

In addition to identifying contemporary classed practices of child rearing, Lareau's study analyzes the social, and broader, consequences of these differing cultures. Starting in grade school, poor and working-class children suffer adverse effects because of differences between their home culture and its values and those of the dominant culture, especially within institutions: school, health care organizations, and state agencies. School staff perceive poor and working-class parents' deferential behavior—their deliberate noninterference with teachers' authority—as evidence of a lack of engagement, and they divest their energies from such families. The children's own deferential behavior toward adults—a sign of good training and source of pride within their communities—is a key factor in perpetuating their disadvantages in institutional contexts. Middle-class children, by contrast, are socialized from earliest childhood to engage with adults as equals. Their eye-to-eye negotiation skills allow them to articulate their views and wishes to those in power, and they learn a sense of entitlement that is reinforced at school and in other institutional settings. Such advantages—and, on the other side, disadvantages—have been shown to compound substantially over time, in social, cultural, and economic dimensions.

The sociologist Jeannie Thrall studied upper- and lower-middle-class parents in the university town of Ann Arbor, Michigan, and found, as both Kusserow and Lareau did with their class-disparate samples, differing ratios of individualism to sociocentrism between the groups. Upper-middle-class families in Thrall's study placed cultivation of children's individual distinction ahead of social interaction. These families sacrificed family group interaction and development of children's family responsibilities, and limited children's social interaction with peers—viewing the latter (along with pop-culture exposure) as a downward-mobility threat—in favor of their pursuit of elite individual achievement, the subsidized and heavily supported pursuit of "passions and gifts." By contrast, lower-middle-class parents emphasized personal responsibility for one's actions and a different standard of performance: "do your best." These families were not willing to pursue individual distinctive achievement, which would have prevented family and peer social group interactions.[94]

Preschool students' linguistic practices are the subject of related research by the sociologist Jessi Streib. Her observations find that four-year-olds are already aware of class difference and engaged in behaviors that reproduce it. In Streib's study, the principal means of children's performance of socioeconomic class at a class-diverse (and to that extent, unusual) midwestern preschool is linguistic style. Her results align with several decades' literature on children's classed linguistic styles demonstrating that upper-middle-class children "have larger vocabularies, speak more often, interrupt more, and feel more entitled to speak to teachers than their working-class counterparts." These children's language style "distinguishes them from the working-class children and confers [on] them . . . the power both to direct classroom events and to further improve their own language skills. They 'take the floor' while inadvertently silencing working-class children." With Bourdieu and Lareau, Streib emphasizes that language is "intimately tied to class and power."[95]

In Streib's study, upper-middle-class children often prevailed over working-class children in classroom conflicts. Even when a working-class child was in the right, upper-middle-class children's profuse and confident use of language in the school's preferred style often led teachers to decide matters in their favor. Upper-middle-class children's advantage in preschool begins with the fact that their home linguistic and cultural style and the school linguistic and cultural style are one and the same, with no translation or adaptation required. Streib's observations registered the embodied, implicit communication of one working-class girl's "pleading eyes" directed at the teacher when a toy was snatched away from her, in violation of classroom rules. But in an institutional culture whose motto is "Use your words," implicit communication is not recognized as communication, and a middle-class toy snatcher who talks a good line (the boy in Streib's classroom did) stands a strong chance of winning a favorable verdict from the teacher-adjudicator. Working-class and middle-class children alike, albeit from opposite angles, learn at preschool a model of institutional justice in which often it is not what you do that counts but who you are and where you come from.[96] However early this lesson may be learned, it seems there are people for whom it continues to chafe even many years later. The same scenario of tilted justice provides the grounds for vindication, playing to listeners' identification and catharsis, in "Harper Valley P.T.A." and other country songs of working-class resentment.

CLASSED SUBJECTIVITY AND MUSICAL STYLE

The class-linked styles of subjectivity observed by Kusserow and Lareau in their studies of child socialization match those reported in other research on adults, including two influential major studies by Lamont and recent social psychology research by Alana Snibbe and Hazel Rose Markus.

Like Kusserow, Snibbe and Markus question the universalizing notion, frequently assumed in the social sciences and more broadly, that there is an American style of subjectivity and that it emphasizes expressing uniqueness and exerting control over one's environment. In a 2005 article, they offer several original studies showing that white Americans of different socioeconomic status, either working- or middle-class, engage with different symbolic and material worlds and thus have different ideas about what it means to be a subject in society. Their research suggests that the style of subjectivity most prevalent in middle-class contexts indeed emphasizes expressing uniqueness and exerting outward, environmental control, but that another American style of subjectivity, prevalent in working-class contexts, emphasizes maintaining personal integrity—honesty, loyalty, reliability, and consistency across situations, including acting the same way no matter who one is with—and exerting inward, *self*-control. As the authors put it, being a subject in middle-class contexts "means actualizing and expressing one's unique, internal attributes—actions that often require arranging or changing the world to reflect those attributes." By contrast, being a subject in working-class contexts "means maintaining one's personal integrity—an action that often requires steeling oneself" against the world to deal with the demands of a challenging situation.[97]

Snibbe and Markus also directly address questions of popular music in relation to classed subjectivity. One part of their research uses 2000 U.S. Census data from over 14,000 respondents to establish that the probability of liking country music decreases with educational attainment, while the probability of liking rock increases with educational attainment (results were the same using income in place of education). Their data (cited above) on the rates of country appreciation in differing U.S. regions can be further considered in relation to middle-class cultural omnivorism and Bryson's finding that it excludes country, and also to the "univore" taste that researchers identify as its counterpart, whereby working-class subjects supposedly prefer country (or another style) to the exclusion of other musics.[98] Another part of Snibbe and Markus's study blind-codes the content of hit country and rock song lyrics and finds that country and rock model subjectivities matching, respectively, working-class and middle-class styles (as defined by their review of the relevant research literature). Thus, being a subject in country songs "more frequently means having integrity, controlling the self, and resisting social influence," whereas being a subject in rock songs "more frequently entails being unique, actualizing and expressing that uniqueness, and exerting social influence."[99]

Still another part of the study links these two styles of subjectivity to actual working- and middle-class subjects through a pair of experiments examining individuals' responses to choice. Snibbe and Markus tested responses in two situations, one in which subjects were allowed to choose an object and another in which their choice was solicited and then thwarted when they were given an object other than the one they chose. The first experiment found that middle-class study participants "spread alternatives": they revised their assessments after the fact to elevate (as the best possible choice) the object they chose and devalue the one they rejected. Working-class subjects, by contrast, did not revise their assessment of the chosen object, a CD.[100] In the second experiment, participants chose a free gift—one of several different makes and models of $1 pens—and then received either the chosen pen or a different one. In response to the threat to (what one theory views as) their freedom of choice, preference-thwarted middle-class subjects assessed the unchosen pen below the chosen one in design, function, ink quality, or overall—thus behaving as predicted by psychological theory. Working-class respondents, however, assessed unchosen gift pens equally with chosen pens.[101]

This last response on the part of working-class subjects aligns with an adage cited by Garth Brooks in CD liner notes to his classic hit "Unanswered Prayers" (#1 1991): "Happiness isn't getting what you want; it is wanting what you've got."[102] The results in both experiments jibe, too, with the aims of hard parenting styles as outlined by Kusserow, to the extent that working-class subjects here seem to accept the free gifts that come their way with little fuss and, when the gifts are not what they asked for, a "get over it" attitude. Both experiments lend further support to the "country" and "rock" styles of subjectivity proposed by Snibbe and Markus: the working-class style, also modeled in country lyrics, of maintaining one's integrity despite the world; and the middle-class style, also modeled in rock lyrics, of expressing one's uniqueness in the world. Notably, each experiment finds that a relevant psychological theory applies to middle-class study participants alone, and thus these results suggest that the influential theories falsely universalize—and even ascribe to hard-wired human cognition—what is in fact a middle-class model of subjectivity.

Acknowledging that white working- and middle-class cultures are overlapping and not mutually exclusive, Snibbe and Markus characterize the differences in behavior observed here as differences of relative emphasis between the class cultures. They discuss some of the differences between working-class and middle-class symbolic and material worlds that might account for class groups' differing ideas about subjectivity. Lower class-status occupations generally pay less than higher class-status occupations and afford less choice, autonomy, and control, the authors explain, and they point out that lower class-status adults, "owing in part to less wealth and income," have "fewer and more dangerous places where they can afford to live, . . . less geographic mobility, . . . less leisure time, . . . and worse health outcomes" than higher class-status adults. Snibbe and Markus follow Bourdieu in interpreting their data in relation to material constraints on working-class life—limited resources and foreshortened choices (by welcome contrast to research, much of it from the past, focusing on putative genetic deficiencies in the working class). It is important to note, however, that the culture of any group is always a creative production forged with and against the conditions of its life and environment, and never merely the foreseeable result of those conditions. Working-class culture *as* culture is just as elaborate and coded as middle-class culture and is no more inevitable, utilitarian, or transparent in its own right. It is the two cultures, and the conditions engaged by them, that differ—not their status as full-fledged cultures. Relatedly, Lawler objects to narratives viewing the working class only in terms of lack, not for their determinism per se but for their dehumanizing effect, inasmuch as they "rob the subjects of such narratives of any moral value."[103]

Snibbe and Markus's findings suggest that different forms of subjectivity prevalent in the working and middle classes assign different roles to choice. These results support their hypothesis that working-class subjectivity is focused on controlling a "reliable self" for whom "independence is defined as having integrity." Here, making choices may be less relevant to individual agency than is assumed by universalizing models that operate in psychological theory and in public discourse, including journalism and scholarship. The authors speculate that the reason working-class subjects do not react to the threat to their "freedom" in these experiments is that *exercising choice is not how they conceive of their freedom as independent subjects*. For middle-class subjects, however, "choice is a primary medium through which agency is lived," the means by which unique attributes, preferences, and positions are expressed, and thus the means by which a middle-class self is brought into being.[104]

Such findings are crucial for understanding and interpreting country music, and equally for understanding why many middle-class audiences and critics dislike and misread country music. All popular music models styles of subjectivity, through songs and artists; it speaks to listeners as subjects, about and through their subjective styles, stances, and options; and it is a potent means by which subjects are marked as belonging to certain styles of subjectivity—including, in postwar America, such subject styles as punk, Goth, bobby soxer, and hepcat. Audience affinity with the styles of self associated with a given style of popular music is powerfully linked to fandom. So country music's resonance with working-class subjectivity, culture, and values suggests one reason that working-class subjects might like country more often than middle-class subjects do. Admiration for individuals who behave the same way regardless of who is present, for example, offers further explanation for the persistence of claims like the one cited above about Loretta Lynn: "Even in sequins and chiffon, the pride of Butcher Holler, Ky., will always be the coal miner's daughter next door." Of course, middle-class listeners also face disincentives to engaging with country music, given that its association with the working class can threaten middle-class identity status. Bryson found that middle-class agents of "multicultural capital" excluded country from their fashionably inclusive tastes. And Lawler reminds us that since middle-classness is defined precisely in opposition to working-classness, the first requirement for being middle class is *not* being working class. Looking, or sounding, working class can endanger middle-class status and privilege.[105]

WORKING-CLASS REPERTOIRES AND COUNTRY AESTHETICS

In a revealing follow-up study included in the second edition of *Unequal Childhoods*, Lareau revisited the lives of the middle-class and working-class ten-year-olds from her research sample a decade after their original work together. Discussing the results, she flags signs of America's growing dissatisfaction with the costs and effects of middle-class child-rearing culture, with its intensive investments in talent cultivation and college applications. Lareau urges social researchers to devote attention to the drawbacks of middle-class family life and adds a further injunction: "there should be more studies of the potential advantages of the cultural repertoires of working-class and poor families." She notes that scholars "remain focused on searching out deficits" in working-class and poor parents' child-rearing practices "rather than probing the limits of middle-class cultural practices."[106]

Lareau's proposition that working-class cultural practices might offer advantages over those of the dominant culture is rarely encountered in American academic or policy dialogues. The notion arises often, however, in country music. In "(What This World Needs Is) A Few More Rednecks" (1989), Charlie Daniels advocates "A little less talk and a little more action" as one of the benefits to be derived from having a few more rednecks around—meaning (within the term's race-specific purview) more working people: "What most people call a redneck / Ain't nothin' but a workin' man," the narrator avows. The song thus gives voice to working-class walk-the-walk values while devaluing talk. Another lyric, "I don't believe in mindin' / No one's business but my own," asserts the importance of not judging others within the song's code of working-class values. Daniels's track, like so many others in country, rehearses and celebrates what the narrator stands for, yielding a laundry list of working-class "redneck" values. Middle-class critiques, as we have seen, express irritation and disgust at the professions of "country" values heard repeatedly in this music. But contrary to critics' claims, the countless country records enumerating what it means and why it is important to "be country" (or "redneck," "working people," "common folk") are neither pointless nor nonsensical.

In "A Few More Rednecks" as in many similar songs, being working class is an engaged act, not a passive state of being, and a meaningful cultural practice, not merely an identity. Such songs assert the existence of a subordinated culture, that is, working-class culture; articulate a repertoire of values and practices that define the culture (these vary somewhat from song to song, showing that such definition is dynamic and contested); and insist on the worth of this culture, its repertoires, and its members against the everyday, commonplace pathologizing of all these in the dominant culture. But it is not only "country pride" songs that embody working-class cultural repertoires. Across a wide range of song topics, country music engages with working-class cultural values and practices, sounding the working-class subject in tones that resonate with the classed cultures, rhetorics, and subjectivities discussed in this chapter.

Dominant-culture critiques of country music often complain of its trite-ness, reliance on formula, or lack of innovation. A central factor in these critiques is the practice of othering, which can cause any unfamiliar style of music to sound "all the same." So whereas a knowledgeable country listener might discern something fresh and ingenious in a particular pedal steel gui-tar solo, an unacculturated listener may register little beyond the presence of this "weepy" instrumental timbre that is not merely neglected, but avoided outside of country music. Indeed, Shania Twain rose to crossover fame in the 1990s by releasing alternate versions of her records in which the pedal steel and fiddle tracks that were included for country radio rotation were strategically removed for pop audiences.[107] So marked is the sound of pedal steel that its occurrence, and that of other marked country character-istics like twangy vocals and fiddle sounds, is likely to make a pronounced impression on inexperienced listeners, who may recall the presence of these elements in a song above all else. The marked perception of unfamiliar ele-ments cognitively crowds out other details and leads one to index the music in terms of its perceived differences from other, familiar music.[108] Thus to an uninitiated (or deliberately distanced) listener, a certain country song may be heard as the song with the pedal steel guitar—or twangy vocals, or fiddle, or "being country" theme—and on hearing a few more country songs con-taining the same (from this perspective) salient element, such a listener might wonder why all country songs sound so much alike. Othering of an artistic object is incompatible with critical discernment.

But othering is not the only mechanism at work in charges of triteness in country. Commentators on country music often bring unexamined and culturally incongruous values to the task of criticism. Originality, for exam-ple, is not a universal good, equally prized in all times and places. Rather, it is a cultural construct with a specific history. For contemporary American purposes, that history is rooted in twentieth-century modernism, a cultural movement that, in its self-consciousness toward a weighty past, placed a premium on novelty and, in its anxiety about identifying creative genius, exalted exceptionalism and revered originality. Originality is also, arguably, the supreme principle in rock music. It is not the supreme principle in country. Country is the music, after all, in which a beloved heartbreak song by the Carter Family, "I'm Thinking Tonight of My Blue Eyes" (1929), sup-plied the tune for a major country-gospel (pre-chart-era) hit by Roy Acuff, "Great Speckled Bird" (1937), which was in turn recycled for Hank Thompson's blockbuster plaint against faithless women, "The Wild Side of

Life" (#1 1952), and its answer song, Kitty Wells's proto-feminist megahit, "It Wasn't God Who Made Honky-Tonk Angels." To be sure, the spectacular fourfold appearance of the "Blue Eyes" tune is a singular (and early) instance, but it does suggest the presence of criteria other than originality driving country song conception and audience response.

One of these criteria is feeling. Sample and Fox, and the anthropologist Kathleen Stewart before them, identify the conjuring and intensification of feeling as a central aim of country music. Sample, the working-class theologian, observes that working people tend not to focus on or discuss their interior lives very much by comparison to the middle and, especially, professional middle classes. Country serves an important function for working-class listeners by singing their feelings and rendering them vivid. Hence the country singer Webb Pierce's oft-quoted account of how to make a hit song: "You sing about the things they think about most, but don't talk about." Sample also emphasizes the low cultural status accorded to the feelings of those who are granted low status in society. He cites the sociologist Arlie Russell Hochschild, who notes that the feelings of high-status people tend to be noticed and deemed important, whereas the feelings of low-status people tend to be viewed either as unimportant or as irrational and therefore dismissable. Thus, Sample points out, just as working-class taste is a dominated aesthetic, working-class affect is likewise dominated. He posits that because of these factors it is difficult to appreciate fully the deep significance of country music for working-class fans—that of hearing one's (marginalized) feelings sung in a style consistent with one's (devalued) tastes. In this way, country music feeds what Sample terms a "hunger of soul."[109]

Stewart reads country as embodying a cultural poetics of romance, in which life is a quest. Within this frame, she analyzes country's tearjerkers as neither naive nor literalistic but as knowingly reproducing an old, stylized and conventionalized "poetics of intensification"—and thus practicing an artistic technique for heightening feeling.[110] Fox identifies feeling as a central social and musical concept among the Texas working-class country devotees in his study. These country music lovers place feeling at the pinnacle of their aesthetic, social, and musical evaluations. So a really good night at the honky-tonk (the site of Fox's research) is one when there is a live band on stage, and the musicians and everyone in the place are locked onto the *feeling*. The operative notion of feeling, on Fox's analysis, joins together two dimensions, of deft language—including clever, pretty, and penetrating words—and compelling embodiment, especially through rhythms that inspire movement. In this conception of feeling, a kind of working person's *jouissance*, the whole is greater than the sum of its parts.

For feeling gives rise to another quality entirely, a "third dimension" uniting memory, emotion, sociability, storytelling, and especially the human voice, which is, through speaking and singing, "the very meeting point" of language and embodiment.[111]

Fox finds not only that musical feeling is a medium of sociability that "mediates friendships" for working-class country listeners, but that certain songs and voices can evoke past experiences and bring cherished past feelings into the present.[112] His and Sample's analyses of the workings of feeling in country music can counter the accusation, articulated by Forbis, that country is "disingenuous" in its emphasis on tradition over modernity. In the dominant cultural perspective of Forbis and other commentators, the working-class aesthetic is not so much opaque as it is nonexistent. Since, from this vantage point, working-class culture lacks realness, its products appear phony and disingenuous.

But if the purpose of country music is shared feeling and recapturing past feelings has special social and aesthetic value in working-class country music culture, then it is only logical that country songs often seek, not simply to portray, but to *evoke* the past, through lyrical themes and stylistic elements. Country radio hits like Mark Wills's "19 Somethin'" (#1 2003), Tim McGraw's "Back When" (#1 2004) and "Southern Voice" (#1 2010), and Brad Paisley's "Welcome to the Future" (#2 2009) recite litanies of persons, events, and trends from listeners' lived pasts or an American past known through parents, grandparents, or history. With the lines "Saw *Star Wars* at least eight times / Had the Pac-Man pattern memorized . . . Farrah Fawcett hairdo days / Bell bottoms and eight-track tapes," the narrator in "19 Somethin'" places his childhood in the 1970s, moving forward through other decades to locate his coming-of-age and adulthood and, in closing, to express nostalgia for a simpler time in his own life. Dr. (Martin Luther) King, the space shuttle *Challenger* disaster, Rosa Parks, and the fatal crash of Number Three (Dale Earnhardt) are among the landmark events and personages that parade by in these songs' lyrics. Back When songs (to borrow McGraw's title) are well designed not only for conjuring listeners' past feelings, but for making them the basis of shared collective feeling, experience, and existence.

SUBSTANCE AND SURFACE IN COUNTRY AND THE WORKING CLASS (CONCLUSION)

A similar emphasis on time's passing animates what might aptly be called the Three-Verse Life Cycle song in country, of which "A Father's Love" by

Bucky Covington is one example. Others are Brad Paisley's potent tear-jerker "He Didn't Have to Be" (#1 1999), Alan Jackson's self-penned "Drive (for Daddy Gene)" (#1 2002), and Kenny Chesney's "There Goes My Life" (#1 2003), a song whose title frames the requisite kaleidoscopic chorus (to coin a phrase), offering a vision that shifts with each turn of the verses. The first statement of that chorus punctuates the opening verse, in which a young man learns that he is about to become a father and laments his plans, now dashed, to escape his hometown and travel the country, remarking, "There goes my life." The second verse finds the young man and his partner raising their toddler daughter, and when she climbs the stairs at bedtime, he muses, "There goes my life," his heart brimming. The third verse finds the daughter grown up and leaving home, and in the final chorus "There goes my life" becomes a wistful statement and summation of the protagonist's adult life to that point. Both the Three-Verse Life Cycle and the Back When song genres afford listeners the opportunity to reflect on the significance of ordinary lives, and on ordinary, utterly precedented patterns in their own lives. From a perspective sympathetic to working-class experience, this reveling in shared ordinariness can reflect a rich sociality and humble humanity. From a perspective presuming middle-class values of exceptional individualism, the same scenario is described in terms of conformity, and social intolerance is read into the celebration of ordinariness (construed in terms of an enforced normalcy).

From a middle-class perspective, too, the focus on parent-child relationships in so many country songs—including not only Chesney's "There Goes My Life" but Covington's "A Father's Love (The Only Way He Knew How)," Cash's "A Boy Named Sue," "Fancy" as recorded by both Gentry and McEntire, Haggard's "Mama Tried," and McBride's "Independence Day" (to name just a few)—may seem curious. Grossman's article devotes considerable attention to this element of country thematics and concludes that "Mama is elevated in country music to the level of a god."[113] Her overstatement here may reflect the unexpectedness, from a dominant-culture perspective, of the appreciation accorded to mothers (and fathers) in country music. This may connect in turn to marked differences researchers have observed between working- and middle-class children's tendencies toward empathy for their parents. In her classic study of working-class families, *Worlds of Pain*, the sociologist and psychotherapist Lillian B. Rubin heard "exactly . . . opposite" responses from working-class and professional middle-class adult children concerning their parents, with the middle-class progeny (encouraged by therapeutic culture) expressing anger and resentment about the ways their parents had failed them and their working-class counterparts (despite often painful childhoods) empathizing with their parents in their own difficulties.[114] The studies by Walkerdine and Lucey and by Kusserow registered corresponding differences in child-rearing practices: while working-class parents did not conceal from children the difficulties and sacrifices they faced as parents, middle-class parents invisibilized them. Lareau observed comparable differences between the working- and middle-class ten-year-olds in her study and noted in her follow-up a significant difference between the two groups, now at age twenty, in their recognition of parents' sacrifices on their behalf: working-class youths showed "striking awareness," while middle-class youths were "much less aware."[115]

Ortner observes that middle-class parent-child relations show a "chronic friction and explosive potential," and she explains this, interestingly, as a sign that middle-class parent-child relations carry "much of the burden of introjected 'class struggle' and even class 'war.'" Middle-class families devote enormous effort and resources to ensuring that children maintain middle-class status in their adult lives. Anxious about life-determining issues of education, occupation, and partnering, middle-class parents attempt to control their children's lives and choices well into adolescence and beyond. Seeing their children "as embodying the threat of a working-class future" (Ehrenreich's "Fear of Falling"), the parents seek to impose control, "and the children respond in kind." They criticize their parents' (class) values and rebel precisely by taking on symbols of lower-class affiliation: hair, music, dress, speech, and sometimes relationships. Thus, on Ortner's analysis, the middle-class "discourse of parent-child conflict . . . is simultaneously a class discourse."[116] And this critical, conflictual discourse contrasts with the typically loving, often empathetic child-parent discourse that has long featured prominently in country music.

Elsewhere, we might also flag the note of fatalism in "There Goes My Life," a note that figures in many country song narratives. The song suggests that what once seemed disastrous, the unexpected and early arrival of parenthood, might have been a blessing in disguise. Its narrative accords with the popular saying "Things works out for the best"—or, more deterministically, "Everything happens for a reason." In Garth Brooks's signature song, "The Dance" (#1 1990), the narrator looks back on an ill-fated love and concludes in the refrain that he is better off for having allowed fate to run its heartbreaking course: "Our lives are better left to chance; I could have missed the pain, / But I'd have had to miss the dance." Country lyrics frequently invoke the popular wisdom rehearsed in Trisha Yearwood's "She's in Love with the Boy" (#1 1991), "What's meant to be will always find a way." Similarly, in another No. 1 hit from 1991, Brooks attests that "some of God's greatest gifts are unanswered prayers." The track, "Unanswered Prayers," fleshes out this clincher line with a vignette in which the narrator perceives through a chance encounter that the high school girlfriend he had fervently prayed for would not have been as good a life partner for him as the woman he actually married.

The lyric then takes a turn into another important country genre rehearsing working-class values, the Count Your Blessings genre. In "Unanswered Prayers," the pivotal lyric expressly invokes God: "I looked at my wife / And then and there I thanked the Good Lord / For the good things in my life." Many, if not most, examples of this genre are secular, however. The impulse to count your blessings in these songs is one of opportunity more than obligation, to summon feelings of strength, calm, and joy by taking inventory of the good things one has, especially in the realm of what really matters—family and friends—by contrast, implicit or explicit, to how bad life could be. Jessica Andrews scored a big hit with "Who I Am" (#1 2001), which registers these sentiments while expressly rejecting achievement-based standards of a person's worth. Featuring the fresh, youthful voice of a teenage Andrews, the catchiest "earworm" moment in this track is the chorus's beginning, on the rhythmical couplet, "I am Rosemary's granddaughter / The spitting image of my father," which is followed by further inventorying of the narrator's self-constituting bonds with family and friends who are "all a part of me." Given their love and support, and because they know "where I stand" and "who I am," the narrator can declare, "If I . . . never see the seven wonders / That'll be all right," and "If I don't make it to the big leagues . . . never win a Grammy / I'm gonna be just fine." To count your blessings here is to celebrate, not the ordinariness (or normalcy, or traditionalism) per se, but the richness and sufficiency of an ordinary life and the freedom that comes from recognizing this and from feeling oneself part of a supportive and accepting community.

In another arena, occupational rather than personal, Cyphert's rhetorical analysis identifies similar working-class cultural perspectives. She underscores the productivity of a work crew adept at accommodating changes in the environment, and she challenges the dominant culture's judgment of working-class accommodation as a dysfunctional fatalism and, by classed standards of goal orientation and control, a failure. Snibbe and Markus recognize related class repertoires in their identification of working-class subjects' "non-reactant" acceptance of thwarted choice. Kusserow, Lareau, and other researchers show that working-class families purposefully prepare children to respond to life's inevitable thwartings of desire with appropriate perspective and minimal fuss. This mirroring of country musical themes in social research on the working class does not suggest that all country listeners, or creators, are members of the working class or that all working-class people listen to country music: of course, neither proposition is true. But it does reinforce the notion that country traffics in working-class values and repertoires.

Country music thus performs a type of cultural work that is performed by popular music generally. It models subjectivity in forms relevant to its listeners. In country songs as in working-class worlds, young people learn that they will not always get what they want, and life will not always turn out as they had planned. What is important is to hold onto the dignity, self-, and life preservers of personal values and to maintain personal integrity, so as not to be distracted or derailed by the world's surprises, judgments, and disappointments. The working-class repertoires modeled in country songs offer methods for coping with desires and dreams denied, from an unchosen pen to an unexpected child, and worse. For contemporary country, unusually by popular music standards, treats real-life themes of hard times, including facing serious illness and facing death, one's own and that of loved ones. Country's uniqueness in this regard is emphasized by Brad Paisley in "This Is Country Music" (#2 2010): "You're not supposed to say / The word *cancer* in a song . . . But this is country music, and we do." The term *fatalism* connotes powerlessness, but the cultural and musical messages here are not about that. Neither do they present an all-powerful individual. Rather, these messages stress the power of cultivating a connected, contextual understanding of self within a big picture assuming unknown factors and a time span greater than one's individual present, known reality.

The outlook just described is consistent with the sociocentric (vs. exceptional) style of individualism that structures working-class subjectivity in the findings of Cyphert, Kusserow, Lareau, Thrall, and other researchers. This outlook is also consistent with a larger ethos that ties together instances of working-class cultural logic demonstrated throughout this chapter. It is an ethos of skepticism toward surface appearances—including the labelings and representations crafted by middle-class experts—and a trust in deeper substance. This ethos of substance over surface can be seen in Fillingim's hillbilly humanism, with its rejection of worldly hierarchies and judgments and steadfast focus on the deeper truth of all persons' equal worth; in the emphasis on walk-the-walk action and devaluation of talk demonstrated by Cyphert's concrete crew and Ollivier's study of "useful" occupations, as well as country songs like "When You Say Nothing at All"; in working-class friendship research by Walker and country songs treating friendship, like Tracy Lawrence's "Find Out Who Your Friends Are," stressing material support between friends; in the concern with maintaining internal integrity rather than imprinting one's unique qualities outwardly onto the world, documented by Snibbe and Markus in country (vs. rock) lyrics and in working-class (vs. middle-class) subjects; and in the music-aesthetic evaluative focus, identified by both Sample and Fox, on the soul-level quality of musical *feeling* over other, institutionally sanctioned criteria like innovation and originality.

Two No. 1 country radio hits appreciated for the deep feeling they inspire through their sensitive lyrics and vocal tracks (among other features) are Chesney's "There Goes My Life" and Brooks's "Unanswered Prayers." If the renown of these records depended on achieving distinction through innovation or originality, both would likely be rarities today. "There Goes My Life" presents a narrative and moral that readily bring to mind Frank Capra's classic 1946 film, *It's a Wonderful Life,* whose protagonist also finds his dreams of small-town escape reined in by a web of family and community duties and entanglements, which he, too, eventually embraces as life's most precious treasures. And the climactic chorus in "Unanswered Prayers" is musically reminiscent of that of another major hit, Dionne Warwick's Grammy-winning pop single, "I'll Never Love This Way Again" (#5 Pop 1979), all the more powerfully for being in the same key and similar tempo. For some listeners, such resemblances would constitute evidence of ineptness or illegitimacy, but for listeners attuned primarily to the feeling evoked by a song, these resonances with other works can be acceptable or even, conceivably, an enriching asset. They are likewise compatible with an ethos elevating substance over surface. After all, a good story is a good story, and a good tune is a good tune—never mind the window dressing.

In a similar vein, there is a popular saying that facts can often obscure the truth. The expression bespeaks a relationship to facts and truth that is known to working-class country listeners, people who do not own or produce the facts. Those privileges belong to the middle class, who wield cultural authority and, with powerful institutional backing, articulate official knowledge, including the facts that assert the low value and blameworthiness of working-class people. We might wonder why country music, in its address of working-class themes and topics, does not take issue with this ordering of the world. In fact, it does—as we shall now see.

PART II

Rednecks, Country Music, and the Queer

3. Gender Deviance and Class Rebellion in "Redneck Woman"

In 2004 Gretchen Wilson exploded onto the country music scene with "Redneck Woman." The blockbuster single led to the early release of her first CD, *Here for the Party,* and propelled it to triple platinum sales that year, the highest for a debut in any musical category. "Redneck Woman" shot to No. 1 faster than any country track in the previous decade and held the top spot for five weeks. Wilson garnered a raft of distinctions, including a Grammy for best country song and best female vocalist honors from both the Country Music and American Music Awards (see figure 9).

The record was a milestone in country music and in Wilson's career: she went in a few weeks from struggling Nashville unknown to top-selling Nashville star. In the process, the "Redneck Woman" she had created with cowriter and MuzikMafia crewmate John Rich became not only her signature song but her star persona. "Redneck Woman" was the tagline that served to introduce Wilson in public appearances and media features. The neck of her guitar even proclaimed "REDNECK" in mother-of-pearl inlay. More than a nickname, the handle keyed to a network of images, attributes, and attitudes that Wilson represented and that, for fans, represented her in an essential way. Loretta Lynn was the Coal Miner's Daughter, Johnny Cash was the Man in Black, and now Gretchen Wilson was the Redneck Woman. Anyone curious about the meaning of any of these monikers could simply listen to the eponymous song.

All three songs have served as identity totems for their singers and the fans who have embraced them. All are first-person narrations on themes that have been prevalent in postwar country music, including an identification with humble folk—both the materially impoverished and the socially scorned. "Coal Miner's Daughter" (#1 1970) poignantly chronicles the singer's hardscrabble family origins in a Kentucky holler. Its message is

FIGURE 9.   The cover of Gretchen Wilson's 2006 debut album, *Here for the Party*, pictured the singer as the "Redneck Woman" of her blockbuster single. Courtesy of Country Music Hall of Fame® and Museum.

familiar to country fans: We were poor, but we had love—of God and each other. The narrator in "Man in Black" (#3 1971) explains that he shuns color in his dress to protest poverty, hopelessness, and lives lost to war and imprisonment. That song's lyrics invoke another champion of the down-trodden, Jesus. The persona in "Redneck Woman" acknowledges her own scorned status but frames it with neither poignancy nor righteous protest. Her statement is a defiant apologia for herself and her redneck sisters and their "trashy" social position.

Wilson's breakthrough single, with its extraordinary reception and success in the country music market, remakes white working-class female identity through language, sound, and images and in relation to middle-class/working-class, male/female, and individual/communal affiliations. It is an identity bereft of cachet, or "cultural exchange-value," according to Skeggs, whose work powerfully illuminates the cultural terrain on which the song is produced and received.

Skeggs offers a theory on the workings of the contemporary Western political and symbolic economy—a cultural system that elevates stories of individual subjects and rewards those who can access, use, and display the right identity attributes. The winners here are those who are positioned to access other subjects' "properties." These powerful actors can "use the classifications and characteristics of race, sexuality, class, and gender as resources" by borrowing them, fluidly and according to the circumstances, from the subject positions to which they are seen to belong. Such self-resourcing takes place in a modern neoliberal context of "propertiz[ed] personhood." Here, exchange value attaches not only to objects or the labor that transforms them into possessions (as in Marx), but to "the cultures, experiences, and affects of others" that entitled subjects use as resources for middle-class self-construction.[1]

Less entitled subjects, however, are limited in their ability to trade and convert their characteristics and classifications "because they are positioned *as* those classifications and are fixed by them." So while the criminality that attaches to white working-class males and the cool that attaches (among other characteristics) to their black counterparts can be detached and deployed as resources by white middle-class men to enhance their cultural power, the source subjects are pathologized and essentialized by their criminality and cool. In another example, from the workplace, straight male managers who perform feminine caring enhance their symbolic value and power, but women in the same role are essentialized, perceived as simply being themselves, and derive no special rewards. Indeed, they may be penalized for their (presumed) tendency to caring when toughness or another quality is called for. Certain selves are fixed in place so others can be mobile.[2] Skeggs's analysis underscores the salience of the symbolic in contemporary cultural and economic processes and the emphasis, in prevailing perspectives, on individual agency to the exclusion of prior structural and systematic conditions in society: "Structural inequality is moralized as a pathological effect of the inability to display the correct subjectivity, to resource oneself effectively in a moralscopic economy of recognizable visible difference."[3]

Skeggs also identifies a particular type of misrecognition operating here, a kind of reverse misrecognition. Misrecognition (in Bourdieu's usage) is a spurious attribution of natural, hence legitimate, privilege and power to the privileged and powerful, in which the energies and efforts that endowed an individual with knowledge and talents (e.g., family expenditures and sacrifices and elite education in the child-rearing practice that Lareau calls "concerted cultivation") are hidden and an individual is credited with superior innate gifts. Skeggs's point is that the reverse process also occurs. Subjects inscribed by racial, gender, sexual, and/or class stigma who lack privilege and power "do not have to *achieve* immorality or criminality; they have been positioned and fixed by these values." Skeggs flags this process as another form of misrecognition, "not a hiding of the operations of the powerful, but a hiding of the systems of inscription and classification (which work in the interests of the powerful)." She notes that the powerful hide the illegitimacy of their claims to power not only through Bourdieusian misrecognition, which falsely naturalizes their superior position, but through their "access to systems of symbolic domination, which impose fixity onto those from whom they draw and claim moral distance" and thus establish social power. These symbolic systems of inscription, value, and exchange are central to "how differences (and inequalities) are produced, [and] lived."[4]

"REDNECK WOMAN"

Well I ain't never been the Barbie doll type
No I can't swig that sweet Champagne
I'd rather drink beer all night
In a tavern or in a honky tonk
Or on a 4 wheel drive tailgate
I've got posters on my wall of
Skynyrd, Kid and Strait
Some people look down on me but I don't give a rip
I'll stand barefoot in my own front yard
With a baby on my hip cause

I'm a redneck woman I ain't no high class broad
I'm just a product of my raisin' I say hey y'all and yee-haw
And I keep my Christmas lights on
On my front porch all year long
And I know all the words to every Charlie Daniels song
So here's to all my sisters out there keeping it country
Let me get a big hell yeah from the redneck girls like me
Hell Yeah (Hell Yeah)

Victoria's Secret well their stuff's real nice
Oh but I can buy the same damn thing
On a Wal-Mart shelf half price
And still look sexy just as sexy
As those models on TV

No I don't need no designer tag
To make my man want me
You might think I'm trashy, a little too hard core
But in my neck of the woods I'm just the girl next door

I'm a redneck woman I ain't no high class broad
I'm just a product of my raisin' I say hey y'all and yee-haw
And I keep my Christmas lights on
On my front porch all year long
And I know all the words to every Tanya Tucker song
So here's to all my sisters out there keeping it country
Let me get a big hell yeah from the redneck girls like me
Hell Yeah (Hell Yeah)

I'm a redneck woman I ain't no high class broad
I'm just a product of my raisin' And I say hey y'all and yee-haw
And I keep my Christmas lights on
On my front porch all year long
And I know all the words to every Ol' Bocephus song
So here's to all my sisters out there keeping it country
Let me get a big hell yeah from the redneck girls like me
Hell Yeah (Hell Yeah)
Hell Yeah (Hell Yeah)
I said hell yeah

An ethnographic study of white working-class women by Skeggs found the women's position severely limited in the prevailing symbolic economy. They are inscribed with certain cultural dispositions but none that inspire borrowing by others. Their subject resources are assessed as fixed and worthless, having only use value to themselves and perhaps their communities and no exchange value in the cultural marketplace. Consequently, the women face restrictions on their economic value and their sense of individual value. Skeggs writes of her research subjects that a "daily struggle for value was central to their ability to operate in the world and their sense of subjectivity and self-worth."[5] Her analysis offers a frame for understanding the phenomenal popularity of "Redneck Woman," particularly among fans its chorus calls out as "redneck girls" ("Let me get a big hell yeah from the redneck girls like me").

The record uses self-resourcing techniques (as identified by Skeggs) and song craft to affirm the distinctiveness and legitimacy of the Redneck Woman, and does so in solidarity with redneck men. Indeed, the track trades on the only exchange value Skeggs locates in white working-class identity, male criminality, through allusions to hard-core rock and country icons. "Redneck Woman" positions itself on the hard side of the gendered hard/soft country duality. The song invites comparison with postwar hard country, which Ching analyzes as a "burlesque abjection" of culturally low, ineffectual white masculinity defiantly enacted against the foil of "women and conventionally successful men."[6]

"Redneck Woman" is also defiant but directs its defiance exclusively at the dominant middle-class culture. It offers moments of burlesque in lyrics touting the narrator's unrepentant year-round Christmas displays, barefoot baby-toting, and preference for cheap Walmart lingerie. But it stakes serious claims for her resourcefulness, country affiliations and tastes, desirability, and, especially, agency. Indeed, the song de-essentializes and thus remakes a subjectivity long disowned and devalued in the dominant culture and once labeled the "Virile Female"—by proclaiming it deliberately chosen. This remaking calls upon popular music's capacity to model and create social identity.[7] And it begins at the song's title, with its juxtaposition of clashing identities.

FRAMING THE REDNECK

The first of these clashing identities, redneck, is conspicuously classed. But its working-class valence is also marked in terms of race, as white; locale, as provincial; and sex, with the "redneck" label conventionally attaching to maleness and connoting a rough style of masculinity, often but not exclusively southern.[8]

Several scholars have noted the emergence in the 1970s of a redneck pride phenomenon in the United States, with roots in country music. Peterson documents an early redneck pride moment beginning in 1973, and involving a spate of country songs over the next few years, that helped to redefine the word *redneck* and make it into a label voluntarily claimed and positively associated with "an anti-bourgeois attitude and lifestyle." Malone sees in Jimmy Carter's 1976 election the dawn of a more "benign" view of the South, accompanied by a shift in meanings: "'Redneck' seemed somehow to be overcoming the association with racial bigotry from which it suffered in the early 1960s, and instead was now being used to describe white working-class males. It became a proud self-designation for many white southerners and by the early eighties was appearing frequently in country songs." In fact, these changes extended beyond the South, at the least to the industrial Midwest and other destinations of the many white southerners who migrated north in the twentieth century. Thus the cultural anthropologist John Hartigan notes in connection with his ethnographic work in Detroit that by the late 1980s terms like *redneck, hillbilly,* and *country boy* were claimed with pride and used almost interchangeably to connote "working-class lifestyle and consciousness."[9]

By the early 1990s the comedian Jeff Foxworthy had taken up the torch of redneck pride. Foxworthy launched a thriving redneck comedy industry in U.S. popular culture and in 2000 with three fellow comedians brought the phenomenon to its apex in the Blue Collar Comedy Tour. At the core of Foxworthy's franchise is an ever-growing list of jokes in the form, "If———, you might be a redneck." In live performance Foxworthy's redneck-revealer lines elicit an enthusiastic response from his nearly all-white audience, most of whom, like Foxworthy himself, seem likely candidates for demi-redneck status—or at least once removed from redneck identity. His stand-up comedy expanded the visibility of redneck reclamation and advanced a commercial and cultural redneck pride movement that inspired identification, however ironic, with a persona elsewhere despised and unfashionable.

Foxworthy and company's runaway popularity lent "redneck" a brand currency that undoubtedly helped to set the stage for "Redneck Woman." Here, however, redneck identity was decidedly male. All four comedians on the 2000 Blue Collar tour were male, and their humor centered on a male redneck subject. Foxworthy's "you might be a redneck" gags often hinge on a reference to the redneck's wife or girlfriend or otherwise conjure a male subject implicitly via compulsory heterosexuality ("If you go to the family reunion to meet women, you might be a redneck"). The redneck's maleness is also explicit in the Carter-era context described by Malone and in some late-twentieth-century literary examples given in the *Oxford English Dictionary* under the term *redneck:*

> 1978 J. UPDIKE *Coup* v. 192 Her momma's a washrag and her daddy's a redneck.

> 1974 *New Yorker* 25 Feb. 102/3 He seems Southern redneck—a common man who works outdoors in the sun—to the soul.[10]

Prior to the 2004 release of "Redneck Woman," a turn-of-the-millennium redneck craze had brought to a head three decades of redneck pride. It created an audience for representations of redneck identity perceived as funny or telling while retrenching its male image. Gender is thus foregrounded in "Redneck Woman" beginning at the title, where cross-paired identities create a stereotype-jolting effect like that of "female surgeon" or "lady plumber." Here begins, too, the foregrounding of class and its entanglement with gender. Listeners are likely to be drawn into "Redneck Woman" by the implications of the title, including the implication that the song might shed some light on its gender- and class-freighted contradictions. And it does, through both music and lyrics, in ways that I will examine in some detail. Before opening that examination involving interlinked issues of gender, class, and country music, it will be useful to engage some existing dialogues around and within these three domains, as found in scholarship and in country songs themselves.

CLASS (UN)CONSCIOUSNESS AND COUNTRY MUSIC

Denial of class difference runs high in American society. Several decades of sociological research has documented a tendency "for all but the very rich and very poor to define themselves as middle class."[11] This probably reflects the historical success of U.S. labor unions, which, as Cowie notes, "fostered a relatively affluent industrial working class, which often passed in American political discourse for the amorphous 'middle class.'" Since 1973, that working-class affluence has passed: "Weekly earnings of non-supervisory workers increased 62 percent between 1947 and 1972 before stagnating indefinitely thereafter."[12] But still the middle class is, in Ortner's phrase, "almost a national category." Polling in late 2008 showed that even among Americans with annual family incomes over $150,000, 33 percent identified themselves as middle class, and 41 percent of those with annual family incomes under $20,000 (below the federal poverty line) identified themselves as middle class.[13]

Ortner traces the emergence of this labeling tendency to a postwar "national project" she calls the "middle-classing of (white) America." Directed at improving working-class minds, skills, and consumerism through the GI Bill and other programs, its rationales included defense of capitalism against communist encroachment, defense (in the wake of Nazism) of the populace against ideological vulnerability, and deflection of "the class consciousness and incipient class warfare" that had arisen during the Great Depression.[14] Indeed, amid the economic crisis and populist-left political actions of the 1930s, *working class* was a designation that many Americans wore proudly.

The phrase "middle-classing of (white) America" contains a racial qualification, and it is an important one. The historian and political scientist Ira Katznelson has shown that pre- and postwar federal social initiatives, including Fair Deal and New Deal policies and the GI Bill, strategically excluded African Americans at the behest of the powerful southern Democrats. Lawmakers from Jim Crow states favored various dodges and loopholes to exclude African Americans from social benefits: for example, the 1938 Fair Labor Standards Act excluded maids and agricultural laborers and so effectively excluded African American workers from its important reforms. By these means, the legislators preserved a poverty-wage black service class in the South. In assuaging the southern white politicians, the U.S. government excluded African Americans from the nation's earliest, transformative program of affirmative action and thus engineered a postwar prosperity in which inequality between blacks and whites actually grew.[15]

Katznelson's work can shed light on the mutual entanglement of race and class in the results of what Ortner calls the postwar U.S. middle-classing project. In Ortner's account, the results included "obscuring the older middle class/working-class boundary, especially among white people," and the transformation of *class*, with its linkages to communism, into "a kind of dirty word." Within the national discourse the class boundary was "largely replaced with a race boundary; and everyone white—with a few virtually invisible 'exceptions' at both ends—became, or imagined themselves to have become, middle class." One might add that race and class were conflated, such that people of color were assumed to be poor and working class, and white people middle and upper class.[16] These class-confused notions persist in the United States generally. But might we not expect things to be different in country music, given its legendary links to the white working class?

Peterson addressed this question in his 1992 essay, "Class Unconsciousness in Country Music." He contends that country music engages with and celebrates working-class topics but does so, across all its thematic genres, in a way that is politically regressive and fosters "class unconsciousness." Describing the latter as a "fatalistic state in which people bemoan their fate, yet accept it," Peterson echoes countless critiques of country music as impotently whiny and self-pitying. Reading fatalistic acceptance and hence class unconsciousness in songs that fail to call for collective action against the capitalist owners, Peterson aligns his analysis of country music with the orthodox Marxian notion of working-class consciousness, a recognition of one's group membership and economic interests that finds its definitive expression in proletarian uprising.[17]

In the course of his discussion Peterson reckons that country music offers fewer songs about American dream upward mobility than about what he calls "poverty pride," which asserts that it is better to be poor than rich. This message indeed surfaces often in country (e.g., "Coal Miner's Daughter"), whether the reason offered is that of avoiding emptiness and misery, or of staying humble and real, or that poverty is better in God's eyes. Elsewhere, examining representative country songs' treatment of nation, race, gender, region, rurality, and religion, Peterson concludes of each topic that it is a distraction serving to "deflect . . . considerations of class" and "the emergence of class consciousness." Similarly, when noting the 1980s advent of a country music trope he dubs the "tribute to working people," Peterson underscores its failure to "highlight exploitation or identify an exploiter." Overall he finds that class consciousness in country songs, once evoked, is "diffused" or "explicitly dissipated."[18]

This instance shows once again an analyst neglecting to consider that country music might be engaged in sophisticated artistic processes—here, involving meanings beyond the literal surface sense of song lyrics. By contrast, the American cultural scholar George Lipsitz echoes the country music writer Dorothy Horstman's observation about Hank Williams—that "part of his appeal to audiences came from his ability to infuse songs about failed romance with the injuries of class." In Horstman's attuned reading, "a tragic love affair, then, is the final insult—and perhaps the focus for economic and social frustrations it would be unmanly to admit."[19] This suggests, contra Peterson's implication, that country may not just fool itself out of sheer false consciousness into locating power struggles and economic frustrations in heterosexual gender wars, thus pissing its revolutionary impulse down its leg. Rather, Hank Williams uses deliberate displacement and poetic figuration to register social and economic woes without alienating audience sympathies.

An axiomatic assumption operating throughout Peterson's analysis is the notion that class consciousness should incite the working class to revolution, overthrowing the capitalist system. If Peterson never questions this tenet, others have done so. By 1914 Max Weber had scrutinized the "direct and immediate" link many Marxists then assumed between class and class consciousness, calling it a "pseudo-scientific operation." Neo-Marxist scholars from the "historical sociology camp" (in Ortner's terms) have argued that "we should stop looking at what the working class has only infrequently done, which is become conscious of itself as the vehicle for revolutionary social change . . . [and] look at the extraordinary range of ways in which it has formulated and expressed a distinct identity and a distinct relationship to the rest of society." Walkerdine and Lucey call the expectation for proletarian revolution a projected fantasy of the middle class and charge that the white working class has been abandoned by the popular Left for its failure to realize this fantasy.[20]

Despite various compelling critiques of the classical Marxist conception of working-class consciousness, Peterson neither defends nor questions its use as his central premise. His thesis that country music demonstrates class unconsciousness can thus be readily dispatched by all but those who hold that a conscious working class would, by definition, unite to overthrow capitalism. Malone has directly contradicted the assessment of class unconsciousness in country: "Modern country work songs do not dwell exclusively on nostalgia or pride; they sometimes bristle with anger and class consciousness. They express resentment, not radicalism. Although problems abound, the 'enemy' remains ill-defined."[21]

Malone's phrase "resentment, not radicalism," recalls that "fatalistic state" Peterson calls class unconsciousness, "in which people bemoan their fate, yet accept it." Malone's usage, however, neither trivializes nor condemns country expressions of resentment-sans-radicalism but grants them legitimacy. Such expressions are further legitimated by Ortner's identification of class in the national discourse as "almost entirely a matter of economic gradations of goods and privilege" and "embedded in narratives of snobbery and humiliation," or, as Sennett and Cobb put it, "the hidden injuries of class." Class formation is fought out, not in any "Marxist narrative of irreconcilable differences" between capital and labor (in Ortner's words), but rather "at the level of the symbolic." The focus here—as in "Redneck Woman"—is not on production but on consumption and symbolic exchange in capitalist society.[22]

Bourdieu's writings on class cultures illumine the cultural logic at work in so-called poverty pride songs—and indeed, in the mechanisms of working-class formation. Bourdieu argues that subordinate groups often internalize the limits of their position in society and thus exercise "the choice of the necessary." They exclude from consideration those aspirations and actions that are improbable for members of their group, "either totally without examination, as *unthinkable*, or at the cost of the *double negation*," which inclines subjects "to refuse what is anyway refused [to them] and to love the inevitable," a "virtue made of necessity."[23] Country songs present an endless array of foreshortened working-class tastes and "choices," a love for "the inevitable" including modest or impoverished life conditions, low-status Walmart wardrobes, and being labeled "redneck."

Recent research offers further perspectives on value, taste, and choice in the working class. Snibbe and Markus's experiments suggest that working-class individuals focus less than middle-class individuals on choice and control over the external world and more on personal integrity and self-control. Notably, "Redneck Woman" speaks to both perspectives. The song's narrator also addresses the mutual opacity of the classes (Scott's "class apartheid") when she points out to the listener who "might think I'm trashy, a little too hardcore," the codes and values proper to her "neck of the woods," where she's "just the girl next door." In the context of radically separate social and cultural spheres, country music's working-class reputation and focus often inspire alienation and revulsion in middle-class audiences. But the working class has its own views and values, separate from and unrecognized by the middle-class system of values and symbolic exchange, and (as Bourdieu demonstrates) dominated by it.

Ethnographic research by Lamont shows that American workingmen place moral value above economic value and so, in the terms of their own value system, place themselves above the middle class. This can suggest a subculturally productive function of country's poverty pride songs (We were poor, but we had love) having nothing to do with revolution—of affirming collective self-worth against the dominant culture's devaluations. Fox also posits a transformative process of affirmation whereby country's abject status in the dominant culture allows it to be alchemized into sublime pleasure in shared social rituals of the honky-tonk—which entail music, dancing, alcohol, cigarettes, and working-class sociability. Fox suggests that for working-class devotees, the honky-tonk's inversion of hierarchies of musical value, of country from (dominant cultural) bad to (subcultural) good, implies a similar reversal in the socially prescribed realm of human value.[24]

All of this links to Wilson and "Redneck Woman." The song is a gender-inclusive statement of redneck pride and a call to twenty-first-century working-class consciousness, fine-tuned to distinctions of consumption and self-construction and their social, economic, and affective reverberations. It exemplifies Bourdieu's scenario whereby the "object" of sociology's classifications produces her own "classifying operations" and articulates a polemical view of the other class. For example, the lyric in verse 2 classifies lingerie consumers in terms of Victoria's Secret versus Walmart types and scoffs at those who would pay twice as much at Victoria's Secret for "the same damn thing" Walmart sells, just for the status marker of a "designer tag." Such attention to details of clothing and style has long been feminized, trivialized, and readily condemned as a dissipation of the revolutionary impulse. As Steedman points out, however, fashionable clothing is a necessity for women's and girls' entry into the social world and historically has been an object of working-class women's desires and labors. She contends that the desire and envy of poor and working-class women for "decent clothes" is nothing less than political, a contention borne out by "Redneck Woman."[25] The narrator expresses her interest in attractive clothes in tandem with disdain for the social and cultural tyranny of designer labels, empty status markers of bourgeois individualism, premised on a distinction between the individual and the (here, Walmart-clad) masses.

THE MULTIMEDIA CREATION OF GRETCHEN WILSON'S GENDER AND CLASS PERSONA

Historians and critics of country music have devoted considerable attention to the ways in which country artists convey sincerity and biographical authenticity, or realness, through their songs and public personas. Peterson has examined the creation of country music as a process of "fabricating authenticity," and Jimmie N. Rogers has written of the "sincerity contract" in country as the expectation of rapport between a credible, straightforward artist and her or his audience. The latter ideal finds illustration in Wilson, who since 2004 has cultivated an image as a *real* redneck woman along the lines sketched in her song. We see her in the video muddin' on a four-wheeler and elsewhere, in ads and media reports, modeling jeans and lingerie beside a shiny new Chevy pickup; hanging out with "ol' Bocephus," Hank Williams Jr.; and wielding her "REDNECK" signature guitar.

All of these images encourage us, particularly through gender and class signifiers, to understand Wilson as one and the same with the "Redneck Woman" of her song.[26] So does the biographical information that circulated in the press and media and in the lyrics of the track "Pocahontas Proud" upon the release of her debut album. It emphasized the singer's background as the child of a teenage mother; a resident of trailer parks in rural Pocahontas, Illinois; an eighth-grade dropout who went to work tending bar in a rough country dive. "At fifteen I was tending Big O's Bar / I'd sing till two a.m. for a half full tip jar . . . / And I'll be damned if I'm gonna let 'em down," she sang in "Pocahontas Proud." The elaboration of Wilson as Redneck Woman continued with the 2007 release of an autobiography (with Allen Rucker) titled *Redneck Woman: Stories from My Life.* In early 2010 Columbia Nashville issued *Gretchen Wilson: Greatest Hits* with a rusting, battered mobile home pictured on the cover. And two months later Wilson announced her fourth studio album, *I Got Your Country Right Here,* as the first release on her own label, Redneck Records.

The track "Redneck Woman" asserts multiple affiliations of gender and class, as well as race and taste, through its many shout-outs. These include namechecks and musical references to a pantheon of male hard country and rock gods, along with a few marketplace endorsements (beer, Walmart) and dis-endorsements (Barbie, champagne, Victoria's Secret), all defining a distinct "Redneck Woman" identity profile. Wilson invokes the southern-rock legends Lynyrd Skynyrd, self-proclaimed "American Bad Ass" Kid Rock, "King of Country" George Strait, "Redneck Fiddlin' Man" Charlie Daniels, hard country icon Hank Williams Jr., and one woman: Tanya Tucker, the "bad girl of country" and the only iconic female star associated with the 1970s Outlaw Country movement.[27] Each chorus ends with a "Hell yeah" performed in slightly ragged unison by what we might call the "regular folks' chorus" (here, sounding young and female), a feature of various country songs since the new country era, including Brad Paisley's "Welcome to the Future" (#2 2009) and "Alcohol" (#4 2005); Toby Keith's "Get Drunk and Be Somebody" (#3 2006) and "I Love This Bar" (#1 2003); Martina McBride's "This One's for the Girls" (#3 2003); and what may be the prime instance, Brooks's "Friends in Low Places." The chorus represents collective buy-in of the song's message and promises to enfold the listener in the warmth and vitality of communal embrace—or from another listener perspective, threatens to obliterate the individual distinction that underwrites middle-class subjectivity.

Several sonic signifiers further define the "Redneck Woman" and mobilize a kind of musical cross-dressing. Wilson leads into the "Hell Yeah" section of each chorus with bravura full-voice high notes evoking hard rock and heavy metal male vocality à la Black Sabbath, Led Zeppelin, and AC/DC. These vocals are coupled at the octave below (e.g., 1:09–1:13), a muscular gesture that recalls Kid Rock's 2003 hard-core anthem, "Son of Detroit," and the 1973 hard rock classic "Radar Love." The fiddle in "Redneck Woman" is also referential, its sound and style evoking Charlie Daniels (e.g., 0:54–1:09, 2:30–2:42).[28] And there is an arresting moment when the instruments drop out to underscore Wilson kicking things up a notch (2:48–2:50), echoing uses of the same technique by Lynyrd Skynyrd in the legendary extended guitar solo of "Free Bird" and by Skynyrd's own heroes, the Allman Brothers, in "Whipping Post."

Listeners use popular music for affective and identificatory purposes, to touch places inside and to project signals outside. Relatedly, we might expect the musical references in "Redneck Woman" to operate on a special level, more subliminal and embodied than that of the verbal shout-outs. They might also inspire special admiration from fans by virtue of the skill and craft involved in creating them, especially in a working-class context where "walking the walk" commands more respect than "talking the talk." Wilson's track extends an established genre of self-mythologizing hard country song comparable to the rap genre that the musicologist Adam Krims designates "Mack" rap (the historian Adam Gussow traces both genres to the same centuries-old American braggadocio tradition). In Mack rap, an emcee, characteristically male, struts his sexual prowess and wealth.[29] In the hard country version, a male singer boasts about his class-outlaw excesses, touting his toughness, fearlessness, or indifference; his bad habits of choice; and maybe a favorite car, truck, bike, or freight train. Examples include Merle Haggard's "Mama Tried" (#1 1968), David Allan Coe's "Son of the South" (1986), and Hank Williams Jr.'s "My Name Is Bocephus" (1987).

Another example is Kid Rock's "Son of Detroit," an adaptation of Coe's "Son of the South" that compares to "Redneck Woman" on several counts. Rock claims both "redneck" and "pimp" identities and namechecks Hank Williams Jr., Run DMC, Lynyrd Skynyrd, ZZ Top (also invoked in the guitar riffs), himself, and "Willie, Waylon, George and Merle" to define a special Detroit hybrid persona rooted in both country and hip-hop, white "hillbilly" and urban African American cultures.[30] The track also specifies the narrator's preferences in booze: "I like my whiskey straight up daiquiris / make me ill." And booze leads to ride. The line "I'm a drink a couple dozen beers, / go out and jam some gears" is followed by references to the narrator's "west coast chopper," "pickup truck," "four wheelin'," and street racing.

Wilson's declarations are similarly macho. Her namechecks overlap Kid Rock's and assert a similar hard-core patrilineage. She declares her own intolerance for prissy drinks with "I can't swig that sweet champagne / I'd rather drink beer all night." This leads her to specify her haunts and her ride: "In a tavern or in a honky tonk / Or on a 4 wheel drive tailgate."

THE VIRILE FEMALE PAST AND PRESENT

My close attention to Wilson's "Redneck Woman" and the cross-gender elements in her performance and image construction is not meant to suggest that the persona she conjures is new or unprecedented. On the contrary, Wilson breathes new life into an old gender-class identity with an established cultural presence. It was much the same identity that R. J. Reynolds (RJR) market researchers defined in 1989 and dubbed the Virile Female. RJR had commissioned a study for a marketing strategy targeting young white working-class (and apparently provincial) women, a highly profitable segment for rival Philip Morris's Marlboro brand. Although its ads have featured rugged males exclusively since the birth of the Marlboro Man cowboy image in the 1950s, Marlboro was in 1989 the best-selling cigarette among young female smokers in America. It still is, surely helped by the fact that Reynolds's planned Dakota cigarette never materialized. The company abandoned the campaign in early 1990, when a *Washington Post* reporter exposed "Project V.F." just weeks after the tobacco giant touched off a furor with its launch of Uptown, a cigarette aimed at African Americans.[31]

PROJECT V.F.: 1989 R. J. REYNOLDS MARKET RESEARCH
DEFINES THE "VIRILE FEMALE"

- Young white female with high school education at most
- Service or factory worker
- Likes "partying" and "cruising"
- Significantly male identified: into boyfriend and whatever he is doing, including:

  Hot rod shows
  Tractor pulls
  Concerts, especially by all-male groups

- Smokes Marlboros[32]

Following its fatal disclosure, details of Reynolds's Virile Female report were disseminated, now with a novelty-infotainment slant, to *Harper's Magazine* and National Public Radio audiences. Among these audiences the mere phrase "tractor pull" can elicit a chuckle, serving to distance one from the class and taste community evoked thereby. But the central exhibit offered for armchair anthropologists was more fascinating still, a familiar species of gender-crossed working-class female newly named and classified.[33]

"Redneck Woman" both conforms and talks back to long-standing perceptions of working-class women as excessively or inappropriately gendered. Historical and pop culture examples of "hard" women among provincial poor and working-class whites include Calamity Jane and Annie Oakley, *Li'l Abner's* Mammy Yokum, Loretta Lynn's persona in "You Ain't Woman Enough" (#2 1966) and "Fist City" (#1 1968), and Tanya Tucker's Outlaw Country persona in the 1970s and 1980s (figure 10). Masculine or butch personas among queer women bear long associations, too, with working-class identity. Real-life and fictional examples include the female invert as viewed by nineteenth-century sexologists; 1940s–1950s lesbian bar culture as chronicled by Kennedy and Davis; lesbian butches and transmen as represented in Joan Nestle's and Leslie Feinberg's writings; Brandon Teena, fictionalized in *Boys Don't Cry* (1999); and a 2001 study by the sociologist Sara Crawley confirming the prevalence of working-class identity among late-twentieth-century U.S. butch lesbians.[34]

As these examples might suggest, gender is contingent on class. Working-class women "have always been positioned at a distance" from femininity, a historically specific construction that was indicatively bourgeois from its eighteenth-century beginnings. And at the working-class and rural intersection staked out in "Redneck Woman," gender skews mascu-

FIGURE 10. Martha Jane Burke, "Calamity Jane," ca. 1901. Courtesy of the Collections of the Library of Congress.

line, by comparison with urban norms, for males and females alike. Urban styles of femininity, including male effeminacy, can be conspicuously extravagant in rural American contexts. This has implications for rural queer men, as some writers have noted, and for both queer and straight women. Given the relative masculinity of rural gender norms, many rural queer women are prone to find themselves *less* conspicuous than they would be in the city. By the same token, rural straight women are prone to confuse urban tourists, who sometimes conclude from the women's gender styles that they must be queer.[35]

THE WORKING-CLASS FEMALE PREDICAMENT

The persona under discussion appears so gender-crossed and extraordinary from a dominant culture perspective that it has been dubbed the Virile Female. But this identity seems more normal among young female country artists. In 2005 Jo Dee Messina scored a No. 1 hit by striking a flinty pose toward an ex in "My Give a Damn's Busted." Her cocky, taunting persona in the track and video suggests an aspect of the Virile Female unnoted in Reynolds's marketing report but foregrounded a few days after its exposure, in a *Washington Post* column titled "Cigarettes and Virile Chicks." "I went to high school with girls like this," recalls the author, a self-described "Chaucer major." "We called them 'hitter chicks,' because they liked to hit people, and I adored them for their wild ways." He describes the Virile Females of his 1960s adolescence as Marlboro smokers who were savage in fistfights.[36] The tough persona portrayed and exoticized here resonates with "You Ain't Woman Enough," "Fist City," and other examples previously cited.

A few months after "My Give a Damn's Busted" broke the charts, even Carrie Underwood, an icon of wholesome and glamorous femininity, joined the V.F. club. Following her *American Idol* victory and conquest of country and Christian radio with the inspirational megahit "Jesus, Take the Wheel" (#1 2005), Underwood's next No. 1 single was "Before He Cheats" (2006), a revenge song that has the narrator keying her unfaithful man's "four-wheel drive" pickup and whacking it with a "Louisville Slugger." The latter sends glass shards flying in the video, which cuts between the cheater's seduction scene with the other woman and the singer's cool, unflinching delivery of a verbal and vehicular thrashing.

Underwood's persona here is downscale and belligerent. She appears throughout much of the video in heavy blue eye shadow and a faded black slit-neck tee, shoves strangers in the alleyway without a glance, and imagines her romantic rival performing "white trash . . . karaoke." Her choreography includes menacing looks, sneers, and a "chicken head" gesture by now associated with *Jerry Springer Show* guests, and glass shatters spontaneously wherever she walks. Underwood's publicity has never cast her in the Virile Female mold, and her fashion model looks and frequent magazine cover appearances have helped to prevent anything too hard core or "real" from sticking to her celebrity image. But her foray into Virile Female territory in "Before He Cheats" was well received by country fans and seemed only to bolster her credibility as a country artist amid her stylish image as a TV, newsstand, and musical crossover star.

Reaching back over a half century, we might draw a further comparison with "Redneck Woman"—though not on Virile Female grounds. Kitty Wells was censored by country radio and by NBC and its Grand Ole Opry broadcast because of the perceived radicalism of the message in her own career-making megahit, "It Wasn't God Who Made Honky-Tonk Angels." A riposte to Hank Thompson's plaint against a good-timin' woman who left him to return to "The Wild Side of Life" (#1 1952), the song became country's first No. 1 single and first million-selling record by a female solo

artist.[37] In fact, the lyrics of "Honky-Tonk Angels" presume conjugal heterosexuality and a traditional wifely role for women while the tune reprises
Thompson's (which in turn reprises "Great Speckled Bird" and "I'm
Thinking Tonight of My Blue Eyes"). But the song's implication of male
social-sexual irresponsibility and privilege in defense of "us women" was
heard as threatening in 1952 ("Too many times married men think they're
still single / That has caused many a good girl to go wrong"). However
demure, Wells's track seems no less feminist than Wilson's boisterous 2004
celebration of "redneck girls like me."

Both artists were popular icons for female audiences in their respective
moments. Both of their records were apologias for the same figure of sexually imperiled subjectivity, the white working-class woman. But the songs
deploy different tactics. "Honky-Tonk Angels" makes a gender-separative
appeal, blaming men for some women's loss of middle-class respectability
and thus ultimately affirming bourgeois values. By contrast, "Redneck
Woman" makes common cause with redneck men and draws on cherished
symbols of good ol' boy ideals and prerogatives to articulate its manifesto,
a cross-gender, macho-affirmative rejection of the very standards of hege-
monic middle-class femininity.

Notably, the emphasis on class defiance in Wilson's song does not under-
mine its feminist thrust. Indeed, this setup jibes with contemporary inter-
sectional feminism: the Redneck Woman insists that we apprehend her
situation as concurrently working class *and* female. Wilson asserts the
superior sexiness and late-capitalist savvy of the Redneck Woman, a
monogamous object of heterosexual allure in impostor lingerie from
Walmart. Directing its most explicit critique at middle-class cultural style
and social supremacy, the song makes its feminist case—verbally, visually,
and musically—through masculinity rather than against it and so links
with a central theme in postwar country music, insofar as it rehearses and
props up the terms of white working-class manhood.

That manhood is revisited in this chapter's conclusion. But first let us
take another look at white working-class womanhood vis-à-vis the Redneck
Woman—in the song, the artist image, and the audience and in the inter-
pretive light of social theory. Ortner observes "a general tendency for
working- . . . class culture to embody within itself the split . . . between the
working and the middle class." This split is reproduced in working-class
contexts as "a typology of 'styles'[:] . . . the action seekers versus the routine seekers, . . . the respectables versus the undesirables, . . . [and] overwhelmingly . . . women are symbolically aligned . . . with the 'respectable,'
'middle-class' side of these oppositions and choices."[38]

In other words, women in the working-class world are assigned the role of middle-class moral conservator/killjoy.[39] This is illustrated in countless country songs (as Ching suggests in relation to male hard country) and parodied in the "Redneck Woman" video when Wilson wades into the cluttered living room of a mobile home, dominated by a flat-screen TV and two inert men. As she gathers up empty longnecks, casts a disapproving glance, and snatches away one fellow's fat cigar, we see that the good ol' boys are Kid Rock and Hank Williams Jr. in cameo appearances. Of course, these are the heroes in Wilson's song, the guys she stands with, not against. The gender conflict is thus revealed as a send-up, and class solidarity is reinforced anew.

Now, we might see working-class womanhood, as described by Ortner, in terms of a potentially even exchange: on good days you are the very emblem of respectability; on bad days, by the same token, you are a killjoy drag. But that schema operates only in working-class contexts. In the dominant middle-class frame, working-class women signify disrespectability, with real-world consequences. A study by the social psychologist Bettina Spencer found both women and men, liberal and conservative, more likely to assume it was "her fault" when given evidence indicating that a rape victim was working class than when the evidence pointed to a middle-class woman (here, too, clothing signifies and is political).[40] Skeggs's research shows that in our culture's symbolic economy the working-class woman personifies the "slut" and so functions as ground to the middle-class figure of respectability. In fact, respectability exists only as a function of class distinction. It emerged historically as "a property of middle-class individuals defined against the masses."[41] This class-gender backdrop is precisely what "Redneck Woman" plays out against. The record's lyrics and video images show keen awareness of the pathologizing and abjection of working-class women and men and insist on a kind of reverse valuation. "Redneck Woman" attests for its audience that "the privilege of the dominant classes is that they possess social legitimation which is based on the power of the dominant to impose, by their very existence, a definition of what is valued and authorised which is nothing other than their own way of existing—they are at ease in the social world because they determine the legitimated way of existing in it—it is a self-affirming power."[42]

You can find working-class social and cultural affirmation in many postwar country songs, including (to name a few) Lefty Frizzell, "Saginaw, Michigan" (#1 1964); Dolly Parton, "9 to 5" (#1 1981); Jason Aldean, "Amarillo Sky" (#4 2007), and previously mentioned songs including Johnny Cash's "Oney," Jones and Wynette's "(We're Not) the Jet Set," Reba

McEntire's "Fancy," Aaron Tippin's "Working Man's Ph.D.," Montgomery Gentry's "Something to Be Proud Of," and Eric Church's "How 'Bout You." But fans' record-breaking response to "Redneck Woman" evinces the musical and stylistic appeal with which its message and rhetoric projected a young white working-class female persona that country audiences circa 2004 could embrace, and that sounded the right note for their catharsis and identification. "Redneck Woman" offers catharsis to working-class listeners through acknowledgment of and ammunition against the "rejection of self" that arises from everyday encounters with the dominant culture, a "grasping at a conscious level what has always been known at an unconscious level—that to be what you are is 'not good enough.'"[43]

Knowing that you are deemed wrong or inadequate by others' standards does not necessarily make you want to be like those others. The working-class women in Skeggs's ethnography were ambivalent toward the prospect of attaining the definitively middle-class attribute of respectability.[44] More pointedly, "Redneck Woman" rebukes a downward gaze, challenging "you" who "might think I'm trashy." But ultimately the song, too, seems ambivalent, more intent on trashing the dominant culture's ideal of respectability than extending such respectability to its cast-off "trash." This is not to suggest that "Redneck Woman" lacks cultural ambition or productivity. In its celebration of the Virile Female the song produces a persona resistant to the twofold trap in which working-class women (a) symbolize a revered-and-resented middle-class respectability within their own class, even as they (b) embody disrespectability for the middle class. Rebellion in "Redneck Woman" against both straitjacketing options is flagged (a) in the video, by Wilson's parody of the aspirational house-proud scold and affirmation of her one-of-the-boys affinity with Kid Rock and Bocephus; and (b) in the lyrics, when the narrator champions her sub-bourgeois wardrobe choices and refutes the charge that she's "trashy" or "too hardcore" by invoking her own community standards, by which she's "just the girl next door."

The features of female working-class subjectivity discussed above illustrate Ortner's observation that class conflicts in America are largely denied and often displaced to gender and sexuality.[45] Labeling a woman "slut" is a quintessential instance. It is a class insult misleadingly delivered into the realm of sexuality and gender. In alleging impropriety on the part of an individual woman it denies the structural, classed basis of the judgment. We have begun to learn in recent years how gender intersects with race and must be understood differently across different racial and ethnic locations. But we still have much to learn about the effects of class in relation to gender. These, too, are interwoven with race, ethnicity, geography, and other factors, as we can see in the case of Elvis Presley.

ILLEGIBLE SUBJECTS (CONCLUSION)

In a 1992 essay, the literary and cultural critic Marjorie Garber placed Elvis Presley alongside Valentino and Liberace as a matinee idol who appropriated feminine dress and self-presentation to enhance, paradoxically, his heterosexual appeal. On the analysis of the historian Michael Bertrand, however, Presley's persona traversed, not any gender boundary, but class-specific racial boundaries. In his flashy suits and jewelry, pompadour and aura of cool, the white working-class Memphian drew on midcentury southern (and, we might add, urban) black working-class style, in which impeccable suits, coiffed hair, and manicures heightened heterosexual masculinity and asserted individuality without threatening a segregated social order. Noting that poor whites and African Americans constituted "two underclass groups the southern elite lumped together as lazy, dependent, and biologically inferior," Bertrand posits that Elvis "appropriat[ed] this form of *machismo* for the same reason that black men utilized it, . . . to demonstrate his manhood within a society in which his dignity and self-respect . . . [had] been under constant assault."[46] This suggests the importance of class perspective in conjunction with racial and regional perspectives for understanding the workings of gender and sexuality around Presley's celebrity persona.

Like Presley, Wilson and her Redneck Woman persona are illegible beneath a bourgeois gender lens. Multiple factors—Wilson's iconic status among country fans, the broader history of the Virile Female, the defiantly antibourgeois message of "Redneck Woman"—point to the need for another analytics, one that would acknowledge and investigate the class complaint at the center of the song. It would reckon with Wilson's various male identifications as well as her claim, "In my neck of the woods I'm just the girl next door." Examining "Redneck Woman" in relation to the provincial white working-class world referenced in its music and lyrics yields perspective on the track's message and its eager embrace among fans.

Presley's sensational public persona appropriated cultural resources from his class, gender, and regional peers across society's color line—from working-class southern black male counterparts. Wilson's Redneck Woman persona appropriates cultural resources from her class, racial, geographic, and vocational peers across the gender line—from working-class- and rural-identified white male rock and country icons—while reaffirming her heteronormativity through stereotypically gendered images: lyrics on courting her man's desire and propping a baby on her hip, video cuts to female cage dancers and trailer park moms. "Redneck Woman" thereby puts a new spin on an old, tainted identity, the Virile Female, and, most strikingly, manages to forge an appealing persona out of white working-class female subjectivity. Undoubtedly the persona thus created does not appeal to everyone, but any cultural instance that generates positive or even neutral interest in white working-class womanhood merits notice.

Skeggs notes that forms of self-resourcing and self-marketing that were once the stuff of celebrity are now "a responsibility of the neoliberal individual."[47] In this context, the appreciative reception of "Redneck Woman" surely reflects its deft rebranding of denigrated, essentialized white working-class female subjectivity. Operating on a cultural landscape where choice defines the empowered neoliberal subject, the narrator attests that she *chooses* her working-class, redneck affiliations with hard country and rock artists, beer over champagne, discount intimates, and déclassé front yard spectacles. To this extent, "Redneck Woman" might be heard as staking a claim for power and authority on the terms of the dominant culture. Of course, the song does not take up the values of middle-class neoliberal self-exchange. It affirms working-class identification and ideals, giving voice to perceptions of the middle class as snobbish, elitist, competitive, pretentious, and morally lacking by comparison to working-class values of family attachment, loyalty, personal sincerity, and honor.[48] "Redneck Woman" thus scores its symbolic victory over the class status quo, directing new-bourgeois self-resourcing techniques to antibourgeois ends in a gendered declaration of working-class consciousness lasting three and a half minutes, and—who knows?—perhaps beyond.

CODA: FEMINISM BEYOND THE LABEL

In its address of white working-class female subjectivity, "Redneck Woman" takes an empowering stance that readily draws the description *feminist*. Indeed, I have characterized the song as such and would similarly characterize certain other songs discussed in this chapter, including those of Kitty Wells and Loretta Lynn. But this is not to presume that the artists would embrace the feminist label to describe themselves or their political outlooks. As Malone notes, few female country artists are "overt feminists."[49] And in various instances since the 1970s, *feminist* has been shown to be primarily a white middle-class identification, one that women outside this social group have tended to avoid. Such facts, however, must not be taken to mean that middle-class women's *perspectives* are more feminist than those of working-class women. In psychology research by Abigail Stewart and Joan Ostrove, working-class daughters actually held more skeptical views of middle-class heterosexual norms and gender roles than their generational peers from either middle- or upper-class families.[50]

Among Stewart and Ostrove's subjects, working-class women alone tended to see their mothers' marriages as negative examples, lessons in gender subordination to be avoided. Middle-class women, meanwhile, saw their mothers' marriages as positive examples, and upper-class women expressed marriage-positive values independent of their mothers' models. The authors acknowledge that styles of gender relation differ by class: "A patriarchal ideal dictated women's open subordination to their husbands within working-class families. . . . As [Lillian B.] Rubin . . . stated, 'For the working-class woman, the power and authority of her husband are more openly acknowledged. . . . She knows when he won't let her; it's direct and explicit—too much so for her to rationalize it away.'"[51] Significantly, the working-class women not only distrusted the working-class marriages they grew up with, but distrusted subordination to a husband within genteel middle-class companionate marriage. As Stewart and Ostrove note (again citing Rubin), "in middle-class marriages an ideal of egalitarianism prevented both husbands and wives from recognizing the actual power relations in the family."[52] But no middle-class egalitarian ideal obscured the real gender dynamics of their marriages for working-class women looking on.

Among a subset of the study's subjects who saw the women's movement as important in their lives, working-class women were far more likely to see it as validating their prior views: 83 percent of these women did, compared with none in the middle and upper classes.[53] Still, working-class women rarely call themselves feminist or are seen as such by others. I will now consider a similar situation, for working-class women and men alike, with regard to the label "political."

4. "Fuck Aneta Briant" and the Queer Politics of Being Political

> To be known and recognized also means possessing the power to recognize, to state, with success, what merits being known and recognized.
>
> PIERRE BOURDIEU, *Pascalian Meditations*

> Fuck Aneta Briant! Who the hell is she,
> Tellin' all them faggots that they can't be free?
> Throw that bitch in prison! Maybe then she'll see
> Just how much those goddamn homosex'als mean to me.
>
> DAVID ALLAN COE, "Fuck Aneta Briant"

In 1978, David Allan Coe was at the peak of his career. He opened the year with a songwriting grand slam in Johnny Paycheck's release of "Take This Job and Shove It," which climbed to No. 1, spent eighteen weeks on the country charts, and inspired a 1981 Hollywood comedy of the same name (which introduced monster trucks to the big screen). Coe had previously captured the top spot in 1974 with "Would You Lay with Me (In a Field of Stone)," a song that became both a bona fide hit and a succès de scandale, censored by many country radio stations when recorded by the dusky-voiced teenager Tanya Tucker.[1] As a singer, Coe in 1978 released two new albums and a greatest hits collection on Columbia Records, all three of which went to the Top 50 on the Country Albums Chart. He had enjoyed recent singles success with sly-witted, musically compelling cuts of Steve Goodman's "You Never Even Called Me by My Name" (#8 1975) and the self-penned "Longhaired Redneck" (#17 1975). And he would chart again in the next few years with "The Ride" (#4 1983), "Mona Lisa Lost Her Smile" (#2 1984), and "She Used to Love Me a Lot" (#11 1984), among other records.

Also in 1978 but worlds away from Nashville's Music Row, Coe issued an LP in a limited production run on his private label, D.A.C. Records. Bearing catalog number DAC-0002, the album's low-budget cover featured black block lettering on a plain white background, with added text and graphics scrawled in freehand. The title and opening track proclaimed *Nothing Sacred*, and the phrases "Adults Only," "not recomended for Air-

FIGURE 11. Nothing fancy: An underground album release by the David Allan Coe Band, *Nothing Sacred* was issued in a limited pressing and with DIY cover art on Coe's private label, D.A.C. Records, in 1978. Courtesy of Country Music Hall of Fame® and Museum.

Play," and "Not for Sale in Store's [sic]" adorned the sleeve front and back. Track titles like "Linda Lovelace," "Cum Stains on the Pillow," and "Master Bation Blues," with their openly sexual allusions and often obscene language, clearly warranted such advisories in the context of 1970s country radio. Another title, listed as Track 5, further challenged dominant standards of propriety, presenting not only obscenity but belligerence and bad spelling. Yet even with misspellings, "Fuck Aneta Briant" made its reference clear (figure 11).

WHO THE HELL IS SHE?

After being crowned Miss Oklahoma in 1958, Anita Bryant won the second runner-up title in that year's Miss America pageant and proceeded directly into a singing and recording career. She scored four hits on the pop Top 40 charts in 1959–60 and released over a dozen albums in the 1960s and 1970s. Bryant was Coe's contemporary and in the seventies his label mate at Columbia, but her music fell into two categories far removed from his Outlaw Country: Christian music and the radio format then known as middle of the road, or MOR (now called "adult standards"). Beginning in 1969, Bryant appeared in a series of television commercials for the Florida citrus industry, and for the next seven years she was best known as America's prime promoter of orange juice. But she gained her greatest and most lasting notoriety in a different arena.

In 1977, Bryant spearheaded an antihomosexual crusade in Dade County, Florida. Dade County was where the entertainer and three-time winner of *Good Housekeeping* magazine's "Most Admired Woman in America" poll made her home, in a Miami bayfront mansion she shared with her husband and four children. When the county's board of commissioners voted to add a sexual orientation clause to Dade's civil rights statutes, Bryant launched an organization called Save Our Children and campaigned to repeal it. Alleging that homosexuals recruited children by any means necessary, Bryant positioned herself as protector of the sexuality of children and thus deployed what had been "for over a century," in the words of the cultural anthropologist and sexuality theorist Gayle Rubin, the most reliable "tactic for stirring up erotic hysteria."[2]

Bryant vilified homosexuals as a threat to children, the family, godliness, American freedoms, and the survival of the nation. After defeating the local ordinance in June 1977, she vowed to take her cause national, lobbying for the repeal of antidiscrimination laws in other jurisdictions across the country. Bryant's zealous battle against "the homosexual lifestyle" witnessed over the next few years the loss of her marriage, her lucrative celebrity endorsements, and her career. Her campaign provoked surges of homophobic hatred and violence in Miami, and it sparked a sex and child pornography panic in communities throughout the country. But it also galvanized a national lesbian and gay rights movement—something that the localized and short-lived Stonewall Rebellion had not done. By now, historians view the Dade County episode as the opening battle in a war that still reverberates in U.S. political culture. Writing in 1999, the journalist Dudley Clendinen summarized Bryant's crusade as having "helped build the two great competing movements of the last two decades." He identifies these rival movements as "conservative Christianity and the pursuit of gay rights."[3] Others would refer to them, jointly, as the culture wars.

"FUCK ANETA BRIANT"

The first of a pair of LPs he calls his "X-rated albums" (the second would appear in 1982), Coe's *Nothing Sacred* featured "Fuck Aneta Briant" as its side 1 closer. The album and track were legendary in fan circles. Though the initial pressing of *Nothing Sacred* was minuscule, homemade copies surely circulated in the cassette tape era. And in more recent years, versions of both underground albums have been sold at Coe's concerts and online. "Fuck Aneta Briant" stood well outside the mainstream of contemporary country music by dint of its lyrics, which were potentially offensive from multiple, contradictory angles. Complicating matters further, Coe's song presented an irresistibly catchy tune. Jaunty and upbeat, "Fuck Aneta Briant" opens with a verse (see epigraph, above) that raises the question of homosexuals and their freedom in connection with Bryant and her antigay campaign. The next three verses leave Bryant behind (returning to her only in the last line) in favor of surveying the qualities of what is, in Coe's hands, a far more interesting subject: social-sexual life in a male prison environment.

The non-gay-identified ex-con shows an easy familiarity with the ways of those he calls "faggots" and freely proclaims his appreciation for what "those goddamn homosex'als" offer, sexually, socially, domestically, and pharmacologically, in a prison setting.[4] His lyric flies in the face of middle-class euphemistic speech, and it exemplifies antibourgeois country in the extreme. Tongue-in-cheek and irony feature, too, in "Fuck Aneta Briant"— from the first line, when Coe in a punchy voice drops the title phrase like a bomb into the track's vaguely corny introduction, a vaudeville razzle-dazzle tinged with twang.[5] But however laden with humor and wit, the lyric projects a sincere appreciation of "homosex'al" qualities running the gamut from tender to ferocious. And irony or not, it is worth remarking that the well-known singer and songwriter, who has long inspired a fervent hard-core following, went on record with this lyric apparently without fear of sexually tainting *himself*. The fact that Coe never developed a queer reputation, despite boasting knowledge of how "those" men will "beat your meat," "help you drain your hose," and—perhaps more intimately—"clean your fingernails," raises questions that are pivotal to this chapter (figure 12).

FIGURE 12. David Allan Coe in the 1970s, in the period when he sometimes called himself the "Mysterious Rhinestone Cowboy." Courtesy of Country Music Hall of Fame® and Museum.

One question is whether the taint-free scenario just sketched might bespeak a late 1970s persistence of the gender-based identities that Chauncey documented in New York's street-level male sexual culture from the turn of the twentieth century to the 1950s. In other words, could it be that Coe's song went out into a reception sphere in which his outlaw masculinity guaranteed his "normal" sex-gender status, regardless of same-sex self-incriminations? Masculine performance on the part of soldiers, sailors, and other same-sex-involved "rough trade" in the early-twentieth-century working-class world had indeed served to guarantee those men's status as "normal."[6] Another question that readily arises for twenty-first-century listeners has to do with Coe's language and tone in this song. That is, whose side is he on? And if, as seems to be the case, it is the gays' side, then why does he curse them and call them "faggots"? What do we make of the fact that this apparent gay defender used epithets widely identified as homophobic, while Bryant, an avowed gay enemy, used only the officially legitimate term *homosexual*?

Still another question pertains to the nature of "Fuck Aneta Briant." Is the song simply pornographic, as might be suggested by its underground release on Coe's "X-rated" album and his performance of it on Al Goldstein's *Midnight Blue*—a local access cable show largely about pornography, created by a notorious pornographer? Or might Coe's song be seen as a political gesture, an early statement of anti-Bryant, antihomophobic protest on a terrain virtually devoid of such protest? Indeed, in her groundbreaking 1984 essay "Thinking Sex," Rubin emphasized the broad significance of the 1977 Dade County measure and marveled that "with the exception of [the North American Man-Boy Love Association (NAMBLA) and the American Civil Liberties Union (ACLU)], no one raised a peep of protest."[7] David Allan Coe did.[8] But does a disreputable, obscene, self-implicating manifesto in the form of a country song count as political protest? Why, or why not? Finally, whether or not "Fuck Aneta Briant" qualifies as political, what are the stakes attaching to the question?

WHAT COUNTS AS POLITICAL?

Coe's "Fuck Aneta Briant" is a rare, early, and emphatic statement of opposition to Bryant and her antigay campaign that began in South Florida and would shape American politics and civic culture for decades to come. The song, however, was not heard as a political statement in its original moment, and still today is unlikely to be cited as political within a dominant-culture frame. Nor—albeit for different reasons—is *political* a designation likely to attach to Coe's song when considered in a working-class cultural context. Across a range of styles and periods, many modern American popular songs have been received as political—songs by Woody Guthrie to N.W.A., Joan Baez to Dead Prez, Sweet Honey in the Rock to Rage Against the Machine, and many others. So, we might ask, what distinguishes this music from "Fuck Aneta Briant"? Or we might conversely wonder, does Coe's song share enough in common with such music even to warrant mention in the same breath?

Country songs seldom surface in journalistic or scholarly discussions of protest or political music—except in connection with reactionary politics and, sometimes, working-class dupes. Here, Haggard's "Okie from Muskogee" and Keith's "Courtesy of the Red, White and Blue (The Angry American)" serve as frequent examples. I have already discussed Haggard's "Okie" and will say more shortly about Keith's song. But for now I wish to focus on what I view as a long-running discourse of protest and resistance in modern country music, albeit one that is not usually granted political status. It is found in country's frequent expressions of antibourgeois resistance, which we have glimpsed in various songs and examined up close in "Redneck Woman." Antibourgeois expression in country has sometimes attracted notice in the dominant culture but usually as a sign of bad taste, socially unacceptable behavior, or political impotence. Judge's journalistic country music critique, for example, relegates antibourgeois expression to the distasteful, morally reprehensible realm of "resentment" and thus ridicules, trivializes, and depoliticizes it. And Peterson's scholarly Marxian analysis catalogs and frames representative instances of antibourgeois expression in country as products of false consciousness and hence the antithesis of anything political.

Using different analytical strategies and apparently coming from quite different ideological positions, both Judge and Peterson negate and dismiss white working-class political resistance in country music. Such negation is a political act in its own right, remaking middle-class supremacy. But its political nature can be obscured by the frequent foregrounding of style and aesthetics in musical discussions. This is not to say that critics' talk of style and aesthetics covers up some *real* political content lying elsewhere in the musical commentary—for indeed, stylistic and aesthetic discussion *is* the political content. The problem, rather, is that style and aesthetics, feminized and (supposedly) frivolous topics, are not always recognized as the vehicle of masculinized, "important" political content. The reasons for this failure of recognition include the gender mismatch just flagged and a related mismatch of public/private zones: whereas politics is the most public of topics, aesthetic taste is deemed an individual, personal matter. And so music and arts criticism flies beneath an aesthetics camouflage, allowing critics to drop cultural and political bombshells that may reverberate widely but receive less political scrutiny than they would elsewhere. The notion that you cannot argue with a person's taste, although misplaced in this context, may seep nevertheless into our assessments of music criticism, even when it is doing political and ideological work—for example, attacking and depoliticizing class complaints in country music.

Antibourgeois expression in country music typically involves musical-textual vignettes about social or workplace superiors oppressively breathing down one's neck or, especially, judging one inadequate or wrong. These are protests against the position of working-class people within existing structures of socioeconomic power and value. In line with country song conventions, such protests are presented, not in the language of politics or activism, but in stories of ordinary individual lives, and with an emphasis on feeling. At times, class is invoked through terms like *working people* or *the little man*. For example, Alan Jackson's self-penned "Little Man" (#3 1999) is a commentary on the injuries exacted by the corporate Walmartization and gentrification of white and black small-town America. Jackson's commentary takes the form of a lamentation for "the little man that built this town / Before the big money shut him down" and closes with a succinct prayer, "God bless the little man."[9] Protest in country music is sometimes funny, sometimes angry, frequently stylized and metaphorical, and always focused on things other than revolution. Songs often offer glimpses of insight into, or analysis of, working-class actuality, as "Little Man" does with its four-minute gloss on the causes and effects of 1990s small-town blight and erosion of community. Here as elsewhere, antibourgeois country-musical expression articulates a critique of existing power relations in society. And to that extent, it must be counted as political.

In the dominant culture, however, country's antibourgeois expression is seldom recognized as political. Some of the reasons for this have surfaced in previous chapters. One is the middle class's squeamishness and aversion toward country music and working-class worlds. This limits investigation of country and its messages, particularly in a bourgeois-centric media environment. Another factor is the antagonism between the middle and working classes. Their structural opposition creates a disincentive for the middle class to hear working-class protest or to take it seriously—all the more when such protest indicts the middle class itself. Yet another reason that the political significance of antibourgeois expression in country goes unrecognized in the dominant culture is the middle class's lack of fluency in the working-class codes of meaning and value that circulate in country music.

POLITICAL NONIDENTIFICATION IN COUNTRY MUSIC

A barrier to recognition of antibourgeois expression as political expression lies within the working class itself and is given voice in country music. It is a tendency not to identify with partisan politics or a political self. This is in some ways comparable to the tendency not to identify as feminist, and we should note that neither of these tendencies applies to every country fan or working-class person. But we can perceive a tendency toward political nonidentification in country songs' customary avoidance of political language and topics (an avoidance that does not, however, extend to expression of support for U.S. military troops—which is viewed here in interpersonal more than political terms, as discussed below). This nonpolitical tendency is evident in country lyrics that openly disclaim political partisanship or political engagement generally. For instance, Chely Wright declares, "I'm not Republican or Democrat" in "The Bumper of My S.U.V." (#35 2005), a commentary on political hypersensitization and polarization in American society that was released in the wake of the Iraq invasion. Tim McGraw makes the same nonpartisan declaration, albeit in a different narrative context, on his album track "Who Are They?" (2002). The lyric wonders about the authority of the voices of expertise, the faceless "they" who dispense a barrage of health, safety, and civic advice when invoked in the popular phrase "They say——." The opening verse muses, "They say not to have too much fun . . . not to get too much sun, / Democrat or Republican / Guess I'm screwed, I'm neither one."

A more blanketing statement of political nonidentification features in Alan Jackson's extraordinary hit "Where Were You (When the World Stopped Turning)" (#1 2001, #28 Pop). Written six weeks after the terrorist attacks of September 11, 2001, by the New Year it had become the most successful response to the 9/11 tragedy in popular music and perhaps any popular culture form. Jackson approached the difficult and still raw subject in a space apart from politics, a space of feeling, contemplation, and catharsis. His song asks the listener to recall, "Where were you when the world stopped turning on that September day?" A series of further questions lays out an array of possible emotional responses, from shock to anger to sorrow, joy for the survivors, survivor's guilt, and pride at the heroism of responders. In each instance, the song asks listeners if they felt that feeling and then, if they in turn found themselves weeping, praying, drawing loved ones close, reaching out to a stranger, shutting off media violence, or making plans to buy a gun. Jackson's wide-ranging litany of individual responses to the tragedy also ranges widely within his relaxed, pretty baritone voice, regularly reaching out to the upper and lower limits of a one-octave span and sometimes dropping to the fourth below. The understated accompaniment is texturally transparent, foregrounding an acoustic guitar, punctuating drum fills, and touches of bright, hopeful color from violin and mandolin and from wispy, celestial pedal steel flourishes. "I'm just a singer of simple songs / I'm not a real political man," the chorus begins. "I watch CNN, but I'm not sure I can tell you / The difference in Iraq and Iran." The chorus's closing reflection is a scriptural reference to God's gifts of "faith, hope, and love" and a reminder that "the greatest is love."

"Where Were You (When the World Stopped Turning)" won Jackson a Grammy and other major awards, but it also drew criticism for its avowed political disengagement. Rock and Americana music producer T-Bone

Burnett has criticized the song for its unabashed profession of ignorance. But Jackson stands by his lyric: "I just wrote what I felt. . . . I'm just a singer of simple songs, and that's the truth. And I *don't* know the difference between Iraq and Iran."[10] The singer's unvarnished self-representation was undoubtedly useful for purposes of relating to listeners, most of whom in 2001 did not themselves know as much about Iraq or Iran as they would come to know over the next few years. It is useful, too, for purposes of understanding the meaning of "being political" in country music and in differing sectors of American society.

Jackson is often cited as a role model in country music, and he does not shirk the mantle. By all indications, the country icon and role model did not think it controversial or irresponsible when he freely declared himself non-political in "Where Were You (When the World Stopped Turning)," a song that, he has said, he intended to be healing. And if some observers found his public declaration objectionable, they were probably not country fans: the record was a high point in Jackson's stellar career and one of the biggest country hits of the decade. But then Jackson's statement in "Where Were You" is perfectly consistent with the values celebrated in country songs, where "being political" is not claimed as an aspect of selfhood and indeed is sometimes expressly disclaimed. The nonpolitical selves modeled in country music resonate, too, with Cyphert's observations of the working-class crew she shadowed, who "find the highly articulated rhetoric of the dominant political/social world to be an unpleasant, even indecent way of being."[11] Country songs' disavowal of "being political" may also jibe with research findings on working-class styles of self that value a "get over it" attitude and an ability to play whatever hand one is dealt more than any self-serious investment in the impeccability of one's choices and judgments. Working-class nonpolitical stances seem consistent with Sayer's observation that "in the face of deeply embedded undeserved inequalities, resistance may be more painful and less rewarding than compliance and deference."[12] And we might recall the findings of Bartels, Fiorina, Gelman, and others showing that while many Americans have grown increasingly rigid and intent on ideological issues since the 1980s, the working class overall has not been part of this drift.

The theologian Sample offers further relevant insight in his examination of a "traditional" politics that he describes as "characteristic of many working people and well reflected in country music." He paints a picture of working-class people whose world, often, is their family and the issues affecting them and to whom, in many cases, government seems irrelevant. He argues that neither a conservative nor a liberal label applies to the working-class values in country music and writes of a "wider politics" that is "often missed in interpretations of country music and in approaches to working-class life."[13] Malone similarly describes country as eschewing partisan politics while expressing "a traditional scheme of values" and as frequently exuding compassion while generally remaining "skeptical of organized human solutions" to social and political problems.[14] Emphases in this "traditional" politics, Sample observes, include community solidarity and commitment to "a religious and socio-moral world." But "conservative" and "liberal" are the classifications according to which the dominant culture makes sense of American political life. And of these, "conservative" is the label typically assigned to country music and its constituency. In fact, in recent years working people have been overwhelmingly represented as right-wing partisans and extremists. Sample takes a clear view on such representations. He calls them "bigoted stereotypes."[15]

CLASS, POLITICS, AND PIGEONHOLING

Since gaining notoriety for his 2003–5 feud with the Dixie Chicks and the song that sparked it, "Courtesy of the Red, White and Blue (The Angry American)," Toby Keith has often been held up as the poster boy for country music's conservative, red-state zeal. By now, some people know that he has publicly identified himself as a lifelong Democrat—though, like Alan Jackson in his song lyric, Keith has stated, "I'm not a real political guy."[16] What he clearly is, in both of the previous instances and in his song "American Soldier" (#1 2003, #28 Pop), is a vocal supporter of American troops. Given the makeup of America's twenty-first-century all-volunteer military, this is a working-class-affirmative position, and it is a position that often marks those associated with it as working class.

Chely Wright's "Bumper of My S.U.V.," another country hit of the Iraq invasion era, also defines a pro–U.S. troops position. A protest and lament against pigeonholing assumptions and dualistic thinking in the civic sphere, Wright's track appeared at the height of red- and blue-state rhetoric, in November 2004. In a live performance at the Grand Ole Opry just before the song was released, the singer-songwriter recounted its origins in a real-life occurrence.[17] Her story involved an incident in Nashville traffic in 2003, the year President George W. Bush ordered the invasion of Iraq. A woman driving a minivan inexplicably honked her horn and gave Wright the finger and then at a stop rolled down her window and cursed the singer for her bumper sticker—a Marine Corps insignia her brother had sent her upon deploying to Iraq. The song that Wright wrote in the wake of this experience is a plea against the rush to judgment and simplistic typecasting of people and their politics. Its message is encapsulated in the lyric, "Does she think she knows what I stand for / Or the things that I believe / Just by looking at a sticker for the U.S. Marines on the bumper of my S.U.V.?"

Wright has said that she first performed "The Bumper of My S.U.V." for U.S. military personnel and that she took it into the studio because service members urged her to record it. She is well known for having done hundreds of United Service Organizations (USO) tours entertaining American troops. The lyrics in "The Bumper of My S.U.V." acknowledge the military service and sacrifices of Wright's brother, father, and grandfather and show these family members taking differing approaches to service. Her brother's fourteen years in the Marine Corps contrasts with the naval service of her father, a Vietnam vet who "did his duty, then he got out."

Musically, "The Bumper of My S.U.V." is a subdued, down-tempo track. The acoustic arrangement and the song's placement low in Wright's vocal range help to create a mood more thoughtful and intimate than rousing or heroic. This suits the lyric, which is part narrative and part interior musing expressing, among other things, doubts about war. It tells the story of Wright's road rage encounter, situates the U.S. Marines bumper sticker in the context of the singer's family history and her travels in past and current war zones around the world, and finally wonders aloud about the other driver's basis for judging her. Acknowledging the "bright red sticker" on her bumper, Wright's lyric continues, "that doesn't mean that I want war / I'm not Republican or Democrat / But I've gone all around this crazy world / Just to try and better understand / Yes, I do have questions." The next line, "I get to ask them because I'm free," registers a sentiment that might in some part account for the song's having been labeled in some places as patriotic and even controversial—a labeling that may reflect broad stereotypes about country music more than any specific features of the actual song.

Wright's pro-troops sentiment, deemed provocative circa 2003, is one around which the national discourse soon shifted. By the end of the decade, Americans expressed gratitude for military veterans' service with less fear of thus being linked to any particular political position or party. Indeed, concerning the extreme concentration and class stratification of wartime sacrifice in Iraq and Afghanistan—for example, members of the military comprise just 0.5 percent of the American population, and 78 percent of U.S. casualties in Afghanistan came from the working class—the facts circulated just enough, perhaps, to help motivate those careful expressions of appreciation that have arisen on both the left and the right. Such expressions often deploy the recently established formula, "Thank you for your service."[18]

In 2008, a feature called "Hilariously Hyperbolic Pro-America Songs" appeared in the *Onion*, a humorous pseudonewspaper that hosts the most popular satire site on the Internet. The article offered this synopsis of "The Bumper of My S.U.V.":

> A woman in a minivan gives Wright the finger, and Wright assumes it's because she has a U.S. Marines bumper sticker on her S.U.V. Hey Chely, maybe it's because you're taking up two lanes or wasting what's left of the earth's petroleum. Who knew that pro-America country singers— with especially overwrought Southern accents—hated minivans and private school?[19]

Of course, the *Onion* makes clever snarkiness its business. But here the attempt at cleverness only invokes the same kind of stereotyping that inspired Wright's song in the first place. The article takes a jab at the singer's "Southern" accent (Wright and her accent are actually from Kansas) and places her under a label, "pro-America country singers," that is deaf to her song's express ambivalence. The road-hogging and oil-wasting wisecracks ascribed to the other driver, too, seem inapt and preconceived, given that the song identifies that woman's vehicle as a minivan—typically comparable to an S.U.V. in size and gas guzzling. Overall, the *Onion*'s renowned satire in this instance amounts to no more than a rehashing of stereotypes bound up with a presumption. But, as we have seen, such treatment often suffices where country music is concerned.

Premiering her song at the Opry in 2004, Wright seemed to fight off tears from the start. As she reached the closing lines, her voice finally broke. At the time, Wright's emotionalism would have appeared as a sign of the shock and insult of the song's originary incident. Viewing this performance today, however, many fans might speculate in hindsight that Wright's personal situation added to the difficulty, and even irony, in the event. In 2010, she came out as a lesbian, becoming the first mainstream LGBTQ country artist to come out publicly. Since then she has attested (in a 2010 autobiography and many interviews) to the difficulty of her years of secrecy, even describing a point in 2006 when secrecy combined with a relationship breakup to push her to the brink of suicide. The first thing Wright, a devoted Christian, describes having done after taking her pistol out of her mouth is getting on her knees and praying aloud for peace. She claims that her prayer was granted and in her moment of God-given peace she saw that she had to end her secrecy and live truthfully as the gay person she is, regardless of the consequences for her career.[20] (One consequence, according to a 2012 interview, is that Wright has been snubbed by the USO—which she attributes to the "old school mentality of the [USO] upper brass" and not to the troops, who have continued to support her.)[21]

So the country singer Chely Wright has come out as lesbian and attests that God led her to do it. Toby Keith, architect of the apparently pro-Bush line "we'll put a boot in your ass" (in his Iraqi war–era single, "Courtesy of the Red, White and Blue") and the most politicized figure in contemporary country, identifies himself as a lifelong Democrat who is "not . . . real political." And in so doing, he echoes similar professions of political disengagement on the part of various artists and songs in a realm, country music, that serves in the dominant culture as a prime emblem of political conservatism. As for Wright, it seems possible that she would have added a new sticker to her bumper since 2010, in rainbow colors. Perhaps such a badge would have shielded her from the rage-filled encounter she wrote about in 2003. At the least, it would have stirred no small confusion, the rainbow sticker and the bright red Marine Corps sticker sharing space on the same bumper. Beyond the official meaning of the symbols—of LGBTQ pride and Marine Corps pride, respectively—further, clashing connotations attach to each one: middle-class versus working-class connotations and liberal-progressive versus conservative political connotations.

Chely Wright and (in a more complicated way) Toby Keith thus illustrate in the realm of politics the same problem that Gretchen Wilson and Elvis Presley illustrate in the realm of gender. Their positions are unintelligible on the dominant culture's terms, which presume middle-class cultural logic and values. However meaningfully these artists' messages may resonate among country music audiences, in the dominant culture they are misinterpreted and reduced to broad, static stereotypes and so merely serve to confirm status quo views on country music and its constituency. Because of the recent shift in Wright's public identity, her instance can shine light on the flatness of the frame within which a "country music" story might be interpreted. Before Wright's 2010 coming out, her protest against facile, reductive political stereotyping in "The Bumper of My S.U.V." was itself recouped to facile, reductive political stereotyping in the *Onion*. Wright seems less likely to be seen so two-dimensionally today, since her current status as an open lesbian jams the circuits that reproduce the dominant culture's "country music" type. Her lesbian identity unleashes possibilities for recognition of ambivalence and complexity in her work, and in her person. Possibilities for such recognition have been limited, however, by the fact that Wright's career in the country music spotlight had faded some time before her coming-out moment. Her last appearance in the Top 40 was six years earlier, in 2004.

INTELLIGIBILITY, CLASS, AND QUEER VISIBILITY

This chapter views the underground country track "Fuck Aneta Briant" as (among other things) a time capsule from a past world of sexualities and personas. Listening to "Fuck Aneta Briant" today requires historical frames of interpretation, and it offers historical perspective on class and sexuality and their significant interactions. The present section pursues historical knowledge in order to unlock the time capsule that is "Fuck Aneta Briant" and to situate the song within a relevant historical and cultural context. It discusses the roots of modern gay rights activism in middle-class organizations seeking *respectability* for gay and lesbian people—in large part, by distinguishing them from gender-variant people who were marked by class and, often, race.

In the late 1990s, David Valentine was a safer-sex activist in lower Manhattan, working with communities of young, poor, gay people of color. Or at least they thought they were gay. Social service agencies had another idea, reckoning some "gay" and others "transgender." That is, they classified some members of the community as being at variance with society's hetero norms of sexuality and others—according to a distinction the agencies deemed crucial—at variance with society's gender norms of male masculinity and female femininity. This classificatory scheme served to divide and differentiate where formerly there had been—under an inclusive *gay* self-designation—group unity and shared identity. It also placed community members in the position of having to represent and negotiate their experiences, selves, and needs through someone else's sex-gender worldview. Even so, the impoverished, socially marginalized young people (Valentine describes them by comparison to the subjects in Jennie Livingston's 1990 documentary on Harlem drag ball subculture, *Paris Is Burning*) had reason to take up the transgender paradigm. It rendered them intelligible to social services agencies that used the *transgender* label to administer much-needed safer-sex educational resources and free condoms.

Now a cultural and linguistic anthropologist, Valentine has written about his work with these communities of mostly male-bodied, feminine people, or "queens," in what turns out to have been a transitional moment—for the ensuing years have seen them abandon their local self-understandings as "gay" to adopt the dichotomy, by now thoroughly institutionalized, of gay versus transgender. Valentine's book *Imagining Transgender* examines the early 1990s emergence of transgender as a category distinct from homosexuality, while paying special attention to the crucial, constitutive links between sexual-gender classifications and lived experiences of race and class.[22] The study traces the rise of the transgender concept as (among other things) a product of mostly white, middle-class homosexual activists' efforts since the 1970s "to define homosexuality *against* that which was visible"—in particular, against racially and class-inflected public sexuality and cross-gender behavior.[23]

In other words, Valentine links the advent of transgender to gay activists' push to define homosexuals as people identical to heterosexuals in every way, except that they happen to be attracted to members of their own sex.[24] The catchall transgender category—encompassing gender-variant, transsexual, and transvestite identifications—serves to separate visible sexual and gender others from relatively "normal" homosexual ("gay" and "lesbian") people and so serves to distill a more mainstream homosexual constituency and concept. In Valentine's analysis, transgender functioned particularly to contain the elements that threatened gay men. Indeed, gay men's concerns to decouple male homosexuality from femininity, and thus to privilege sexual identity over gender identity, have been the primary engine driving the politics of "just like you" gay gender normativity.[25]

The forces at work in all this go back well before the 1970s. Throughout much of the twentieth century, middle-class homosexuals cultivated what the British sexuality scholar Alan Sinfield has called the "discretion model" of homosexuality.[26] Distinguished by their undetectability—meaning especially their conformity to dominant gender norms—middle-class homosexuals were the least visible members of the homosexual world. Modern middle-class homosexuality defined itself by contrast to gender inversion, "discovered" by late-nineteenth-century sexologists and famously defined by the German activist Karl Ulrichs as "a woman's soul trapped in a man's body," and (in the case of female inverts) vice versa.[27] U.S. gay and lesbian histories by Chauncey, Lillian Faderman, and others attest that in the first half of the twentieth century, people with same-sex desire "did not constitute themselves as one people but as many . . . distinguished by class, color, sexual practices, and gender style."[28] The array of erotic personas included male fairies, rough trade, jockers, wolves, and husbands and female femmes, butches, kikis, ladies, studs, and bulldaggers. And the worlds that grew up around these personas and practices—including bars, public sex spaces, parties, and balls—were forged along the same diverse lines. Chauncey's study of early-twentieth-century gay New York shows that in the working class, gender performance defined the identities of "fairies" and "trade," but there were also many men who had sex with men without putting any label on it.

From the late nineteenth century through most of the twentieth, sexologists and other experts viewed the working class as the natural home of homosexuality. In the introduction to his influential and widely circulated volume *Sexual Inversion* (1896), the British sexologist Havelock Ellis discussed instances of homosexuality among racially and culturally othered peoples in places including Zanzibar and New Guinea before summarizing that "among lower races homosexual practices are regarded with considerable indifference, and the real [i.e., congenital] invert ... generally passes unperceived or joins some sacred caste which sanctifies his exclusively homosexual inclinations." Ellis's next sentences reveal a conceptual blurring of racial-cultural others with class others:

> Even in Europe today a considerable lack of repugnance to homosexual practices may be found among the lower classes. In this matter, as folklore shows in so many other matters, the uncultured man of civilization is linked to the savage. In England, I am told, the soldier often has little or no objection to prostitute himself to the "swell" who pays him, although for pleasure he prefers to go to women; and Hyde Park is spoken of as a center of male prostitution.[29]

Slightly further on, Ellis quotes an unidentified correspondent on the "patent" fact that "simple folk" often show no more disgust for "the abnormalities of sexual appetite" than for "its normal manifestations." And he articulates the notion, widely registered throughout Euro-American culture, that "true sexual inversion can be traced in Europe from the beginning of the Christian era ... especially among two classes." That is, one finds "an undue tendency to homosexuality" among "criminals, and, to a much less extent, among persons of genius and intellect."[30] Chauncey notes that various observers in the early twentieth century found working-class straight men more tolerant of gay men and more open to their advances than were their middle-class counterparts: "After interviewing thousands of men in the 1930s and 1940s, Alfred Kinsey was surprised to reach a similar conclusion. Men at the highest and lowest social strata ... were more likely than those in the middle classes to tolerate other men's homosexual activity. Even those men in the lower-status group who did not engage in homosexual activity themselves rarely tried to prevent other men from doing so."[31]

Around the turn of the twentieth century, American middle-class "queer" men increasingly defined their queerness on the basis of their sexuality, apart from gender. And "normal" middle-class men had begun to define themselves as "heterosexual" on the basis of renouncing behaviors and feelings that might be perceived as homosexual.[32] Even beyond the middle class, diversely conceived communities of same-sex desire were, by the middle decades of the century, moving to become simply a "world of homosexuals and heterosexuals" through a "complex, uneven process, marked by substantial class and ethnic differences."[33] At midcentury, Valentine writes, gay- and lesbian-identified people, mostly white and middle class, "insisted on gender-normative presentation as the hallmark of homosexual identification and rejected other sexual/gender subcultures as 'deviants.'" Valentine cites the anthropologist Esther Newton's pioneering ethnography of mid-1960s drag queens, *Mother Camp*, in claiming that the "deviant" group was largely working class and poor, included most sexually and gender-variant people of color, and harbored such conspicuous and (so-called) flamboyant persons as femme and butch lesbians, male fairies and queens, and homosexual sex workers.[34]

The historian John D'Emilio has influentially argued that homosexual collective identity coalesced in the 1950s, with the development of a definition of homosexuality framed solely in terms of object choice.[35] This development arose from "homophile" activist groups' pursuit of strategies for middle-class respectability, which included an insistence on defining homosexuality as purely a matter of "object choice"—a preference for partners belonging to the same sex as oneself.[36] This vision of gay politics would be challenged briefly by the 1969–73 gay liberation movement. In an article titled "The Class-Inflected Nature of Gay Identity," the sociologist Steve Valocchi discusses the tensions in this moment between gay liberationists, who included race, class, power, sexual style, and gender performance in their view of gay political concerns, and homophile activists, who insisted on the single-issue focus of gay civil rights, where "gay" was defined in terms of object choice alone.[37] Tension between these two views of gay activism faded after 1973, however, with the triumph of largely white, male, middle-class homophile groups like the National Gay Task Force. Their ascendancy "reinforced the middle-class nature of the movement and reinscribed the hetero/homo binary that had been briefly called into question by gay liberation."[38]

Histories of twentieth-century U.S. homosexual activism reveal parallel efforts, then, between 1950s and 1990s middle-class homosexual cohorts. Both sought to distinguish themselves from more visible poor and working-class sexually and gender-variant people and thus to claim the benefits of respectable middle-class identity status. On Valocchi's analysis, gay identity was forged in the twentieth century in "a structural context of state control of 'threatening' sexualities and middle class anxieties over gender non-conformity. These class-inflected influences on the emergence of a collective gay identity affected the recruitment strategies, the organizations, and the political issues of the lesbian and gay movement."[39] Indeed, in the mid-twentieth century, discreet middle-class "homosexuals" distinguished themselves from more visible poor and working-class, racially marked, and gender-variant people and designated them "deviants" by contrast. And in the 1990s, relatively mainstreamed middle-class "gays" and "lesbians" distinguished themselves from more visible gender-variant, transsexual, and transvestite people and designated them "transgender" by contrast. By now, however, transgender identity, like other formerly déclassé sex-gender practices and personas—for example, drag performance, femme and butch lesbianism—has been annexed to contemporary middle-classed queerness.

Valentine's study illustrates how middle-class institutions imposed their conceptual and linguistic regime du jour in one late 1990s instance—through social service agencies' use of power and resources to "correct" young, poor, gender-variant African Americans' and Latinos' self-designation as gay. Valentine emphasizes here that advocates of the transgender versus homosexual paradigm have come to believe with certainty in its correctness and even its natural realness, though it is, of course, a constructed notion.[40] I would add that such certainty contributes to the situation whereby, in matters of social identity, those who fail to brandish the dominant culture's current conceptual model and terminology risk being judged unsophisticated, backward, or worse. Ehrenreich notes that the professional middle class is the class "privileged to do the discovering and naming of [socioeconomic] classes" in society.[41] Indeed, the professional middle class is privileged to do the discovering and naming of identities and groups in society generally. Of course, other classes possess their own categories and labels, but the PMC is distinguished as possessing the right ones, the ones that carry cultural authority and are immune to accusations of ignorance, bias, and bigotry.

THE WORKING CLASS AND THE QUEER: A CENTURY-LONG ASSOCIATION

Chapter 1 examined several cultural instances demonstrating a prevailing contemporary ideology. This ideology maintains that the white working class is a (or even *the*) mother lode of homophobia, a pathologized attribute, and links to a more sweeping ideology positioning the white working class as America's bigot class. By same token, it positions homosexuality and homosexual "tolerance" as progressive, enlightened properties of the middle class.

The present chapter shows that past ideology posited just the opposite associations and values. From its scientific designation circa 1870 through most of the twentieth century, homosexuality was pathologized in the dominant culture, and both homosexuality and acceptance of it were attributed, negatively, to the working class. Shunning and renouncing homosexuality were lauded and associated, virtuously, with the middle class. But in a process that has become increasingly evident since the 1970s, America has seen a shifting of ideological poles in the realm of sexuality and class. Homosexual acceptance has gone from being working class and bad to middle class and good, while homosexual aversion—what we now call homophobia—has gone from being middle class and good to working class and bad.

Even across these 180-degree reversals of meaning, however, a signal feature is conserved: the values attaching to the classes. Despite an about-face in cultural perspectives on homosexuality and homophobia, the position perceived as middle class (formerly, averse to homosexuality, and now, accepting of it) retains a positive value, and the position perceived as working class (formerly, accepting of homosexuality, and now, averse to it) retains a negative value. This scenario underscores how cultural beliefs about sexuality help to uphold and remake the established hierarchy of class status and power. It also speaks to the essential role of class in the making of cultural meanings—including those of sexual identities—and in determining social, moral, and political value.

Indeed, histories of twentieth-century U.S. sexual cultures reveal quite different conceptions of sexual identities and practices in different class worlds. Boyd highlights such differences in the introduction to *Wide-Open Town*, her history of queer San Francisco circa 1900–1965. She notes that the early-twentieth-century working-class sexual landscape of urban fairies, as documented by Chauncey in *Gay New York*, fostered "development of identities that did not function within a homo/hetero binary," the sexual regime now dominant in American culture overall and dominant already then in the middle class. Thus, Boyd emphasizes, the grassroots "constituents of 'Gay New York' did not express the same *kinds of identities*" that would define "the world inhabited by [middle-class] homophile activists" of the 1950s and 1960s.[42]

Boyd's study looks at working-class sociosexual culture, not in the New York male street scene, but among male and female sexual and gender deviants who constituted the social world of San Francisco gay bars and taverns. Kennedy and Davis explore related terrain in their history of Buffalo's postwar lesbian community, *Boots of Leather, Slippers of Gold*. They argue that in this moment when what might constitute the best "degree of 'obviousness'" was a topic of debate in the lesbian community, working-class femmes and butches "came down on the side of asserting difference, despite the consequences"—which included oppression, violence, and police action.[43] Kennedy and Davis thus align with the author and activist Joan Nestle in viewing 1950s lesbian femmes and butches as "sexual heretics" who were "front-line warriors against sexual bigotry."[44] But middle-class contemporaries, and homophile activists in particular, saw femmes and butches—as well as male fairies, queens, and trade—as liabilities in the quest for homosexual respectability and as obstacles to acquiring homosexual rights. In their daily public defiance of sexual and gender norms, these working-class deviants (putatively) stood in the way of freedom and advancement. By the 1970s, some middle-class lesbian feminists and others would view femmes and butches as retrograde heterosexual wannabes and so, once again, as obstacles to freedom and advancement.

Kennedy and Davis's account, however, ascribes historical significance to the lives and actions of midcentury femme-butch lesbians. They underscore the "prepolitical" resistance of lesbians in Buffalo's bar scene, arguing that femme-butch lesbians, like gay liberationists, worked to effect social change but, unlike them, did so outside of organizations. Indeed, Kennedy and Davis identify the boldly visible femme-butch roles enacted by working-class lesbian bar habitués as "the primary prepolitical institution of resistance against oppression"—borrowing Hobsbawm's notion of "prepolitical" agitation, a "primitive" mode of rebellion he defines by contrast to modern social movements.[45]

Building on Kennedy and Davis's insights, Boyd develops the argument for the significance within the history of LGBTQ activism of postwar working-class femmes and butches and other queer or gender-transgressive groups. Her community study rejects the emphasis, central in much LGBTQ historiography, on midcentury homophile organizations as the crucial precursor leading to post-Stonewall liberation movement gay activism.[46] Boyd argues that in San Francisco "the social worlds—the pockets of cultural resistance—that evidenced the greatest amount of [wider] community interaction and mounted the heaviest challenge to mainstream law and order were *not* factions that clearly articulated same-sex sexual identities or aligned themselves with overtly political organizations."[47] Rather, she identifies the roots of LGBTQ activism in the nonorganizational, day-to-day *gender* transgression of working-class queers—which she views in specifically political terms.

In the 1950s, Boyd notes, as "homophile activists began to articulate new social identities (i.e., as sex variants, homophiles, homosexuals, and lesbians), they distanced themselves from the working-class and transgender culture of queer bars and taverns. With monthly publications, they promoted gender-normative identities and worked to connect homophile communities to a practice of political integration and social assimilation." During this time, femme-butch bar communities constituted a "competing social world," which framed a "cultural politic . . . of lesbian visibility and queer social resistance in San Francisco that stressed their differences from members of mainstream heterosexual society, rather than their similarities to them."[48] Thus, in Boyd's assessment, the working-class world of queer bars and taverns was histori-cally significant in its own right and not "simply . . . a stepping-stone for the more important project of homophile activism." "The communities forged inside bars and taverns," she continues, "functioned politically and, ulti-mately, offered practical and ideological responses to policing that were dis-tinct from those of San Francisco's homophile (or lesbian and gay civil rights) organizations."[49]

The 1950s appear in these historical accounts as a time when U.S. queers were visible and defiant in the working class and discreet and assimilative in the middle class. This scenario entailed class differences in not only queer society, but society at large. Indeed, class status was associated with differ-ing relations between queerness and the nonqueer majority: slack and per-missive in the working class, critical and more distant in the middle class. The extensive and visible early-twentieth-century New York gay world that Chauncey revealed was working class in its geographic location and in the forms it took, its saloons, social clubs, and dress-up balls mirroring the working-class social institutions of the time. "Although middle-class gay men participated in the gay world," Chauncey notes, "its public sites were restricted at the turn of the century to the working-class neighborhoods of the Bowery and waterfront, their very existence contingent on the ambiva-lent tolerance afforded them by working-class men."[50] By midcentury the working class was still viewed as accepting of deviance—lacking "repug-nance" toward it, in Ellis's phrase—in contrast to the middle class. And queer residents and businesses, including bars, restaurants, and sex clubs, found quarter not in posh or prosperous areas of American cities and towns but in lower-rent districts.[51] In working-class neighborhoods, queers, overt and gender nonconforming, were a visible presence.

WHO SAYS WE DON'T NEED THEM HOMOSEX'ALS?

Unlike various other country musical instances we have seen, David Allan Coe shows no bourgeois aspirational tendencies in "Fuck Aneta Briant"—

or anywhere else, for that matter. The hard-core cast of Coe's music and lyrics, and of his star persona generally, is consistent with Outlaw Country, a 1970s movement that he was part of. Outlaw Country was a species of hard country understood as a reaction against the Nashville sound and countrypolitan style. In addition to Coe, the movement encompassed Willie Nelson, Waylon Jennings, Johnny Cash, Billy Joe Shaver, Merle Haggard, Kris Kristofferson, Tanya Tucker, and Jessi Colter, among other artists.

In "Fuck Aneta Briant," Coe displayed intimate knowledge of the domestic charms and sexual favors afforded by other men in a prison setting, yet managed not to raise queer suspicion around himself. This fact is striking in light of the twentieth-century economy of the homosexual open secret, wherein "the social function of secrecy," on the analysis of the literary critic and queer theorist D.A. Miller, "is not to conceal knowledge, so much as to conceal knowledge of the knowledge."[52] But Coe maintained a nonqueer identity and reputation despite his richly descriptive litany in "Fuck Aneta Briant" extolling "them faggots" and their diverse attributes, which ranged between the high and low, cerebral and visceral. In Coe's portrayal, these guys both "read and write" and "fuck all night," can "help you dress" or "play you chess," may "be your wife" or "take your life." They are big, small, and in between, some of them "yellow-bellied queers" and others mean, and they include killers, thieves—even singers. Hence the climactic turnaround at the end of the fourth verse, "In fact, Aneta Briant, some act just like you!"

In 1978, when Coe retorted in "Fuck Aneta Briant," "Who says we don't need them homosex'als?" (thus closing verse 3), he refuted the authority of those who would judge certain debased groups in society as worthless and expendable. And he did so with a credibility, an antiauthority, deriving from his own dishonorable social status. This status, known to fans and partially rehearsed in "Fuck Aneta Briant," was not that of a queer but that of a redneck, ex-con Outlaw Country singer and songwriter. Coe wielded cred concerning "faggots" via a shared social position of disreputability and marginality—in his case, as a member of the working class, and in particular its "hard-living" sector, and as a former inmate versed in the ways of male prison society.[53]

But this is not to say that Coe crafted his public image at great distance from same-sex eroticism. That was certainly not the case in his appearance in about 1984 on *Midnight Blue,* a long-running sex-themed New York public access cable show (1974–2003) created and hosted by the publisher of *Screw* magazine, Al Goldstein. Coe opened his dual-episode guest stint with a solo performance, live and unplugged, of the first verse of "Fuck Aneta Briant."[54] With the salient themes thus broached, Goldstein asked

Coe about his murder of a fellow inmate who had tried to have sex with him. The rumor that he had killed a man in prison circulated widely in Coe's heyday, apparently promoted by the singer himself. *Rolling Stone* went after the story and questioned its veracity in a 1976 article.[55] But whether or not apocryphal, the tale is intriguing and, particularly in Coe's *Midnight Blue* embroiderings, provocative for present purposes.

Goldstein began, "You killed a homosexual in prison. What motivated that kind of a violent response?" Coe stumbled on the characterization he had been handed. "I'm not sure he *was* a homosexual. Well, I guess he was a hom—he wanted to fuck me in *my* ass. You know?" Perhaps for Coe here, as for Chauncey's early-twentieth-century working-class men, the "manly," insertive sexual role did not link to a deviant labeling. But as he attempted to clarify the nature of the incident, Coe also struggled with the word *homosexual* itself. The middle class's concept and term somehow did not fit the story he needed to tell. He finally abandoned it in favor of the explanation, "He wanted to fuck me in *my* ass." Remarkably, Coe then continued with this account of his reason for (allegedly) killing the man: "I mean, it woulda been—I might not have killed him if he wanted me to fuck him in *his* ass. But, you know, it was a different situation. It was basically because he was trying to force me to do something I didn't wanna do."[56]

So, David Allan Coe, hardest of the hard country outlaws, stated on Al Goldstein's cable show that he might have been amenable to, or at least unbothered by, a solicitation for anal sex from a fellow male inmate—so long as he himself figured in the insertive role. Later in the interview, Coe averred, too, that his erotic aesthetic, developed while he was in juvenile detention, focused on "the guy in prison with the nice ass." This male-bodied ideal was for him the exclusive marker of femininity, he explained, such that even up to that day he liked only small-breasted women.[57] All told, Coe's declarations on *Midnight Blue*, and likewise his lyrics in "Fuck Aneta Briant," seem completely, and perhaps (for a public figure) danger-ously, out of step with dominant hetero-masculine standards of the late 1970s to mid-1980s. In his overt expressions of awe and affection for "fag-gots"; his profession of need for their social, sexual, and domestic attentions in a prison context; and his disregard for the homo/hetero paradigm and his defining emphasis on gender role in male sexual match-ups, Coe conjures the historical working-class same-sex worlds documented by Chauncey and Boyd.[58]

But Coe's utterances date from 1978–84, well beyond the documented era of gender-based "prehomosexual" cultures. Chauncey shows that "it was easier for workingmen" than for middle-class men "to engage in [same-sex] activity because the conventions of their sexual world tended to categorize only one of the men involved as 'queer'"—the one who took the "womanly" role. He views these conventions, however, as persisting into the 1950s at the latest.[59] Perhaps this suggests that we should not pay too much attention to Coe's claims and imaginings. For one thing, his outlook is rooted in prison society, which bears certain connections but is by no means equivalent to life on the outside. And Coe's perspectives are likely to be most relevant not only to prison society, but to that of the mid-1940s to mid-1960s, when, by his own account, he did his time. Moreover, Coe has sustained a nearly forty-year reputation for being boastful, self-mythologizing, and outrageous, and he came under scrutiny as such early on.

Granting all this, however, there is still the matter of Coe's reception by his hard country audience—which in his commercial prime included many mainstream fans but since the 1990s has condensed into a fervent and loyal following that may be the most hard-core, rough, dangerous crowd in all of American country music. Despite the underground release of "Fuck Aneta Briant" and surely, too, because of it, the song has made the rounds among Coe's audiences, through his concert and other appearances, fans' bootleg recordings, and, now, eBay sales of the original *Nothing Sacred* LP and YouTube postings of the album track. In the years since its appearance, the song, even in its first-person and autobiographical framing, has never queered Coe in the reception sphere. But neither, despite its sharp, prescient targeting of Bryant and her consequential antigay crusade, has it ever politicized Coe's image.

Today, "Fuck Aneta Briant," in all its familiarity with and fondness for "faggot" social and sexual practices, stands as an artifact of a past social order, an order at odds with current cultural narratives and fast disappearing from collective memory. It was a social order rooted in ideology equating the primitive, the criminal, and the disreputable with the working class; equating these same stigmatized qualities with sexual and gender queerness; and, by similar logic, equating the working class with the queer. In current ideology, it is the middle class that is equated with the queer, following a different logic having to do with, not stigma, but ideals of enlightenment, tolerance, and liberation. Hence what I have termed the middle-classing of the queer—and hence the present homonormative moment, in which bourgeois concerns around marriage and child rearing dominate the LGBTQ political agenda, and queerness often seems to bolster, more than challenge, the social, political, and economic status quo. Left commentators have often bemoaned this state of affairs, and it may be telling that one of the hottest recent releases in LGBTQ nonfiction is Justin Spring's *Secret*

Historian: The Life and Times of Samuel Steward, Professor, Tattoo Artist, and Sexual Renegade (2010), a story of middle-class gay writer and professor Steward's exotic adventures in the working-class male social-sexual underground of the mid-twentieth century. Readers' and critics' fervent embrace of Spring's book evinces fascination with a past queer world markedly more colorful and edgy than contemporary homonormalized, middle-classed queer life.

RECOGNITION, NAMING, AND POWER (CONCLUSION)

In 1978, the Outlaw Country artist David Allan Coe recorded "Fuck Aneta Briant," a ribald condemnation of Anita Bryant and her antigay crusade and a paean to the diverse attributes of prison queers. Over thirty years later, in 2011, the alternative rock band Foo Fighters recorded "Keep It Clean (Hot Buns)," a mildly ribald redneck-inflected gay joke in the form of a mock-country song. The Foo Fighters song was widely lauded as a political statement on behalf of gay tolerance, particularly in a Kansas City performance before antigay protesters from Westboro Baptist Church. We might ask now why Coe's song has not been recognized as a political statement.

There are undoubtedly many factors at work here. Among them, we should note that Coe's song predates the Internet and the 24/7 news cycle, which were the means of notoriety for the Foo Fighters song. We could also observe that "Fuck Aneta Briant" was released only on an underground record, while "Keep It Clean (Hot Buns)" was never released as a record—and both tracks are now available online on YouTube. Recalling the histories rehearsed in this chapter might bring us to other observations. First, given that middle-class respectability was the pivotal strategy behind the political gains of the U.S. homophile movement and its successors, the disreputable Coe is clearly the wrong messenger for any queer-related statement destined for "political" recognition. Second, the queerness that the singer invokes is not the political kind: it is not gender-normative homosexuality (Coe tripped on the word) distinguished by same-sex object choice alone, advanced by activists, and belonging to the middle class. Rather, the kind of queerness Coe invokes is gender based and prehomosexual and has been the property of the working class. Kennedy and Davis went so far as to call this latter kind of queerness prepolitical, granting recognition of its historical importance in catalyzing social change. Extending this assessment, Boyd has labeled it political, without qualification. But these scholars' interpretations knowingly fly in the face of dominant ideology.

I observed just above that Coe is the wrong messenger for a pro-LGBTQ political statement. Clearly the singer's hard-core, déclassé persona is counterproductive in the context of a lesbian and gay rights movement built on bourgeois respectability. But that is not the only issue. The British theorists John Clarke and Stuart Hall and their colleagues' analysis of youth subculture suggests that another messenger would fare no better, so long as the medium is working-class culture. On their view, the dominant culture renders working-class culture as delinquent no matter how emphatically political and middle-class culture as political even when antipolitical.

> The objective oppositional content of working-class subculture expresses itself socially. It is therefore often assimilated by the control culture to traditional forms of working-class "delinquency," defined as Hooliganism or Vandalism. The [middle-class hippie and other post-1965] counter-cultures take a more overtly ideological or political form. They make articulate their opposition to dominant values and institutions—even when, as [has] frequently occurred, this does not take the form of an overtly political response. Even when working-class subcultures are aggressively class-conscious, this dimension tends to be repressed by the control culture, which treats them as "typical delinquents." Even when the middle-class counter-cultures are explicitly anti-political, their objective tendency is treated as, potentially, political.[60]

More recent analyses of the workings of contemporary politics underscore the centrality of the neoliberal individual and of claims to individual rights. Skeggs points out that contemporary queer political advocacy is based on a "recognition politics" involving individual rights claims. But research reveals that recognition politics are available exclusively to middle-class individuals. And so in this framework, too, working-class queer politics appear as a conceptual impossibility.[61]

The celebratory media reception of "Keep It Clean (Hot Buns)" stood on images of the hillbilly pervert and the redneck homophobe—that is, on both the twentieth- and twenty-first-century scripts pathologizing the working class through the queer. These ideological scripts are, of course, opposite and contradictory to each other. The new one gradually overtook the old one in the final decades of the twentieth century—though, as Foo Fighters demonstrate, the priapic hillbilly can still resurface and even appear in tandem with the redneck homophobe. Coe's "Fuck Aneta Briant" emerged in this moment of transition as a cultural utterance that was legible by the old optics—of prehomosexual, gender-based queerness understood as a working-class phenomenon—and was rather puzzling by the new optics of middle-class, gender-normative homosexuality. Such puzzlement can be useful in our own moment. The cultural amnesia, or presentism, of our time fosters the belief, not simply that the working class is the homophobic bigot class, but that things have always been so. Listening to "Fuck Aneta Briant" impels us to question both propositions.

By thus challenging presentist notions, the song can provoke us, further, to revisit the history of twentieth-century LGBTQ activism and social-cultural change. In the process, we might conclude that the homophile activists were right to get their hands on some respectability. Doing so allowed them, eventually, to retain their middle-class status without denying their homosexuality—hence, to be recognized as individuals with legitimate rights claims and so to be marked as political rather than sexual. Homophile activists' sustained tactics of respectability ushered in (what I have called) the middle-classing of the queer, and the queer cultural category forged thereby is, definitively, both middle-classed and political. The contemporary politicized queer exists apart from the working class and its members, no matter how political. Indeed, the working class today serves as a prime foil against which the middle-classed, politicized queer is defined. So just as the white working class has become coded as hyperwhite and racist after having long been stigmatized for its insufficient whiteness, this group that was so long deemed deficient in respectable, *hetero* sexuality is now too an emblem of pathological hyperstraightness and homophobia.[62]

Social and cultural values change over time following upon changes in the dominant middle class, which dynamically adapts its self-constructions in ways that preserve its social dominance. This consequential self-fashioning is grounded in distinction from an othered working class, whose image in the mainstream culture is radically reductive and pathologized. Nonrecognition of working-class culture, in its existence and intricacies, enables nonrecognition of working-class political expression and its complexities. And both are instrumental to middle-class power.

Outro

David Allan Coe was a top-selling singer and songwriter in his 1970s prime, but his antibourgeois and antihomophobic 1978 underground album track "Fuck Aneta Briant" stands apart, in its ribaldry and blatant obscenity, from mainstream country music. By 1992, Garth Brooks had sounded a more earnest, even churchy, antihomophobic note with "We Shall Be Free." More recent antihomophobic and queer-friendly country releases include Toby Keith's "I Love This Bar" (#1 2004, #26 Pop), whose video features a comically sympathetic transwoman in its colorful cast of characters, and Willie Nelson's contribution to the *Brokeback Mountain* sound track, "Cowboys Are Frequently Secretly Fond of Each Other" (2006). Phil Vassar's "Bobbi with an I" (#46 2010) is a gently humorous ode to a regular Joe, one-of-the-guys transvestite that urges, "live and let live." Rascal Flatts' title line in "Love Who You Love" (2009) signified to many listeners in much the same way as Brooks's "free to love anyone we choose" had done years earlier. In "All Kinds of Kinds" (2011) Miranda Lambert presents a set of vignettes on fringy and eccentric characters, including a cross-dressing congressman, that unfolds over a compelling and equally eccentric two-against-three polyrhythmic groove. The refrain, "Ever since the beginning, to keep the world spinning / It takes all kinds of kinds," is extended in the coda to call out those who "point a finger," making the song's ultimate message one of hillbilly humanism.[1] Her fellow Texan singer-songwriter Kacey Musgraves's #1 country album, *Same Trailer, Different Park* (2013), elicited comparisons to Lambert and includes a track, "Follow Your Arrow," exhorting listeners to "Love who you love" (echoing Rascal Flatts) and to pursue their own paths "When the straight and narrow / Gets a little too straight."

A salient theme in these queer-affirmative country songs is LGBTQ characters' belonging within an everyday, regular-folk social world. The realm of regular folk may be marked as socioeconomically low (e.g., "Fuck Aneta Briant"), as small-town or rural (e.g., "Cowboys Are Frequently Secretly Fond of Each Other"), or as both (e.g., "Bobbi with an I"). This book's discussion of country music and the queer has focused primarily on the social and political workings of socioeconomic class—whose high/low opposition is often represented symbolically in urban/rustic oppositions. But the rustic and provincial meanings associated with country music also link to another analytic perspective on the queer, one that asks how queerness operates in actual social spaces structured, not by urban anonymity, but by small-town familiarity. These are spaces in which everybody knows everybody's business via networks of relationship and exchange tracing an individual's history back across years, often from birth. Rural and small-town sites have long been imagined as antithetical to LGBTQ life, the very places one must escape in order to realize queer desires. But current research on LGBTQ life in rural America complicates and questions prevailing assumptions.

Recent studies of rural LGBTQ people by the sociologist Emily Kazyak and the anthropologist Mary Gray, among others, suggest that established presence in the community and adherence to moral values like loyalty, honor, and personal sincerity come before all else—including sexual identity—in rural social life. The rural cultural logic of social coexistence and interaction involves being known and trusted, accepted in the community as "a good person."[2] Then, according to some queer locals, you can be whatever you want to be. In the words of one rural gay man, "Most people really don't give a damn."[3]

We need more research to know the extent to which such findings on rural social life might jibe with class-based traits in social life. I would note, however, that Lamont has flagged the same qualities identified here with the rural—of loyalty, honor, and personal sincerity—as paramount values in the American working class.[4] Pursuing these resonances between rural and working-class repertoires, we might observe that another way of viewing the rural social ethos described here—in which being a "good person" takes priority over identity labeling—is as a species of walk-the-walk values, in which actions speak louder than words and substance trumps surface. In this connection we might recall Ollivier's study identifying greater working-class respect for "useful" occupations than for others designated prestigious, Walker's research finding walk-the-walk values in working-class friendship, Ehrenreich and Valentine's revelations of social identity labeling as an important tool of middle-class domination, and the testimony of Cyphert and of various songs regarding the highly developed and highly valued arts of nonverbal communication in working-class and country music realms. We might further note that Peterson identified a resistance to social division and exceptionalist, special-interest claims in country song lyrics.[5] Given the apparent overlaps between rural and working-class values and perspectives concerning sociality and the queer, perhaps a broader aegis could be useful here, like the "traditional" rubric that Sample applied to political culture.

In any case, an ethos of establishing oneself as a known and valued member of the local community—specifically apart from acknowledgment of any LGBTQ identity status—is clearly at odds with current dominant ideals of LGBTQ visibility. That is, we can see a mismatch between the workings of rural and, perhaps, working-class queerness and the contemporary visibility-based coming out standard for LGBTQ identity and legitimacy, a visibility standard through which urban and middle-class "homonorms" have been exported, universalized, and globalized. The politics of LGBTQ visibility—built on the *invisibility* of racially and class-marked gender-variant people—comes out of a middle-class logic involving claims to individual rights. What we "know" of working-class and rural communities, in the larger world and the academy (including LGBTQ studies), typically issues from middle-class and urban perspectives that regard these communities as the breeding grounds of homophobia and bigotry. Under a middle-class, "metronormative" lens, the absence of visible LGBTQ difference here is evidence of backwardness and intolerance.[6] The standard by which working-class and rural communities are judged and found lacking is that of rights claims, based on a recognition politics that is available only to middle-class individuals.[7] As social theory demonstrates, the middle class is blind to the social and cultural systems of the working class, and vice versa: although middle-class perspectives and values are dominant, they are anything but transparent from a working-class standpoint.[8]

The examples in this book have framed the dominant culture's metrics as ill calibrated to working-class values, practices, and histories. But dominant middle-class understandings of the world are nevertheless imposed on the working class, which is thereby proved deficient and at fault in various ways, particularly in its taste and its politics. Prominent here since the 1970s is the white working class's alleged fervent bigotry, which, according to Thomas Frank's analysis and others, allows this group to be used as a tool of the American Right. The Right, by this account, deploys racism, sexism, and homophobia to attract working-class votes, even as it crafts economic and social policies that benefit the rich and devastate the working class. The white working class, on this view, place a higher value on venting their antagonisms than protecting their own interests.

But it is not only the white working class who suffer under policies favoring the rich and powerful. Recent liberal and progressive dialogues have taken notice of dramatic, at times unprecedented, increases in American income and wealth disparity since the early 1980s, separating the rich and super rich from the rest of society—including the middle and professional middle classes. In this environment, middle-class liberals and progressives have much to gain by making common cause with the working class and seeking out the places where their values and interests might align. By various gauges, however, the divisions between the two groups appear to be growing wider and deeper.[9] Too often it seems middle-class liberals and progressives would rather maintain moral and cultural superiority over the white working class than build alliances with them. They seem, that is, to place a higher value on venting their antagonisms than protecting their own interests.

Those who wish, however, to understand American culture and politics might benefit from taking a look at, and a listen to, working-class cultural expression—beyond the dominant middle-class narratives that interpret, represent, and often misrepresent it.

Notes

INTRO

1. Video posted at http://hotbuns.foofighters.com (accessed September 21, 2011). I am grateful to Nancy Guy for bringing this video to my attention.

2. Video posted at www.youtube.com/watch?v=6e5hRLbCaCs#t=28 (accessed August 22, 2013).

3. George Chauncey Jr., "Christian Brotherhood or Sexual Perversion? Homosexual Identity and the Construction of Sexual Boundaries in the World War I Era" (1985), in *Hidden from History: Reclaiming the Gay and Lesbian Past*, ed. Martin Bauml Duberman, Martha Vicinus, and George Chauncey Jr. (New York: New American Library, 1989), 294–317. See also Lawrence R. Murphy, "Cleaning Up Newport: The U.S. Navy's Persecution of Homosexuals after World War I," *Journal of American Culture* 7, no. 3 (1984): 57–64.

4. Pierre Bourdieu, *Distinction: A Social Critique of the Judgement of Taste*, trans. Richard Nice (Cambridge, MA: Harvard University Press, 1984).

5. Bethany Bryson, "'Anything but Heavy Metal': Symbolic Exclusion and Musical Dislikes," *American Sociological Review* 61, no. 5 (1996): 884–99.

6. See Beverley Skeggs, *Formations of Class and Gender: Becoming Respectable* (London: Sage, 1997), 3.

7. As Aaron A. Fox argues, country music is regarded as racially "contaminated" in connection with its white working-class audience, who are seen as the vectors of a bad, "unredeemed" whiteness: "White Trash Alchemies of the Abject Sublime: Country as 'Bad' Music," in *Bad Music: The Music We Love to Hate*, ed. Charles J. Washburne and Maiken Derno (New York: Routledge, 2004), 44. I discuss his analysis further in chapter 1.

8. One institution that was powerful in defining twentieth-century homosexuality, its meanings, and its implications on social, legal, and medical fronts was the American Psychiatric Association (APA). The APA removed homosexuality from its list of psychiatric disorders only in 1973, following an internal battle among psychiatric authorities whose professional success and theoretical investments were riding on the decision. See Dudley Clendinen and

Adam Nagourney, *Out for Good: The Struggle to Build a Gay Rights Movement in America* (New York: Simon & Schuster, 1999), 199–217.

9. See Alfred Kinsey et al., *Sexual Behavior in the Human Male* (Philadelphia: W. B. Saunders, 1948).

10. The term *homonormativity* originates in Lisa Duggan, *The Twilight of Equality? Neoliberalism, Cultural Politics, and the Attack on Democracy* (Boston: Beacon Press, 2003), where it is defined as "a politics that does not contest dominant heteronormative assumptions and institutions, but upholds and sustains them, while promising the possibility of a demobilized gay constituency and a privatized, depoliticized gay culture anchored in domesticity and consumption . . . [and a politics produced] through a double-voiced address to an imagined gay public, on the one hand, and to the national mainstream constructed by neoliberalism on the other" (50–51).

11. Beverley Skeggs, *Class, Self, Culture* (New York: Routledge, 2004), 4. Skeggs's important and influential work theorizes the centrality of respectability in contemporary class dynamics.

12. A lesser-known designation ascribes political agency: Stonewall Rebellion. Accounts describe the bar patrons and police resisters as racially diverse and including many poor and working-class people. But they differ regarding the number and types of queens involved. David Carter, *Stonewall: The Riots That Sparked the Gay Revolution* (New York: St. Martin's, 2004), argues that drag queens' involvement, in particular, has been exaggerated, but other accounts, including Martin Duberman, *Stonewall* (New York: Dutton, 1993), accord drag queens an important role. See David Valentine, *Imagining Transgender: An Ethnography of a Category* (Durham, NC: Duke University Press, 2007), 45 ff., for further discussion of these debates.

13. The "prepolitical" impact of working-class lesbians' bar-based culture and resistance, including femme-butch visibility, and its historiographic overshadowing by the organized, institutional activism of the middle-class homophile organizations are underscored in Elizabeth Lapovsky Kennedy and Madeline D. Davis, *Boots of Leather, Slippers of Gold: The History of a Lesbian Community* (New York: Routledge, 1993); and Nan Alamilla Boyd, *Wide-Open Town: A History of Queer San Francisco to 1965* (Berkeley: University of California Press, 2003). Also relevant here is John Howard's observation, from his oral histories of gay black and white men—many working class—who were active in Mississippi in the 1960s, "that gay identity in Mississippi (surely as elsewhere) existed alongside multiple queer desires that were not identity based or identity forging": John Howard, ed., *Carryin' On in the Lesbian and Gay South* (New York: New York University Press, 1997), 29. The definitive history of the homophile movement is John D'Emilio, *Sexual Politics, Sexual Communities: The Making of a Homosexual Minority in the United States, 1940–1970* (Chicago: University of Chicago Press, 1983). On visibility politics, see Beverley Skeggs, "Uneasy Alignments: Resourcing Respectable Subjectivity," *GLQ: A Journal of Lesbian and Gay Studies* 10, no. 2 (2004): 294, who cites Nancy Fraser's and Charles Taylor's work on the politics of recognition in formulating

her arguments on this point. Perhaps comparably, Gayatri Gopinath points to a mismatch between visibility projects and postcolonial subjects' conditioned tendency to avoid visibility, categorization, and enumeration, which have been associated with colonial surveillance and legal apparatuses: *Impossible Desires: Queer Diasporas and South Asian Public Cultures* (Durham, NC: Duke University Press, 2005), 151.

14. Bill C. Malone, *Country Music U.S.A.*, 2nd rev. ed. (Austin: University of Texas Press, [1968] 2002), long the definitive source for the history of country music from its origins to the present, dates the birth of commercial country to 1923 (37–38). Katie Stewart refutes the distanced critique of country music as a massifying corruption of some earlier, more authentic folk form into the "naive schlock" of a failed realism and reads country as embodying the cultural poetics of romance—Northrup Frye's "vision of . . . life as a quest": "Engendering Narratives of Lament in Country Music," in *All That Glitters: Country Music in America*, ed. George H. Lewis (Bowling Green, OH: Bowling Green State University Popular Press, 1993), 221–25. For an account of the role of commercialism in country music, see Diane Pecknold, *The Selling Sound: The Rise of the Country Music Industry* (Durham, NC: Duke University Press, 2007).

15. Chart figures refer to the Billboard Country Songs Chart: www.billboard.com.

16. Richard A. Peterson, "Soft Shell vs. Hard Core: The Vagabonds vs. Roy Acuff," in *Creating Country Music: Fabricating Authenticity* (Chicago: University of Chicago Press, 1997), 137–58. Peterson's account builds on Malone's identification of the two historical practices in *Country Music U.S.A.* Peterson does not explicitly identify the two practices in class terms, but his detailed, many-faceted taxonomy suggests clearly the correlation of hard/soft to working class/middle class. Neither Malone nor Peterson develops a gender analysis in connection with the hard/soft stylistic binary, but Barbara Ching does so in *Wrong's What I Do Best: Hard Country Music and Contemporary Culture* (New York: Oxford University Press, 2003).

17. Berman, quoted in Heather Nelson, "A New Shine: Silver Jews Tunesmith/Poet Moves to Town," *Nashville Scene,* January 13, 2000, www .nashvillescene.com/nashville/a-new-shine/Content?oid = 1183887 (accessed April 12, 2012).

18. *Rolling Stone*'s "100 Greatest Singers of All Time" was published in print on November 27, 2008, and online at www.rollingstone.com/music /lists/100-greatest-singers-of-all-time-19691231 (accessed January 10, 2012).

19. Chuck Klosterman, *Sex, Drugs, and Cocoa Puffs: A Low Culture Manifesto* (New York: Scribner, 2003), 167. The definitive text on bluegrass is Neil V. Rosenberg, *Bluegrass: A History* (Urbana: University of Illinois Press, [1985] 2005). Thanks to Daniel Party for bringing Klosterman's discussion of country music here to my attention.

20. Richard A. Peterson and Russell Davis Jr., "The Fertile Crescent of Country Music," *Journal of Country Music* 6 (1975): 19–27; Gerald W. Haslam, *Workin' Man Blues: Country Music in California* (Berkeley: University of

California Press, 1999), 16–17; northern migration figures in the biographies of several midwestern country musicians, a group that includes Bobby Bare, Jerry Brightman, David Allan Coe, Diamond Rio, Jerry Douglas, Janie Fricke, Crystal Gayle, Josh Gracin, Harlan Howard, Alison Krauss, Martina McBride, Johnny Paycheck, Rascal Flatts, Roy Rogers, Connie Smith, Gretchen Wilson, Chely Wright, and Dwight Yoakam, among others.

21. On shifting country audience demographics, see Richard A. Peterson and Paul DiMaggio, "From Region to Class, the Changing Locus of Country Music: A Test of the Massification Hypothesis," *Social Forces* 53, no. 3 (1975): 497–506, esp. 500–503.

22. See, for example, the country scholar and Albuquerque, NM, native Jocelyn Neal's account of the long-standing "sense of ownership" of country music in the Albuquerque region, "equally native" and often blended with Tejano and Norteño music. Jocelyn R. Neal, "Dancing around the Subject: Race in Country Fan Culture," *Musical Quarterly* 89, no. 4 (2006): 572.

23. These figures are based on quantitative analysis of 2000 U.S. Census data from over 14,000 respondents, in Alana Conner Snibbe and Hazel Rose Markus, "You Can't Always Get What You Want: Educational Attainment, Agency, and Choice," *Journal of Personality and Social Psychology* 88, no. 4 (2005): 706–8.

24. Snibbe and Markus, "You Can't Always Get What You Want." The authors review the relevant literature (706–7) and report results of their own studies demonstrating correlation between popular song lyrics and certain social groups (708–9).

25. Malone, *Country Music U.S.A.*, 298; for similar perspectives, see also Malone's *Don't Get above Your Raisin': Country Music and the Southern Working Class* (Urbana: University of Illinois Press, 2002); Mary A. Bufwack and Robert K. Oermann, *Finding Her Voice: The Saga of Women in Country Music* (New York: Crown Publishers, 1993), ix–x; David Fillingim, *Redneck Liberation: Country Music as Theology* (Macon, GA: Mercer University Press, 2003); and Tex Sample, *White Soul: Country Music, the Church, and Working Americans* (Nashville, TN: Abingdon Press, 1996), 70–77. Aaron A. Fox, *Real Country: Music and Language in Working-Class Culture* (Durham, NC: Duke University Press, 2004), dust jacket blurb.

26. Chapter 1 discusses Bryson's findings that country's associations with the least-educated audiences exclude it from the tastes of entitled agents of "multicultural capital": "'Anything but Heavy Metal,'" 884–99. Her conclusions underscore music's importance to "group identity and social differentiation" (885). Relatedly, Stephanie Lawler shows that disgust toward the working class is essential to middle-class identity and constitutive of middle-class subjectivity: "Disgusted Subjects: The Making of Middle-Class Identities," *Sociological Review* 53, no. 3 (2005): 429–46. Chapter 1 also examines perceptions of racism and homophobia in country music and the white working class.

27. Bourdieu, *Distinction*, identifies the middle class as dominant in late-capitalist culture, and the working class as dominated.

28. On post-1980 U.S. and country-musical suburbanization, see Malone, *Don't Get above Your Raisin'*, 47–48, 168–69.

29. Bryson, "'Anything but Heavy Metal'"; and Snibbe and Markus, "You Can't Always Get What You Want," 707–8.

30. Quoting Bourdieu, *Distinction*, 45; see also Paul Fussell's perspectives on bourgeois euphemism and other characteristic discursive habits of the upper (and working) class in "The Life of the Mind," in *Class: A Guide through the American Status System* (New York: Touchstone, 1983), 128–50. On the history and meaning of redneck identity, see Patrick Huber, "A Short History of *Redneck:* The Fashioning of a Southern Masculine Identity," in *Southern Cultures: The Fifteenth Anniversary Reader*, ed. Harry L. Watson and Larry J. Griffin, with Lisa Eveleigh, Dave Shaw, Ayse Erginer, and Paul Quigley (Chapel Hill: University of North Carolina Press, 2008), 303–27; on its complex social and cultural functions, see John Hartigan Jr., "Who Are These White People? 'Rednecks,' 'Hillbillies,' and 'White Trash' as Marked Racial Subjects," in *White Out: The Continuing Significance of Racism*, ed. Ashley W. Doane and Eduardo Bonilla-Silva (New York: Routledge, 2003), and his other works cited here. On redneck pride, see Richard A. Peterson, "Class Unconsciousness in Country Music," in *You Wrote My Life: Lyrical Themes in Country Music*, ed. Melton A. McLaurin and Richard A. Peterson (Langhorne, PA: Gordon and Breach, 1992), 57–58; and Malone, *Don't Get above Your Raisin'*, 46.

31. Bryson, "'Anything but Heavy Metal.'"

32. Snibbe and Markus, "You Can't Always Get What You Want," 706–8, again using 2000 U.S. Census data from over 14,000 white respondents. See also Bryson, "'Anything but Heavy Metal.'" Peterson and DiMaggio surveyed country radio audiences in 1968–72: see "From Region to Class, the Changing Locus of Country Music," 503.

33. Some working-class subjects defined themselves by contrast to "unreal" middle-class others they referred to as "Barbie and Ken people," in Michèle Lamont, *The Dignity of Working Men: Morality and the Boundaries of Race, Class, and Immigration* (Cambridge, MA: Harvard University Press, 2000), 109, 148. "People of Walmart" is the name of a website hosting anonymous contributors' photos of unsuspecting shoppers at Walmart stores in all fifty U.S. states and their mocking and abusive comments on the shoppers' bodies and styles of self-presentation, including tattoos, hair, clothing, and cars.

34. Bourdieu, *Distinction*, 871.

35. Bourdieu, *Distinction*, 871.

36. Pierre Bourdieu, "The Forms of Capital," trans. Richard Nice, in *Handbook of a Theory of Research for the Sociology of Education*, ed. John G. Richardson (Westport, CT: Greenwood Press, 1986), 241–58.

37. In an important and influential analysis along these lines, George Lipsitz views whiteness in the U.S. context as having a "cash value": *The Possessive Investment in Whiteness: How White People Profit from Identity Politics*, rev. and expanded ed. (Philadelphia: Temple University Press, [1998] 2006), vii.

38. A U.S. sociologist's early review of Bourdieu's work identifies misrecognition in similar terms and locates the original source in a 1973 French journal article by Bourdieu, Luc Boltanski, and Monique de Saint Martin: Paul DiMaggio, "On Pierre Bourdieu," *American Journal of Sociology* 84, no. 6 (1979): 1464, 1466.

39. Pierre Bourdieu, *Practical Reason: On the Theory of Action* (Cambridge: Polity Press, 1998), 25 ff.

40. Alfred Lubrano, *Limbo: Blue-Collar Roots, White-Collar Dreams* (Hoboken, NJ: Wiley, 2004).

41. Bourdieu, *Distinction*, 372.

42. Sherry B. Ortner, *New Jersey Dreaming: Capital, Culture, and the Class of '58* (Durham, NC: Duke University Press, 2003), 41.

43. Mike Savage, Gaynor Bagnall, and Brian Longhurst, "Ordinary, Ambivalent and Defensive: Class Identities in the Northwest of England," *Sociology* 35, no. 4 (2001): 877, characterizing John H. Goldthorpe.

44. Bourdieu, *Distinction*, 56.

45. Skeggs, *Class, Self, Culture*; Sherry B. Ortner, *Anthropology and Social Theory: Culture, Power, and the Acting Subject* (Durham, NC: Duke University Press, 2006); Barbara Ehrenreich, *Fear of Falling: The Inner Life of the Middle Class* (New York: Pantheon Books, 1989). Malone, *Don't Get above Your Raisin'* (and other works); Fox, *Real Country*; George Chauncey Jr., *Gay New York: Gender, Urban Culture, and the Makings of the Gay Male World, 1890–1940* (New York: Basic Books, 1994); Kennedy and Davis, *Boots of Leather, Slippers of Gold*; Boyd, *Wide-Open Town*.

46. Drawing from empirical data, one prominent class scholar, the labor and political economist Michael Zweig, views the poor not as a separate class, "not some persistent lump at the bottom of society," but as working-class people who have fallen on hard times. He estimates the proportion of working-class Americans in the overall population at 62 percent: *The Working Class Majority: America's Best Kept Secret* (Ithaca, NY: Cornell University Press, 2000), 86. Others emphasize differences in the identity and experience of poor Americans by contrast to members of the working class. The literary, gender, and class scholar Vivyan C. Adair argues convincingly for the latter view in "US Working-Class/Poverty-Class Divides," *Sociology* 39, no. 5 (2005): 817–34.

47. Chauncey, "Christian Brotherhood or Sexual Perversion?," 294–317; and Valentine, *Imagining Transgender*.

CHAPTER 1

1. See Malone, *Country Music U.S.A.*, 40–42, for discussion of the ambivalence surrounding the use of "hillbilly" and the negative and positive associations attaching to hillbilly music in the early days of country music.

2. Eric Drott, "What Inclusiveness Excludes," in "Colloquy: Musicology beyond Borders?," ed. Tamara Levitz, *Journal of the American Musicological Society* 65, no. 3 (2012): 827.

3. Bryson, "'Anything but Heavy Metal,'" introduces the term *multicultural capital* and follows on the work that introduced the concept of the contemporary "cultural omnivore": Richard A. Peterson, "Understanding Audience Segmentation: From Elite and Mass to Omnivore and Univore," *Poetics* 21 (1992): 243–58; and Richard A. Peterson and Albert Simkus, "How Musical Tastes Mark Occupational Status Groups," in *Cultivating Differences: Symbolic Boundaries and the Making of Inequality,* ed. Michèle Lamont and Marcel Fournier (Chicago: University of Chicago Press, 1993), 152–86. The 1975 study of country listeners, analyzing data collected in 1968–72, was Peterson and DiMaggio, "From Region to Class, the Changing Locus of Country Music."

4. The phrase appears in "Foo Fighters 'Hot Buns' Video: Band Nude in the Shower (NSFW VIDEO)," www.huffingtonpost.com/2011/08/29/foo-fighters-hot-buns-video_n_941033.html (accessed September 21, 2011).

5. "Foo Fighters: Westboro Baptist Church Counter-Protest With 'Keep It Clean (Hot Buns),'" September 18, 2011, www.huffingtonpost.com/2011/09/18/foo-fighters-westboro-baptist-church_n_968395.html (accessed September 21, 2011); Jeremy Kinser, "Foo Fighters Sing about Tolerance before Westboro Protesters," September 19, 2011, www.advocate.com/News/Daily_News/2011/09/19/Foo_Fighters_Sing_About_Tolerance_Before_Westboro_Protesters (accessed September 21, 2011); Kevin O'Donnell, "Foo Fighters Announce Tour with NSFW Clip," August 29, 2011, www.spin.com/articles/foo-fighters-announce-tour-nsfw-clip (accessed September 21, 2011).

6. In another apparent rock-historical allusion, "Keep It Clean" shares its title with a 1977 song by the The Vibrators, new wave–punk pioneers of the straight edge movement that is carried on by the members of Rise Against (among others), who joined Foo Fighters on their fall 2011 tour.

7. As of September 21, 2011, viewings were about 275,000 and 150,000, respectively.

8. In Foo Fighters' video of the Kansas City street event, behind-the-scenes cutaways show Grohl singing this line with evident relish backstage in the lead-up to the band's performance (and add still more scatological footage, now showing a band member using a urinal).

9. Quoted phrases are from Jeremy Kinser, "Foo Fighters Sing about Tolerance before Westboro Protesters"; and *Huffington Post,* "Foo Fighters: Westboro Baptist Church Counter-Protest With 'Keep It Clean (Hot Buns),'" respectively.

10. *Tobacco Road* is a 1932 novel by Erskine Caldwell, later made into a hugely successful Broadway play (1933–41) and film (1940). *Deliverance* is a 1970 best-selling novel by James Dickey that was made into a blockbuster 1972 film by John Boorman. Both stories feature poor white characters marked by physical grotesqueries and sensational, animalistic sexuality. The term *priapic hillbilly* originates with the British cultural studies scholar David Bell in "Farm Boys and Wild Men: Rurality, Masculinity, and Homosexuality," *Rural Sociology* 65, no. 4 (2000): 547–61, but echoes J. W. Williamson's discussion of the hillbilly as priapus in *Hillbillyland: What the Movies Did to the Mountains*

and What the Mountains Did to the Movies (Chapel Hill: University of North Carolina Press, 1995), 61–64.

11. The quote draws on two comments dating from September 19, 2011, and signed by truckdawg43, www.youtube.com/watch?v=EWSeDYTHtiQ (accessed November 16, 2011).

12. After performing the song across from the Westboro protest on September 16, 2011, Grohl spoke on mic in Jed-face: "God Bless America! It takes all kinds! I don't care if you're black or white or purple or green, whether you're Pennsylvanian or Transylvanian, Lady Gaga or Lady Antebellum."

13. Joel Whitburn, *The Billboard Book of Top 40 Hits*, 6th ed. (New York: Billboard, 1996), 806.

14. The album, *In a Metal Mood: No More Mr. Nice Guy* (Hip-O Records 40025), peaked at #125. In the realm of singles, Boone had fifty-three career Top 40 hits, of which thirty-eight landed on the U.S. pop charts (all in 1955–62), ten on adult contemporary (1961–75), four on R&B (1955–57), and one on the country charts, a record called "Texas Woman" that peaked at #34 in 1976: see www.musicvf.com/Pat+Boone.art (accessed November 7, 2011).

15. See HRC's website: www.hrc.org/about_us/who_we_are.asp (accessed February 18, 2009).

16. The blog entry, at World Net Daily, was posted on December 6, 2008, at www.wnd.com/2008/12/82830 (accessed January 5, 2012).

17. www.wnd.com/2008/12/82830 (accessed January 5, 2012).

18. Malone, *Don't Get above Your Raisin'*.

19. Bourdieu, *Distinction*.

20. Tina Gianoulis, "Country Music," in *glbtq: an encyclopedia of gay, lesbian, bisexual, transgender, and queer culture* (article published 2002, updated December 1, 2005), 2, www.glbtq.com/arts/country_music.html (accessed May 1, 2012). The queer critic Martha Mockus, too, reads country as conservative, strict in its gender roles, and homophobic, in "Queer Thoughts on Country Music and k.d. lang," in *Queering the Pitch: The New Gay and Lesbian Musicology*, 2nd ed., ed. Philip Brett, Elizabeth Wood, and Gary C. Thomas (New York: Routledge, [1994] 2006), 257–74.

21. The Australian literary and cultural theorist John Frow, following Antonio Gramsci, advocates a broad construal of knowledge workers in "Knowledge and Class," *Cultural Studies* 7, no. 2 (1993): 240–81.

22. See, for example, the 1996 report, "The Knowledge-Based Economy," by the Organisation for Economic Co-operation and Development: www.oecd.org/dataoecd/51/8/1913021.pdf (accessed September 28, 2011).

23. These figures come from Alan Abramowitz and Ruy Teixeira, "The Decline of the White Working Class and the Rise of a Mass Upper-Middle Class," *Political Science Quarterly* 124, no. 3 (2009): 391–422. The 2–3 percent figure is my estimate, based on the authors' information.

24. Barbara Ehrenreich and John Ehrenreich formulated the notion in "The Professional-Managerial Class" (pts. 1 and 2), *Radical America* 11, nos. 2 and 3 (March–April and May–June 1977): 7–31; 7–22. Many writers and thinkers on

class in the United States have adopted the Ehrenreichs' concept, which by now often appears under the equivalent label "professional middle class," or simply PMC. Notably, the concept departs from orthodox Marxian theory, in which there are only two classes, proletariat and bourgeoisie. Martha E. Gimenez argues that the PMC is analytically unhelpful and "alien to Marxism" and that it romanticizes a working-class past: "The Professional/Managerial Class: An Ideological Construct," unpublished manuscript (1977), available at www .colorado.edu/Sociology/gimenez/work/pmg.html (accessed October 17, 2011).

25. Abramowitz and Teixeira, "The Decline of the White Working Class."

26. Sean F. Reardon and Kendra Bischoff, "Growth in the Residential Segregation of Families by Income, 1970–2009," report of the US2010 Project (Russell Sage Foundation American Communities Project of Brown University, 2011), 3–5, 8, http://graphics8.nytimes.com/packages/pdf/national/Russell SageIncomeSegregationreport.pdf (accessed November 16, 2011). Affluence is defined here as having a family income greater than 1.5 times the median family income of the local neighborhood.

27. Lamont, *The Dignity of Working Men*, 2, 269 n. 4. Matthijs Kalmijn, "Status Homogamy in the United States," *American Journal of Sociology* 97, no. 2 (1991): 496–523.

28. Barbara Ehrenreich noted in 1989, "Left and right, we are still locked in by a middle-class culture that is almost wholly insular, self-referential, and in its own way, parochial." *Fear of Falling*, 257.

29. Ehrenreich, *Fear of Falling*, 7. Lawler, "Disgusted Subjects," 431, coins the phrase "public bourgeoisie" to refer to academics, journalists, social commentators, and others "with access to means of representation."

30. James Davison Hunter, *Culture Wars: The Struggle to Define America* (New York: Basic Books, 1991), 42–44.

31. David Brooks, *Bobos in Paradise: The New Upper Class and How They Got There* (New York: Simon & Schuster, 2000).

32. Reader's comment 505 (TK Sung / Seoul, Korea / August 31, 2011) on editorial, "The New Resentment of the Poor," *New York Times*, August 31, 2011, http://community.nytimes.com/comments/www.nytimes.com/2011 /08/31/opinion/the-new-resentment-of-the-poor.html (282 recommendations; accessed October 18, 2011). The editorial reached #1 on the *Times* list of most emailed articles.

33. Reader's comment 6 (Bill / Fairfax, VA / September 20, 2011) on A.G. Sulzberger, "In Small Towns, Gossip Moves to the Web, and Turns Vicious," *New York Times*, September 20, 2011, http://community.nytimes.com /comments/www.nytimes.com/2011/09/20/us/small-town-gossip-moves-to-the-web-anonymous-and-vicious.html (312 recommendations; accessed October 18, 2011).

34. Reader's comment 12 (Anon /NY/ October 10, 2011) on Paul Krugman, "Panic of the Plutocrats," *New York Times*, October 9, 2011, http://community. nytimes.com/comments/www.nytimes.com/2011/10/10/opinion/panic-of-the-plutocrats.html (1,360 recommendations; accessed October 18, 2011).

35. Morris P. Fiorina, Samuel J. Abrams, and Jeremy Pope, *Culture War? The Myth of a Polarized America*, 3rd ed. (Boston: Longman, [2004] 2011).

36. Jerome L. Himmelstein and James A. McRae Jr., "Social Conservatism, New Republicans, and the 1980 Election," *Public Opinion Quarterly* 48, no. 3 (1984): 592–605. Thanks to Brandon Biswas Phillips for bringing this research to my attention.

37. Andrew Gelman, Boris Shor, Joseph Bafumi, and David Park, "Rich State, Poor State, Red State, Blue State: What's the Matter with Connecticut?," *Quarterly Journal of Political Science* 2, no. 4 (2007): 354; Andrew Gelman, *Red State, Blue State, Rich State, Poor State: Why Americans Vote the Way They Do* (Princeton, NJ: Princeton University Press, 2008), 68.

38. Gelman, *Red State, Blue State, Rich State, Poor State*, 36.

39. Ezra Klein, review of Andrew Gelman, *Red State, Blue State, Rich State, Poor State*, http://bnreview.barnesandnoble.com/t5/Reviews-Essays/Red-State-Blue-State-Rich-State-Poor-State-Why-Americans-Vote/ba-p/673 (accessed September 14, 2011).

40. Larry M. Bartels, "What's the Matter with *What's the Matter with Kansas?*," *Quarterly Journal of Political Science* 1, no. 2 (2006): abstract. See also Abramowitz and Teixeira, "The Decline of the White Working Class." Unlike Bartels, Abramowitz and Teixeira see a dramatic decline in Democratic identification in the white working class. But they disagree with Frank's contention that this is linked to Republican positions on cultural issues—which, they argue, have had far more effect on voters in the upper classes.

41. Matt Thompson, "Shifting Gears: When It Comes to Presidential Elections, There May Be More to the NASCAR Set than Meets the Eye," *American Prospect Online*, February 1, 2004, http://prospect.org/article/shifting-gears (accessed November 28, 2011); at the time he wrote this piece, Thompson held a Naughton Fellowship in the Poynter Institute, an internship for new college graduates. On the inadequacies of media treatments of the white working class, see Barbara Ehrenreich, "The Silenced Majority: Why the Average Working Person Has Disappeared from American Media and Culture," in *Race, Class, and Gender: An Anthology*, 4th ed., ed. Margaret L. Andersen and Patricia Hill Collins (Belmont, CA: Wadsworth, 2001), 143–45; Julie Bettie, "Class Dismissed? *Roseanne* and the Changing Face of Working-Class Iconography," *Social Text* 14, no. 4 (1995): 125–49; and Richard Butsch, "Ralph, Fred, Archie and Homer: Why Television Keeps Recreating the White Male Working-Class Buffoon," in *Gender, Race, and Class in Media: A Text-Reader*, ed. Gail Dines and Jean McMahon Humez (Thousand Oaks, CA: Sage, 1995), 575–85.

42. Ehrenreich, *Fear of Falling*, 133.

43. Lawler, "Disgusted Subjects," 431. On universalization of middle-class norms, see also Mike Savage, "A New Class Paradigm?," *British Journal of Sociology of Education* 24, no. 4 (2003): 535–41; and Bev Skeggs, Helen Wood, and Nancy Thumim, "'Oh Goodness I *Am* Watching Reality TV': How Methods Make Class in Audience Research," *European Journal of Cultural Studies* 11, no. 1 (2008): 5–24.

44. Fox, *Real Country*, 108.

45. Pierre Bourdieu, "Distinction: A Social Critique of the Judgement of Taste," in *Social Stratification: Class, Race, and Gender in Sociological Perspective*, 3rd ed., ed. David B. Grusky (Boulder, CO: Westview, 2008), 871; James C. Scott, *Domination and the Arts of Resistance: Hidden Transcripts* (New Haven, CT: Yale University Press, 1990), 133.

46. Lawler "Disgusted Subjects," 442, citing Gayatri Spivak, with Ellen Rooney, "'In a Word': Interview," in *The Second Wave: A Reader in Feminist Theory*, ed. Linda J. Nicholson (New York: Routledge, 1997), 356–78.

47. Mark Judge, "The Decline of Country Music," *Daily Caller*, June 22, 2011, http://dailycaller.com/2011/06/22/the-decline-of-country-music (accessed October 11, 2011). Judge has written frequently on rock 'n' roll music.

48. Wil Forbis, "Interesting Motherfuckers: David Allan Coe," *Acid Logic*, January 1, 2006, www.acidlogic.com/im_davidallancoe.htm (accessed October 11, 2011); reprinted in Wil Forbis, *Acid Logic: A Decade of Humorous Writing on Pop Culture, Trash Cinema and Rebel Music* (Bloomington, IN: AuthorHouse, 2008).

49. Joanna Kadi, "Still Listenin' to That Sentimental Twang," in *Thinking Class: Sketches from a Cultural Worker* (Boston: South End Press, 1996), 96.

50. The classic work in the field is Bourdieu's *Distinction*.

51. Lawler, "Disgusted Subjects," 442, 440, 443; Bourdieu, *Distinction*, 56.

52. Sample, *White Soul*, 76.

53. Fox, "White Trash Alchemies of the Abject Sublime," 44.

54. Patricia A. Turner, "Dangerous White Stereotypes," *New York Times*, August 29, 2011, A23.

55. Joel Williamson, *The Crucible of Race: Black/White Relations in the American South since Emancipation* (New York: Oxford University Press, 1984).

56. Hartigan, "Who Are These White People?," 111.

57. Lawler (citing 2001 research by Chris Haylett and by Angela McRobbie), "Disgusted Subjects," 430.

58. Hartigan, "Who Are These White People?," 111.

59. The same argument was made persuasively by the historian William Henry Chafe as early as 1980 in *Civilities and Civil Rights: Greensboro, North Carolina, and the Black Struggle for Freedom* (New York: Oxford University Press, 1980), drawing in part on even earlier scholarship demonstrating the speciousness of such scapegoating and its efficacy in perpetuating racial injustice.

60. Bryson, "'Anything but Heavy Metal,'" 895–96 (emphasis in original). We can only wonder whether more recent data concerning exclusion of rap would match Bryson's 1993 data. The big story in popular culture of the mid-1990s through mid-2000s was hip-hop's phenomenal popularity among not only urban and of-color but also suburban, middle-class, and white youth. For a related account, see Jason Tanz, *Other People's Property: A Shadow History of Hip-Hop in White America* (New York: Bloomsbury, 2007).

61. Diane Reay, "Psychosocial Aspects of White Middle-Class Identities: Desiring and Defending against the Class and Ethnic 'Other' in Urban Multiethnic Schooling," *Sociology* 42, no. 6 (2008): 1075.

62. Demographic, including educational, data on *New York Times* readers across various circulation platforms are published at http://nytmarketing .whsites.net/mediakit (accessed November 13, 2011).

63. A related form of boundary anxiety manifests in the practice Kirby Moss calls micro-othering, in which, for example, trailer park residents monitor their own and their neighbors' class status according to the relative size of their mobile homes, whether they own or rent the land they sit on, and so on, in "a never-ending process": *The Color of Class: Poor Whites and the Paradox of Privilege* (Philadelphia: University of Pennsylvania Press, 2003), 85.

64. By Ehrenreich's account in *Fear of Falling*, the middle-class media in the late 1960s "discovered" the working class—as racist and reactionary.

65. Ehrenreich, *Fear of Falling*, 123.

66. Lawler, "Disgusted Subjects," 431 (emphasis in original).

67. Bourdieu, *Distinction*, 479.

68. Bourdieu, *Distinction*.

CHAPTER 2

1. This definition follows Fox, *Real Country*, 107.

2. Snibbe and Markus, "You Can't Always Get What You Want," 703–20.

3. Judge, "The Decline of Country Music"; Forbis, "Interesting Motherfuckers."

4. "Should've Been a Cowboy" received this designation and industry recognition for 3 million airplays in 2007: Craig Shelburne, "Toby Keith Jams, Notches 50 Million Airplays," CMT.com, March 1, 2007, www.cmt.com/news /country-music/1553672/toby-keith-jams-notches-50-million-airplays.jhtml (accessed January 10, 2012).

5. Citing Welch's 2001 release *Time (The Revelator)* as #64 on its list, *Rolling Stone* also called the album "a lovely exercise in anachronism": www.rollingstone .com/music/lists/100-best-albums-of-the-2000s-20110718/gillian-welch-time- the-revelator-19691231#ixzz1jFooSHWH (accessed January 12, 2012).

6. Berman, quoted in Nelson, "A New Shine."

7. See, for example, Pamela Fox, *Natural Acts: Gender, Race, and Rusticity in Country Music* (Ann Arbor: University of Michigan Press, 2009); Pecknold, *The Selling Sound;* Joli Jensen, *The Nashville Sound: Authenticity, Commercialization, and Country Music* (Nashville, TN: Vanderbilt University Press, 1998); and Peterson, *Creating Country Music*.

8. Lisa Gitelman, "Reading Music, Reading Records, Reading Race: Musical Copyright and the U.S. Copyright Act of 1909," *Musical Quarterly* 81, no. 2 (1997): 266–67.

9. Ching, *Wrong's What I Do Best*, 30, 4, 18. John Hartigan Jr. discusses these usages in working-class speech in *Odd Tribes: Toward a Cultural Analysis of White People* (Durham, NC: Duke University Press, 2005), 124.

10. The attribution continues: "—one of those guys who can make his prepuce mime the Pledge of Allegiance when his boner is right." Christgau's brief review is reprinted on his website: www.robertchristgau.com/get_artist.php?name = McGraw (accessed April 24, 2012).

11. See Roseanne Barr attesting to this point; also Bettie's commentary in "Class Dismissed?," 134–35.

12. Mario Tarradell, "Country Music Queen Loretta Lynn Sounded Regal during Winspear Opera House Concert," *Dallas News.com*, www.dallasnews.com/entertainment/columnists/mario-tarradell/20120123-country-music-queen-loretta-lynn-sounded-regal-during-winspear-opera-house-concert.ece (accessed February 28, 2012).

13. Bryson, "'Anything but Heavy Metal'"; Snibbe and Markus, "You Can't Always Get What You Want."

14. Fox, "White Trash Alchemies of the Abject Sublime," 44.

15. Geoff Mann, "Why Does Country Music Sound White? Race and the Voice of Nostalgia," *Ethnic and Racial Studies* 31, no. 1 (2008): 73–100. On race and country, see also Neal, "Dancing around the Subject."

16. Such fixity is discussed further, in connection with Skeggs's social theory, in chapter 3.

17. The title of Judge's article, again, is "The Decline of Country Music," and his comments attribute some of the changes he laments in "modern country" to "the last 20 years"—and thus regard it as a recent development.

18. Judge, "The Decline of Country Music."

19. In 2010, the United States witnessed the greatest disparity between rich and poor since 1917, and the average male worker was making less (adjusted for inflation) than he did in 1969. The Berkeley economist and expert on international income and wealth inequality Emmanuel Saez summarized current U.S. income disparity in 2010: "After decades of stability in the post-war period, the top decile [10 percent] share has increased dramatically over the last twenty-five years [1983–2007] and has now regained its pre-war level. Indeed, the top decile share in 2007 is equal to 49.7 percent, a level higher than any other year since 1917 and even surpasses 1928, the peak of stock market bubble in the 'roaring' 1920s." Emmanuel Saez, "Striking It Richer: The Evolution of Top Incomes in the United States," 2; July 17, 2010, update of an article that appeared in *Pathways* (Winter 2008): 6–7, http://elsa.berkeley.edu/~saez/ (accessed July 24, 2011). U.S. wealth inequality is even more extreme. In 2009, when the top 1 percent received 21 percent of all income, they owned 35 percent of net worth. The top 10 percent of Americans that year received 47 percent of income and held a whopping 73 percent of wealth (including over 80 percent of stock market assets). Although U.S. wealth inequality is long-standing, the share of wealth held by the bottom 80 percent worsened significantly between 1983 and 2009, shrinking by nearly one-third, from 18.7 percent to 12.8 percent. And the 225:1 ratio in 2009 between the net worth of households in the top 1 percent and median households was the largest on record, nearly double the 1962 figure. Sylvia A. Allegretto, "The State of Working America's Wealth, 2011," EPI Briefing Paper 292 (Economic Policy

Institute, Washington, DC, 2011), 1–10, 15, http://epi.3cdn.net/2a7ccb3e9e618f0
bbc_3nm6idnax.pdf (accessed March 14, 2012).

20. Moss, *The Color of Class*, 31–32, 34–36, 40–42, 53–54. Moss, an African
American ethnographer of poor whites, conducted the research for his 2003
book in the mid-1990s.

21. Forbis, "Interesting Motherfuckers"; Judge, "The Decline of Country
Music."

22. See, for example, Skeggs, *Class, Self, Culture*, 2.

23. Michael Marmot, *The Status Syndrome: How Social Standing Affects
Our Health and Longevity* (New York: Henry Holt, 2004).

24. Butsch, "Ralph, Fred, Archie and Homer," 404.

25. Butsch, "Ralph, Fred, Archie and Homer," 403–4. On working-class representations in the American sitcom, see also Bettie, "Class Dismissed?"

26. The political theorist Nancy Fraser emphasizes that the exclusionary
(white, male) modern bourgeois public sphere, as theorized by Jürgen Habermas,
was never *the* public but that publicity, virtually from its beginnings, also comprised multiple, competing counterpublics: "Rethinking the Public Sphere: A
Contribution to the Critique of Actually Existing Democracy," *Social Text*
25–26 (1990): 56–80.

27. Curtis W. Ellison, *Country Music Culture: From Hard Times to Heaven*
(Jackson: University Press of Mississippi, 1995); Sample, *White Soul*; and
Fillingim, *Redneck Liberation*, emphasize country's importance to its fans, even
to a salvational degree.

28. Wendy Fonarow, *Empire of Dirt: The Aesthetics and Rituals of British
Indie Music* (Middletown, CT: Wesleyan University Press, 2006), 55–62, points
out that indie music fans are effectively a body of critics, arbiters of elite taste—
"the elect who can recognize *the truth in music*" (56; emphasis in original)—
which in turn, via Romantic ideology, makes them arbiters of spiritual value.

29. Richard Goldstein, "My Country Music Problem—and Yours,"
Mademoiselle, June 1973, 114–15.

30. Eric J. Hobsbawm, *Age of Extremes: The Short Twentieth Century, 1914–
91* (London: Michael Joseph, 1994); Ellen Willis, "Escape from Freedom: What's
the Matter with Tom Frank (and the Lefties Who Love Him)?," *Situations:
Project of the Radical Imagination* 1, no. 2 (February 19, 2006): 18; Jefferson
Cowie, *Stayin' Alive: The 1970s and the Last Days of the Working Class* (New
York: New Press, 2010), 24; and Derek Nystrom, *Hard Hats, Rednecks, and
Macho Men: Class in 1970s American Cinema* (New York: Oxford University
Press, 2009), 4.

31. Malone, *Don't Get above Your Raisin'*, 239; Peterson, "Class
Unconsciousness in Country Music," 57–58; Bruce J. Schulman, *The Seventies:
The Great Shift in American Culture, Society, and Politics* (New York: Free
Press, 2001), 116–17; and Goldstein, "My Country Music Problem—and Yours,"
185. On country music's linkages to conservative politics in this moment, see
also J. Lester Feder, "When Country Went Right," *American Prospect Online*
(February 16, 2007), http://prospect.org/article/when-country-went-right

(accessed January 26, 2012), and "'Song of the South': Country Music, Race, Region, and the Politics of Culture, 1920–1974" (PhD diss., University of California, Los Angeles, 2006), 5–6; and Thomas Ruys Smith, "'Bring Our Country Back': Country Music, Conservatives, and the Counter-Culture in 1968," *Studies in American Culture* 34, no. 1 (2011): 103–12.

32. Paul DiMaggio, Richard A. Peterson, and Jack Esco Jr., "Country Music: Ballad of the Silent Majority," in *The Sounds of Social Change: Studies in Popular Culture*, ed. R. Serge Denisoff and Richard A. Peterson (New York: Rand McNally, 1972), 39; Goldstein, "My Country Music Problem—and Yours," 115; Robert Christgau, "Obvious Believers" (review of Bob Dylan, *Nashville Skyline*), *Village Voice*, May 1969; reproduced at Christgau's website, www.robertchristgau.com/xg/bk-aow/dylan.php (accessed May 16, 2012).

33. On the perhaps satirical origins and phenomenal reception of Haggard's "Okie from Muskogee" see Peter La Chapelle, *Proud to Be an Okie: Cultural Politics, Country Music, and Migration to Southern California* (Berkeley: University of California Press, 2007); Malone, *Don't Get above Your Raisin'*, 210–52; and Feder, "'Song of the South,'" chapter 5. Undue emphasis has been given over the years to a sentence from John Sinclair's countercultural, pro-cannabis underground paper, the *Ann Arbor Sun* (long lost to readers and researchers but now available, in part, online), which in fact quoted Haggard only as "allegedly" having delivered the "now immortal line," "Son, the only place I don't smoke it is Muskogee!," and only in an album review, not an interview: Carson X. Napier, review of *I Love Dixie Blues*, by Merle Haggard and the Strangers with special guests the Dixieland Express, *Ann Arbor Sun* 1, no. 2 (January 11–25, 1974): 17.

34. None of Haggard's seven No. 1 country hits from 1966 to November 1969 had ever before used just two chords. The verses and chorus in "Okie" play out over an uncommonly square groove and simple 16-bar changes: I (6 bars)—V7 (8 bars)—I (2 bars). "Fightin' Side" uses a similar groove and fits the same changes to a 12-bar verse: I (2 bars)—V7 (3 bars)—I (1 bar)—repeat. The chorus in "Fightin Side," however, introduces more harmonic variety. The songs were also performed in the same tonal range: in Haggard's 1970 television appearance on *The Porter Wagoner Show*, "Okie" was played in D modulating to E-flat, and then "Fightin' Side" in E-flat. Both numbers from this broadcast are included on *Legendary Performances: Merle Haggard* (Los Angeles: Shout! Factory, 2008), DVD. Haggard and the Strangers' (including wife Bonnie Owens's) detached, possibly smirking delivery and comical guitar fills do nothing to dispel ambiguity.

35. Sources for this account of events include Tony Scherman, "The Last Roundup," *Atlantic* 278, no. 2 (1996): 79–83; and Andy Mclenon and Grant Alden, "Merle Haggard—Branded Man," *No Depression* 48 (November–December 2003), https://archives.nodepression.com/2003/11/branded-man/3/ (accessed May 15, 2012). "Irma Jackson" was included on Haggard's 1972 album *Let Me Tell You about a Song* (Capitol 882).

36. Patrick Doyle, "Exclusive: Merle Haggard on His Kennedy Center Honor, Meeting Obama and Oprah and More," *Rolling Stone Online*, December

28, 2010, www.rollingstone.com.proxy.lib.umich.edu/music/news/exclusive-merle-haggard-on-his-kennedy-center-honor-meeting-obama-and-oprah-and-more-20101228 (accessed February 3, 2012); Merle Haggard, with Tom Carter, *My House of Memories: An Autobiography* (New York: It Books, [1999] 2011), 192. An audio clip of Haggard performing "Hillary" live in concert was posted in a March 6, 2007, *New York Times* political blog entry by Patrick Healy at http://thecaucus.blogs.nytimes.com/2007/03/06/waxing-lyrical/ (accessed May 15, 2012).

37. Malone, *Country Music U.S.A.*, 318–19.

38. Daniel Geary, "'The Way I Would Feel about San Quentin': Johnny Cash and the Politics of Country Music," *Dædalus: Journal of the American Academy of Arts & Sciences* 142, no. 4 (2013): 65–66 (emphasis mine).

39. Geary, "'The Way I Would Feel about San Quentin,'" 67, 71, 69. Geary borrows the phrase "politics of empathy" from Michael S. Foley, "A Politics of Empathy: Johnny Cash, the Vietnam War, and the 'Walking Contradiction' Myth Dismantled," *Popular Music and Society* (2013). http://dx.doi.org/10.10 80/03007766.2013.798928.

40. Charles F. Gritzner, "Country Music: A Reflection of Popular Culture," *Journal of Popular Culture* 11, no. 4 (1978): 857 (emphasis mine).

41. Schulman, *The Seventies*, 117.

42. Willis, "Escape from Freedom," 17–19, 11 (emphasis mine); Cowie, *Stayin' Alive*, 221–24.

43. See Peterson, "Class Unconsciousness in Country Music," 37–39; and Karl Hagstrom Miller, *Segregating Sound: Inventing Folk and Pop Music in the Age of Jim Crow* (Durham, NC: Duke University Press, 2010), 4–11.

44. See Gitelman, "Reading Music, Reading Records, Reading Race," esp. 276–79.

45. See the accounts of the wide variety of blues, Broadway, and parlor music presented by southern musicians and rejected by record industry talent scouts in George H. Lewis, "The Color of Country: Black Influence and Experience in American Country Music," *Popular Music and Society* 25, nos. 3–4 (2001): 107–19; and Miller, *Segregating Sound*. Both sources discuss the music industry's racial segregation of which Miller's book provides the most complete history and analysis to date. The basic facts of this history have been known to scholars for decades and have been available in Malone, *Country Music U.S.A.*, and Peterson, *Creating Country Music*, among other sources.

46. Wes Bunch, "Lesley Riddle's Music Finally Gaining Recognition," *Kingsport Times-News*, February 21, 2009, //www.timesnews.net/article.php?id = 9011949 (accessed March 29, 2012); Colin Escott, with George Merritt and William MacEwen, *Hank Williams, the Biography* (New York: Little, Brown, [1994] 2004), 10–11. The influential guitarist and sometime singer Merle Travis was another country musician who claimed an important African American musical mentor. I will also mention the great singer and accordionist Amédée Ardoin (1896–ca. 1941), who had considerable influence on Cajun music, which was created and danced to by black and white Southeast Louisianans—sometimes

together, in defiance of Jim Crow—and came at times under the heading of hill-billy music: see Ann Allen Savoy, *Cajun Music: A Reflection of a People,* vol. 1 (Eunice, LA: Bluebird Press, 1984), 65–68 ff.

47. The 1923 records were made in Atlanta on the Okeh label by Fiddlin' John Carson: Malone, *Country Music, U.S.A,* 37–38.

48. Miller, *Segregating Sound,* 8, 19, 72, 103, 119. On country musicians' down-dressing and rube wear, see the discussion and many photographs in Peterson, *Creating Country Music.*

49. Maxine L. Grossman, "Jesus, Mama, and the Constraints of Salvific Love in Contemporary Country Music," *Journal of the American Academy of Religion* 70, no. 1 (2002): 83–115. Salvific love is a form of Christian salvation that comes through connection to another person or to God and involves sacrifice and transformation.

50. Grossman, "Jesus, Mama, and the Constraints of Salvific Love in Contemporary Country Music," 107.

51. The song's lyric makes clear only that the mother burns down the house and her daughter becomes a ward of the state, but the video strongly suggests that both parents perished in the fire.

52. Although country radio bans in various instances have involved songs deemed racy in terms of gender or sexuality or otherwise offensive to conservative sensibilities, country radio stations have also sometimes banned songs, like Tim McGraw's "Indian Outlaw" (#8 1994, #15 Pop), that were offensive to progressive sensibilities. To this extent, it seems more accurate to say that country radio is averse to controversy or conflict than simply to label it conservative, though surely station managements' actions have often served conservative purposes.

53. Grossman, "Jesus, Mama, and the Constraints of Salvific Love in Contemporary Country Music," 107. For a survey of homoerotic themes in country song lyrics ca. 1982, see Stan Leventhal, "Stand by Your Man: The Rise of Gay C & W Lyrics," *New York Native,* March 15–23, 1982, 23, 31.

54. Grossman, "Jesus, Mama, and the Constraints of Salvific Love in Contemporary Country Music," 106.

55. Grossman, "Jesus, Mama, and the Constraints of Salvific Love in Contemporary Country Music," 106.

56. In 2003, about 60 percent of Americans polled had positive opinions of gay men if they thought that homosexuality was immutable, whereas opinions were about 70 percent negative among subjects who believed that homosexuality could be changed. An understanding of homosexuality as immutable correlated to acceptance of gays and lesbians more strongly than other factors surveyed, including level of education, personal acquaintance with a homosexual person, and general ideological beliefs. Pew Research Center, "Religious Beliefs Underpin Opposition to Homosexuality" (Pew Research Center, Washington, DC, 2003), 8.

57. Grossman, "Jesus, Mama, and the Constraints of Salvific Love in Contemporary Country Music," 106–7 (emphasis mine).

58. Fillingim, *Redneck Liberation,* 20; and www.shorter.edu (accessed February 24, 2012).

59. Fillingim, *Redneck Liberation,* 6, quoting Williams's "You got to have smelt a lot of mule manure" statement, first published in an interview for *Nation's Business* and quoted in Roger Williams, *Sing a Sad Song: The Life of Hank Williams,* 2nd ed. (Urbana: University of Illinois Press, [1973] 1981), 107.

60. Fillingim, *Redneck Liberation,* 6.

61. Fillingim, *Redneck Liberation,* 144–45; see also 30.

62. Fillingim, *Redneck Liberation,* 112, 142. He also notes that southern "gospel songs and cheatin' songs similarly struggle with basic existential questions, especially the question of theodicy"—that is, how could God allow such suffering and injustice? "They are texts of theological *liberation* because they respond to experiences of oppression and marginalization" (26). (Emphasis in original.)

63. Fillingim, *Redneck Liberation,* 145.

64. Fillingim, *Redneck Liberation,* 105, 109; Loretta Lynn with George Vecsey, *Coal Miner's Daughter* (New York: Vintage Books, [1976] 2010), 55.

65. Monica Prasad, Andrew Perrin, Kieran Bezila, Steve Hoffman, Kate Kindleberger, Kim Manturuk, Ashleigh Smith Powers, and Andrew Payton, "The Undeserving Rich: 'Moral Values' and the White Working Class," *Sociological Forum* 24, no. 2 (2009): 251.

66. See this book's Outro, 159, for relevant recent song examples.

67. Dale Cyphert, "Rhetoric on the Concrete Pour: The Dance of Decision Making," in *Who Says? Working-Class Rhetoric, Class Consciousness, and Community,* ed. William DeGenaro (Pittsburgh: University of Pittsburgh Press, 2007), 153. Cyphert cites prior literature documenting comparable group-cognition processes in organizations working under hazardous conditions.

68. Cyphert, "Rhetoric on the Concrete Pour," 152, 148.

69. Cyphert, "Rhetoric on the Concrete Pour," 153, 155 *[sic]*.

70. Cyphert, "Rhetoric on the Concrete Pour," 145, 153. In the context of Cyphert's discussion, the phrase "real men" appears primarily to emphasize class connotations—that is, to emphasize "real," indicating workers as opposed to managers, or "suits." Surely the phrase also includes gender connotations, but these are secondary, inflecting the class meaning by suggesting less than optimal masculinity on the part of white-collar workers who would talk about rather than implement solutions.

71. Cyphert, "Rhetoric on the Concrete Pour," 146, 154. The lyric is from "Que Sera, Sera (Whatever Will Be, Will Be)," a No. 2 pop hit for Doris Day in 1956.

72. Cyphert, "Rhetoric on the Concrete Pour," 153, 159.

73. Cyphert, "Rhetoric on the Concrete Pour," 159.

74. Cyphert, "Rhetoric on the Concrete Pour," 155, 158.

75. Cyphert, "Rhetoric on the Concrete Pour," 144–45.

76. Karen Walker, "'Always There for Me': Friendship Patterns and Expectations among Middle- and Working-Class Men and Women," *Sociological Forum* 10, no. 2 (1995): 273–96.

77. R. Andrew Sayer, *The Moral Significance of Class* (Cambridge: Cambridge University Press, 2005), 56.

78. Walker, "'Always There for Me.'"

79. Michèle Ollivier, "'Too Much Money off Other People's Backs': Status in Late Modern Societies," *Canadian Journal of Sociology* 25, no. 4 (2000): 441–70.

80. Adrie Suzanne Kusserow, "De-Homogenizing American Individualism: Socializing Hard and Soft Individualism in Manhattan and Queens," *Ethos* 27, no. 2 (1999): 210–12. Ehrenreich demonstrates in the opening of *Fear of Falling* (3–6) how representations of "the American people" are actually based on the professional middle-class minority.

81. Carolyn Kay Steedman, *Landscape for a Good Woman: A Story of Two Lives* (New Brunswick, NJ: Rutgers University Press, 1986), 7, 123.

82. Richard Sennett and Jonathan Cobb, *The Hidden Injuries of Class* (New York: Vintage Books, 1972), 27.

83. Pierre Bourdieu and Jean-Claude Passeron, *Reproduction in Education, Society, and Culture*, trans. Richard Nice (Newbury Park, CA: Sage, in association with *Theory, Culture & Society*, Dept. of Administrative and Social Studies, Teesside Polytechnic, [1977] 1990).

84. Sennett and Cobb, *The Hidden Injuries of Class*, 30.

85. Scott, *Domination and the Arts of Resistance*, 23.

86. Two of the communities were predominantly white, and one was racially mixed, but in order to isolate class as a variable, Kusserow's study focused on white subjects across all three sites: "De-Homogenizing American Individualism," 214.

87. Savage, Bagnall, and Longhurst, "Ordinary, Ambivalent and Defensive," 882.

88. Kusserow, "De-Homogenizing American Individualism," 222–25, 228.

89. Valerie Walkerdine and Helen Lucey, *Democracy in the Kitchen? Regulating Mothers and Socialising Daughters* (London: Virago, 1989).

90. Kusserow, "De-Homogenizing American Individualism," 217–19; Walkerdine and Lucey, *Democracy in the Kitchen?*, 89–96.

91. Kusserow, "De-Homogenizing American Individualism," 221.

92. Kusserow, "De-Homogenizing American Individualism," 227, 230 n. 7.

93. Annette Lareau, *Unequal Childhoods: Class, Race, and Family Life*, 2nd ed. (Berkeley: University of California Press, [2003] 2011). This book's importance in the field is attested by its ranking among the top ten most cited sources in professional sociology journals for 2008–12: see http://nealcaren.web.unc.edu/the-most-cited-articles-in-sociology-by-journal/ (accessed June 16, 2012).

94. Jeannie S. Thrall, "Strategic Parenting: Making the Middle Class through Distinction and Discipline" (PhD diss., University of Michigan, 2010), 42–43, 231.

95. Jessi Streib, "Class Reproduction by Four Year Olds," *Qualitative Sociology* 34, no. 2 (2011): 341–42. The classic study here is Basil B. Bernstein, "Social Class,

Language and Socialization," in *Class, Codes and Control,* ed. Basil B. Bernstein (London: Routledge and Kegan Paul, 1971), 170–89.

96. Streib, "Class Reproduction by Four Year Olds," 349.

97. Quoted material from Snibbe and Markus, "You Can't Always Get What You Want," 703, 705. Snibbe and Markus index working- and middle-class status by educational attainment of a high school diploma or bachelor's degree, respectively. Michèle Lamont, *Money, Morals, and Manners: The Culture of the French and American Upper-Middle Class* (Chicago: University of Chicago Press, 1992); and *The Dignity of Working Men.* See Snibbe and Markus for a review of further relevant literature.

98. Notably, Ollivier criticizes researchers' definitions of omnivorism and cultural openness for focusing on "cultural domains that are themselves socially valued" while ignoring areas in which working-class subjects often demonstrate cultural breadth and openness. Despite researchers' labeling of working-class subjects as "univores," many working-class respondents "express a strong desire to learn and to improve themselves, but in domains that are not of particular interest to governments and cultural institutions carrying out the surveys used in omnivore research." To counter class bias in such research, Ollivier recommends that "practical competences such as gardening, plumbing, and interior decoration should be considered as a specific component of cultural capital," positing, too, that such "practical" openness "rests on a lack of the symbolic resources that constitute the model of agency valued by upper and middle class European Americans" and by theories (e.g., Ulrich Beck's) of modern, class-free, DIY construction of a unique self through lifestyle and consumption choices: Michèle Ollivier, "Modes of Openness to Cultural Diversity: Humanist, Populist, Practical, and Indifferent," *Poetics* 36, nos. 1–2 (2008): 143.

99. Snibbe and Markus, "You Can't Always Get What You Want," 707–9; Peterson, "Understanding Audience Segmentation," identifies the cultural omnivore and univore. Coding of the song lyrics in Snibbe and Markus emphasized songs from 1968 to 1998 and was done by student research assistants who had no knowledge of the hypotheses being tested; the authors' identification of classed styles of subjectivity derived from a review of relevant social science literature.

100. Free-choice dissonance theory assumes that when people are allowed to choose between two equally attractive options, they spread alternatives.

101. Snibbe and Markus read the results of this experiment in relation to psychological reactance theory, which is focused on freedom of choice and how subjects respond when they feel swayed or manipulated to choose one option over others. The theory posits that when an individual's "free behavior" is threatened, the individual presents with "reactance," an emotional reaction against the threat to freedom.

102. Garth Brooks, *The Hits* (Capitol Records 2247, 1994), liner notes.

103. Lawler, "Disgusted Subjects," 434.

104. Snibbe and Markus, "You Can't Always Get What You Want," 705, 715–16, 712.

105. Lawler, "Disgusted Subjects."

106. Lareau, *Unequal Childhoods,* 307. Compare Cyphert's remarks, above, on the perpetuation of power among the Western literary elite through presumption of the superiority of their values. Compare also Snibbe and Markus: "In a society less dominated by individualism than the United States, with more of an emphasis on the group, the sense of constraint displayed by working-class and poor children might be interpreted as healthy and appropriate. But in this society, the strategies of the working-class and poor families are generally denigrated and seen as unhelpful or even harmful to children's life chances": "You Can't Always Get What You Want," 13.

107. Alan Jackson reportedly refused even to listen to a remix of his hit "Where Were You (When the World Stopped Turning)" from which the fiddle and pedal steel guitar tracks had been removed at the request of adult contemporary radio stations. "If it's offensive, they just shouldn't play [the record], I guess": Chris Willman, *Rednecks and Bluenecks: The Politics of Country Music* (New York: New Press, 2005), 118–19. Jackson's term *offensive* is appropriate here. Steel guitar and fiddle serve for some audiences as sonic cues for visceral disgust—which in this country-musical context points to disgust at working-class existence, along the lines set forth by Lawler, "Disgusted Subjects."

108. Robert S. Hatten, *Musical Meaning in Beethoven: Markedness, Correlation, and Interpretation* (Bloomington: Indiana University Press, 1994), theorizes the semiotics of markedness in music, though in a "pure" musical and cognitive context more than the sociomusical one invoked here.

109. Sample, *White Soul,* 74–75; Pierce quote from Dorothy Horstman, *Sing Your Heart Out, Country Boy,* rev. and expanded ed. (Nashville, TN: Country Music Foundation, [1975] 1996), 151.

110. Stewart, "Engendering Narratives of Lament in Country Music," 221–25 (Stewart's 1993 essay was published under the name Katie, but her more recent work is published under Kathleen).

111. Fox, *Real Country,* 155–56. In this context, it may be relevant to note that Stewart was a member of the doctoral committee under whose advisement Fox wrote the dissertation that was the basis of his book.

112. Fox, *Real Country,* 167, 162.

113. Grossman, "Jesus, Mama, and the Constraints of Salvific Love in Contemporary Country Music," 90. The interpretation seems unlikely to be shared by many country listeners, who seem more likely to characterize country's perspective on mothers in terms of love and respect than deification. Grossman's primary examples include two songs by Confederate Railroad, a country band that flourished in the 1990s with songs that were often self-parodying. From one of these, "She Never Cried," Grossman draws the claim that "offending Mama is the one permanent taboo . . . in the country music world." But the mama turn in this lyric is a gag, an old joke about country song themes—as it is even more unmistakably in David Allan Coe's version of "You Never Even Called Me by My Name" (#8 1975). Coe attests here in a recitation passage that the song as originally written could not be called the

perfect country song because it "hadn't said anything at all about mama, or trains, or trucks, or prison, or getting drunk." He then proceeds to a hilarious final verse that contrives spectacularly to pack in all of these elements.

114. Lillian B. Rubin, *Worlds of Pain* (New York: Basic Books, 1976), 25–29.

115. Lareau, *Unequal Childhoods*, 304–7 (quotes 304–5).

116. Ortner, *Anthropology and Social Theory*, 31–32. Here, the working class is introjected into the middle class through adolescents, just as the middle class is introjected into the working class through women. On Ortner's analysis, the working and middle classes define themselves always in relation to each other, and so "each contains the other(s) within itself, though in distorted and ambivalent forms" (27).

CHAPTER 3

1. Skeggs, "Uneasy Alignments," 296, 293; *Class, Self, Culture*, 153.

2. Skeggs, "Uneasy Alignments," 292–93 (emphasis in original); *Class, Self, Culture*, 55, 153.

3. Skeggs, "Uneasy Alignments," 296.

4. Skeggs, *Class, Self, Culture*, 4 (emphasis mine).

5. Skeggs, *Class, Self, Culture*, 2.

6. Peterson, "Soft Shell *vs.* Hard Core"; Ching, *Wrong's What I Do Best*, 30, 4.

7. Mann argues that popular music is no mere reflection but a powerful producer of society and subjectivity and that country contributes to the U.S. production of particular, racialized kinds of subjectivity: "Why Does Country Music Sound White?" 83–84.

8. See Huber, "A Short History of *Redneck*," 303–27.

9. Peterson, "Class Unconsciousness in Country Music," 57–58; Malone, *Don't Get above Your Raisin'*, 46. On northern migration, see James N. Gregory, *The Southern Diaspora: How the Great Migrations of Black and White Southerners Transformed America* (Chapel Hill: University of North Carolina Press, 2005); and "Southernizing the American Working Class: Post-war Episodes of Regional and Class Transformation," *Labor History* 39, no. 2 (1998): 135–54. Hartigan, *Odd Tribes*, 124. This was also the moment of Ernest Matthew Mickler's best seller *White Trash Cooking* (1986), but as Hartigan notes, "white trash" retains deep stigma and contempt and has not found redemption even in country music, "a domain of popular culture . . . where the badge of social scorn is often worn proudly" (124).

10. S.v. "Redneck," *Oxford English Dictionary*, 2nd ed. (Oxford: Clarendon Press, 1989).

11. Thomas J. Gorman, "Cross-Class Perceptions of Social Class," *Sociological Spectrum* 20, no. 1 (2000): 100. Ortner, *Anthropology and Social Theory*, 71.

12. Cowie, *Stayin' Alive*, 28.

13. Pew Research Center, "Middle Class, by the Numbers," October 6, 2008, http://pewresearch.org/pubs/983/middle-class-by-the-numbers (accessed October 29, 2011).

14. Ortner, *New Jersey Dreaming,* 28.

15. Ira Katznelson, *When Affirmative Action Was White: An Untold History of Racial Inequality in Twentieth-Century America* (New York: W.W. Norton, 2005), shows also that the GI Bill excluded southern blacks by delegating benefits administration to local governments. Allan Bérubé reveals the history of "blue" discharges, neither honorable nor dishonorable, whereby U.S. World War II military veterans were denied the benefits of the GI Bill, and he notes that these were issued to African American veterans in addition to veterans alleged to be homosexual: *Coming Out under Fire: The History of Gay Men and Women in World War Two* (New York: Free Press, 1990).

16. Ortner, *New Jersey Dreaming,* 28. On this race-class conflation, see Moss, *The Color of Class,* 34–35 ff.

17. Peterson, "Class Unconsciousness in Country Music," 60. On class consciousness, see especially György Lukács, *History and Class Consciousness: Studies In Marxist Dialectics* (Cambridge, MA: MIT Press, [1920] 1971).

18. Peterson, "Class Unconsciousness in Country Music," 48; 50, 51, 55; 59; 36, 47.

19. George Lipsitz, *Rainbow at Midnight: Labor and Culture in the 1940s,* rev. ed. (Urbana: University of Illinois Press, [1981] 1994), 28–29; citing Horstman, *Sing Your Heart Out, Country Boy,* 140.

20. Anthony Giddens, "The Class Structure of Advanced Societies," in Grusky, *Social Stratification,* 133–34 (citing Max Weber, "Class, Status, Party"). Ortner, *Anthropology and Social Theory,* 23–24. Walkerdine and Lucey, *Democracy in the Kitchen?,* 13–14. See also Lipsitz, *Rainbow at Midnight,* esp. 9.

21. Malone, *Don't Get above Your Raisin',* 48.

22. Ortner, *New Jersey Dreaming,* 41; Sennett and Cobb, *The Hidden Injuries of Class;* Skeggs, *Class, Self, Culture,* 5; Bourdieu, *Distinction,* 372.

23. Pierre Bourdieu, *Outline of a Theory of Practice,* trans. Richard Nice (New York: Cambridge University Press, 1977), 77 (emphasis in original); and *Distinction,* 177.

24. Skeggs, *Class, Self, Culture,* 153; Bourdieu, *Distinction;* Lamont, *The Dignity of Working Men.* See also Fillingim, *Redneck Liberation;* Fox, "White Trash Alchemies of the Abject Sublime."

25. Steedman, *Landscape for a Good Woman,* 121.

26. Peterson, *Creating Country Music;* Jimmie N. Rogers, *The Country Music Message, Revisited* (Fayetteville: University of Arkansas Press, 1989), 17 ff. See Amy Green, "Even with Fame and Riches, Wilson Says She's Still a 'Redneck Woman,'" *CMA Closeup News,* February 15, 2005, www.gactv.com /gac/nw_cma_close_up/article/0,,GAC_26068_4729456,00.html (accessed February 21, 2007). Wilson has now recorded more titles and appeared with guitars other than her REDNECK acoustic but has not dropped the tag.

27. With reference to Tucker, "bad girl" carries connotations of sexual disrepute that our society ascribes exclusively to women and particularly those of the working class. The singer was notorious for having been censored by country radio stations in 1974, when she was fifteen, in connection with her No. 1 hit "Would

You Lay with Me (In a Field of Stone)," and for her intergenerational relationship in the early 1980s with the country star Glen Campbell.

28. Song timings sync with the video at www.cmt.com/videos/gretchen-wilson/141009/redneck-woman.jhtml (accessed June 25, 2013).

29. Adam Krims, *Rap Music and the Poetics of Identity* (New York: Cambridge University Press, 2000). Adam Gussow, "Playing Chicken with the Train: Cowboy Troy's Hick-Hop and the Transracial Country West," *Southern Cultures* 16, no. 4 (2010): 41–70, argues that such stylized braggadocio fused black and white cultural influences long before the country-rap hybridity of MuzikMafia's Cowboy Troy.

30. Track 9 on the *Kid Rock* CD is "Hillbilly Stomp," cowritten by Rock. As John Hartigan Jr. shows, "hillbilly" functions in Detroit as a rhetorical identity that distinguishes "between proper and improper behavior for whites" (34) when the latter threatens to blur the color line; still actively in play around Detroit, this hillbilly identity connects to a history of black and white southerners' migration to the city dating to the 1920s: *Racial Situations: Class Predicaments of Whiteness in Detroit* (Princeton, NJ: Princeton University Press, 1999), 26–37. Rock's cultivation of a public identity with linkages to hillbilly and white trash identities connects him to moral impropriety and racial ambiguity, both of which seem desirable for purposes of an edgy outlaw and hip-hop redneck image. Cultural significations here are complex, given that redneck, white trash, and hillbilly identities are popularly linked to both racial blurring (esp. white trash) and racial bigotry (esp. redneck). Rock himself (*né* Robert J. Ritchie, son of a prosperous auto dealer in Detroit's northern exurbs) flaunts the Confederate battle (a.k.a. "Rebel") flag even as he provides the face of what he calls "rap rock" and fronts his racially mixed Twisted Brown Trucker band.

31. Edith D. Balbach, Rebecca J. Gasior, and Elizabeth M. Barbeau, "R.J. Reynolds' Targeting of African Americans: 1988–2000," *American Journal of Public Health* 93, no. 5 (2003): 824.

32. Michael Specter, "Marketers Target 'Virile Female': R.J. Reynolds Plans to Introduce Cigarette," *Washington Post*, February 17, 1990, A1.

33. "Stalking the Virile Female," *Harper's Magazine*, May 1990, 26–27. Marjorie Garber, *Vested Interests: Cross-Dressing and Cultural Anxiety* (New York: Routledge, 1992), 156–57, also refers to Reynolds's Virile Female episode in a discussion of gendering and eroticism in past and present images of smoking and flags its mention in a column (featuring self-distancing tractor-pull levity) by William Safire, "On Language; Virile Women Target Tobacco Men," *New York Times Magazine*, March 11, 1990, 18. National Public Radio is now known as NPR.

34. For related discussion of Hollywood's mannish portrayals of hillbilly women, including Yokum and Calamity, see Williamson, *Hillbillyland*, esp. "Mannish Misfits," 242–47. On butch and gender-queer women, see Lillian Faderman, "The Contributions of the Sexologists," in *Surpassing the Love of Men: Romantic Friendship and Love between Women from the Renaissance to the Present* (New York: William Morrow, 1981), 239–53; Kennedy and Davis,

Boots of Leather, Slippers of Gold; Joan Nestle, *A Restricted Country* (Ithaca, NY: Firebrand Books, 1987); Joan Nestle, ed., *The Persistent Desire: A Femme-Butch Reader* (Boston: Alyson, 1992); Leslie Feinberg, *Stone Butch Blues: A Novel* (Los Angeles: Alyson, [1993] 2003); and Sara L. Crawley, "Are Butch and Fem Working-Class and Antifeminist?," *Gender and Society* 15, no. 2 (2001): 175–96. Skeggs, *Formations of Class and Gender,* 105, 98–117, recaps the classed history of femininity.

35. Among the accounts Will Fellows collected from midwestern rural gay men who moved to the city are some respondents' reports that they were struck by the effeminacy of urban gay men, a trait they had not necessarily expected: *Farm Boys: Lives of Gay Men from the Rural Midwest* (Madison: University of Wisconsin Press, 1996). See also Bell, "Farm Boys and Wild Men," among other studies.

36. Tony Kornheiser, "Cigarettes and Virile Chicks," *Washington Post,* February 23, 1990, B2.

37. Emily C. Neely, "Charline Arthur: The (Un)Making of a Honky-Tonk Star," in *A Boy Named Sue: Gender and Country Music,* ed. Kristine M. McCusker and Diane Pecknold (Jackson: University Press of Mississippi, 2004), 48–49.

38. Ortner, *Anthropology and Social Theory,* 28.

39. Cf. Merle Haggard, "I Can't Be Myself (When I'm with You)" (#3 1970); and Montgomery Gentry, "She Don't Tell Me To" (#5 2006).

40. Bias was greatest among male and conservative subjects in Bettina Spencer, "Classism in the Court System: Perceptions of Low-Income Rape Victims" (paper presented at the conference How Class Works, Stony Brook, NY, June 2008).

41. Skeggs, *Formations of Class and Gender,* 3; see also Ortner, *Anthropology and Social Theory,* 34.

42. This passage cites Bourdieu, *Distinction,* and can be read as a gloss of a central revelation of that study. Elizabeth McDermott, "Telling Lesbian Stories: Interviewing and the Class Dynamics of 'Talk,'" *Women's Studies International Forum* 27, no. 3 (2004): 184.

43. Diane Reay, "Dealing with Difficult Differences: Reflexivity and Social Class in Feminist Research," *Feminism & Psychology* 6, no. 3 (1996): 452.

44. Skeggs, *Formations of Class and Gender,* 3.

45. Ortner, *Anthropology and Social Theory,* 26.

46. Garber, "The Transvestite Continuum: Liberace-Valentino-Elvis," in *Vested Interests,* 353–74. Michael T. Bertrand, "I Don't Think Hank Done It That Way: Elvis, Country Music, and the Reconstruction of Southern Masculinity," in McCusker and Pecknold, *A Boy Named Sue,* 84, 76, 75.

47. Skeggs, *Formations of Class and Gender,* 56–57.

48. Lamont, *The Dignity of Working Men,* 97–131, 146–48.

49. Malone, *Country Music U.S.A.,* 431.

50. Abigail J. Stewart and Joan M. Ostrove, "Social Class, Social Change, and Gender: Working-Class Women at Radcliffe and After," *Psychology of Women Quarterly* 17, no. 4 (1993): 489.

51. Stewart and Ostrove, "Social Class, Social Change, and Gender," 479.

52. Stewart and Ostrove, "Social Class, Social Change, and Gender," 479.

53. Stewart and Ostrove, "Social Class, Social Change, and Gender," 493. This was a subset of one of two generational cohorts studied, this one born ca. 1942 and the other born ca. 1925.

CHAPTER 4

The transcription of "Fuck Aneta Briant" lyrics in the chapter epigraph is mine, following the audio track from the 1978 album, including its spelling of the track title.

1. In *Wrong's What I Do Best,* Ching faults the literalism of the stations' response and frames this instance centrally in her argument against narrowly literal interpretations of hard country music. She claims that Coe wrote "Would You Lay with Me" for his brother's wedding and that he insisted on its metaphorical meaning, concerning a love that endures beyond death (14; Coe source uncited). Whether Ching's or Coe's, however, this account does not do justice to the complexity of the song, in which multiple meaning is crucial—as it is, too, in "Fuck Aneta Briant." "Would You Lay with Me" juxtaposes marital steadfastness and spiritual love to carnal desire and thus (in my reading) symbolically fuses the three elements. The song heightens ambiguity by conveying the everlasting and spiritual love themes abstractly (with "Field of Stone" representing the grave, hence death, and in Tucker's recording, southern gospel harmonies suggesting spirituality), while evoking sensuality more materially and immediately (through images like lips, blood, midnight, bathing, and the moon and phraseology like "Would You Lay with Me").

2. Gayle S. Rubin writes of the Dade County campaign as inaugurating a 1977 child porn panic and an enduring "wave of violence, state persecution, and legal initiatives" against sexual minorities and commercial sex: "Thinking Sex: Notes for a Radical Theory of the Politics of Sexuality" (1984), in *Social Perspectives in Lesbian and Gay Studies: A Reader,* ed. Peter M. Nardi and Beth E. Schneider (New York: Routledge, 1998), 102–5.

3. Quote is from Dudley Clendinen, "Floridian: Anita Bryant, b. 1940, Singer and Crusader," *St. Petersburg Times Online,* November 28, 1999, www.sptimes.com/News/112899/news_pf/Floridian/Anita_Bryant__b_1940_.shtml (accessed August 13, 2011). My sources on Bryant's campaign and gay activists' response include Clendinen and Nagourney, *Out for Good;* and John D'Emilio, "Dade County, USA" (2008), *OutHistory,* www.outhistory.org/wiki/John_D'Emilio:_%22Dade_County,_USA,%22_1977 (accessed August 12, 2011).

4. For a reassessment of modern histories of homosexuality in the light of prison sexuality, see Regina G. Kunzel, *Criminal Intimacy: Prison and the Uneven History of Modern American Sexuality* (Chicago: University of Chicago Press, 2008).

5. With this phrase I mean to evoke this tune and arrangement whose idiom is that of vaudeville razzle-dazzle and that could pass for ragtime if played on,

say, clarinet and banjo but is played here by a twangy country band: Telecaster lead guitar, acoustic rhythm guitar, bass, and drum kit.

6. Chauncey in *Gay New York* (1994) identifies the "rough trade" persona as gender-based and deemed "normal" in its working-class home environment and as having operated in New York male sexual culture into the 1950s. Notably, Esther Newton, based on her research in Chicago and (to a lesser extent) Kansas City, had described in 1972 the same cultural persona *in the present tense*—and contrasted it, as Chauncey would over two decades later, with the middle-class notion that men who have sex with men are "queer" regardless of the sexual role they take: *Mother Camp: Female Impersonators in America* (reprint Chicago: University of Chicago Press, [1972] 1979), 102 n. 4.

7. Rubin, "Thinking Sex," 103.

8. The women's music album *Lesbian Concentrate: A Lesbianthology of Songs and Poems* released by Olivia in 1977 was another response to Anita Bryant's campaign. Presented as an "energetic affirmation of lesbian identity and culture" (per the liner notes), the LP is a collection of lesbian-themed tracks by various Olivia artists, including one that specifically addresses Bryant, the opening track "Don't Pray for Me," by Mary Watkins. Comments at the website http://archive.org/details/LesbianConcentrate clearly position this album as political and significant. Thanks to Lucas Hilderbrand for sharing this link and reminding me of the existence of the LP.

9. The video images in "Little Man" include white and black common folk in small-town Georgia, apparently actual residents, and the song lyrics make explicit reference to a black man, known to the narrator in his childhood, who did business as an independent contractor.

10. Willman, *Rednecks and Bluenecks*, 116–20.

11. Cyphert, "Rhetoric on the Concrete Pour," 159.

12. Sayer, *The Moral Significance of Class*, 3.

13. Sample, *White Soul*, 123, 120.

14. Malone, *Country Music U.S.A.*, 299–301; see also 431.

15. Sample, *White Soul*, 113.

16. Keith made these statements in a September 10, 2006, interview with Cynthia Bowers on *CBS Sunday Morning*, summarized at www.cbsnews.com/2100-3445_162-1990758.html (accessed July 9, 2012).

17. Wright's Opry appearance was on October 23, 2004. Video available at http://youtu.be/4mtVU_IcL8M (accessed June 8, 2012).

18. The figure 0.5 percent (referring to a given moment) comes from Pew Research Center, "War and Sacrifice in the Post-9/11 Era: The Military-Civilian Gap" (Pew Research Center, Washington, DC, 2011), http://pewresearch.org/pubs/2111/veterans-post-911-wars-iraq-afghanistan-civilian-military-veterans (accessed June 19, 2012). Some media (including Pacifica Radio) reported on a study of casualties in Afghanistan showing that Native American and, especially, white working-class young people are overrepresented (and African American and Latino groups underrepresented) in what is now America's longest war. The authors identify 78 percent of the casualties in Afghanistan as

members of the working class, compared to 62 percent of the U.S. population overall. Michael Zweig, Michael Porter, and Yuxiang Huang, "American Military Deaths in Afghanistan, and the Communities from Which These Soldiers, Sailors, Airmen, and Marines Came," Center for Study of Working Class Life, October 2011, www.stonybrook.edu/workingclass/publications /afghan_casualties.shtml (accessed October 6, 2011). The website of Queers for Economic Justice raises questions of social-economic justice surrounding facts like these, with its proclamation that the U.S. military is "the nation's de facto jobs program for poor and working-class people": http://q4ej.org/military-job-is-not-economic-justice-qej-statement-on-dadt (accessed September 18, 2011).

19. The minivan bears the sticker of a local private school, and in her final verse Wright expresses a hope that the driver will hear her song "As she picks up her kids / From their private school" and might then understand, in her safety and prosperity, Wright's reason for supporting U.S. service members. Excerpt *[sic]:* Amelie Gillette, Steven Hyden, Genevieve Koski, Josh Modell, Noel Murray, Keith Phipps, Nathan Rabin, Tasha Robinson, Kyle Ryan, and David Wolinsky, "Baseball, Apple Pie, and Kicking Your Fucking Ass: 21 Hilariously Hyperbolic Pro-America Songs," *Onion*, June 30, 2008, www. avclub.com/articles/baseball-apple-pie-and-kicking-your-fucking-ass-21,2364 / (accessed June 8, 2012).

20. Chely Wright, *Like Me* (New York: Pantheon, 2010). "We have yet to see an openly gay artist in hip hop and R&B," Clay Cane points out in his *BET* movie blog, in a review of *Wish Me Away*, a documentary on Wright and her 2010 coming out: see "Chely Wright: *Wish Me Away*," *BET: What the Flick*, June 1, 2012, http://blogs.bet.com/celebrities/what-the-flick/movie-review-chely-wright-wish-me-away/#comments (accessed June 10, 2012). See also Chris Willman, "Chely Wright Comes Out, as a . . . Thinker," *Huffington Post*, May 3, 2010, www.huffingtonpost.com/chris-willman/chely-wright-comes-out-as_b_561103.html (accessed June 9, 2012); Willman, *Rednecks and Bluenecks*, 133–39; and Tom Roland, "John Rich Aghast at Chely Wright Conversation," *GAC Blog*, May 5, 2012, http://blog.gactv.com/blog/2010/05/05 /john-rich-aghast-at-chely-wright-conversation/ (accessed June 10, 2012).

21. Bambi Weavil, "In-Depth Interview with Chely Wright: 'It's Really Our Collective Story,'" OutImpact.com, August 21, 2011, www.outimpact.com /entertainment/celebrity-interviews/indepth-interview-chely-wright-its-collective-story/#axzz1VhNyfoPy (accessed June 10, 2012).

22. Valentine, *Imagining Transgender*, 31.

23. Valentine, *Imagining Transgender*, 56 (emphasis in original).

24. For an extended critique of this "just like you" ideology, see David M. Halperin, *How to Be Gay* (Cambridge, MA: Harvard University Press, 2012), which contends that gay male culture, specifically, is "a cultural practice, expressive of a unique subjectivity and a distinctive relation to mainstream society" (dust jacket).

25. Valentine, *Imagining Transgender*, 238–39. Valentine points out that this politics also privileges a simplistic binary conception of gender that merely

provides an opposite to sexuality, displacing richer notions of gender that would illumine issues central to lesbian self-formation and racialized public sexuality.

26. Alan Sinfield, "Private Lives/Public Theater: Noel Coward and the Politics of Homosexual Representation," *Representations* 36 (1991): 59.

27. Valentine, *Imagining Transgender*, 43.

28. Steve Valocchi, "The Class-Inflected Nature of Gay Identity," *Social Problems* 46, no. 2 (1999): 211, citing Chauncey, *Gay New York*, and Lillian Faderman, *Odd Girls and Twilight Lovers: A History of Lesbian Life in Twentieth-Century America* (New York: Columbia University Press, 1991).

29. Havelock Ellis, *Studies in the Psychology of Sex*, vol. 2: *Sexual Inversion* [1896], 3rd ed. (Philadelphia: F.A. Davis, 1915), 21.

30. Ellis, *Sexual Inversion*, 23, 24, 212. I explore the cultural linkage of queerness and genius in *The Queer Composition of America's Sound: Gay Modernists, American Music, and National Identity* (Berkeley: University of California Press, 2004). Andrew Elfenbein, *Romantic Genius: The Prehistory of a Homosexual Role* (New York: Columbia University Press, 1999), identifies shared key attributes linking the notions of eighteenth-century creative genius and nineteenth-century homosexual.

31. Chauncey, *Gay New York*, 110.

32. Chauncey, *Gay New York*, 100–101.

33. Chauncey, *Gay New York*, 127.

34. Valentine, *Imagining Transgender*, 43; Newton, *Mother Camp*, esp. 51–52. Valentine's account concurs with Valocchi's 1999 argument that "the social construction of gay identity in the twentieth century took place in a structural context of state control of 'threatening' sexualities and middle class anxieties over gender non-conformity": "The Class-Inflected Nature of Gay Identity," 208. I might note here that homosexuals of the upper class and artistic bohemia were also open in their ambiguous "eccentricity" but still typically less visible than the poor and working-class "deviants" and, anyway, few in number.

35. D'Emilio, *Sexual Politics, Sexual Communities*.

36. D'Emilio, *Sexual Politics, Sexual Communities*, chapter 4, reveals that the homophile movement started out radical under the leadership of Harry Hay and others with backgrounds in communist organizing but shifted politically and tactically when it was taken over by different leaders.

37. Valocchi, "The Class-Inflected Nature of Gay Identity," 211–12.

38. Valocchi, "The Class-Inflected Nature of Gay Identity," 218.

39. Valocchi, "The Class-Inflected Nature of Gay Identity," 207–8.

40. Valentine, *Imagining Transgender*, 45.

41. Ehrenreich, *Fear of Falling*, 199.

42. Boyd, *Wide-Open Town*, 13–14.

43. Kennedy and Davis, *Boots of Leather, Slippers of Gold*, 188–90.

44. Joan Nestle, "The Femme Question," in Nestle, *The Persistent Desire*, 140, 138.

45. Kennedy and Davis, *Boots of Leather, Slippers of Gold*, 188–90; E.J. Hobsbawm, *Primitive Rebels: Studies in Archaic Forms of Social Movement in*

the 19th and 20th Centuries, 3rd ed. (Manchester: Manchester University Press, [1959] 1971).

46. Boyd cites D'Emilio, *Sexual Politics, Sexual Communities;* and Marc Stein, *City of Sisterly and Brotherly Loves: Lesbian and Gay Philadelphia, 1945–72* (Chicago: University of Chicago Press, 2000), as work that emphasizes homophile groups in the history of gay activism.

47. Boyd, *Wide-Open Town,* 14 (emphasis mine).

48. Boyd, *Wide-Open Town,* 14, 6, 13.

49. Boyd, *Wide-Open Town,* 14. We might contrast Boyd's findings, too, with Judith (now Jack) Halberstam's reading of an aspect of Fellows's *Farm Boys:* that the gay sons of rural Wisconsin he interviewed, when they went away (in the 1970s and 1980s) to the city, were struck not only by urban gay men's effeminacy but also by the equation of gay with "activist." Halberstam, *In a Queer Time and Place* (New York: New York University Press, 2005), 41, reads this separation of sex from ideological critique as a "legacy of the history of whiteness that marks the communities the gay rural men left behind"—thus, in relation to race and rurality, with no attention to class. Her interpretation naturalizes the combination of the queer with activism, a move that stands upon a universalizing of middle-class subjectivity and individual rights ideology. It also concentrates whiteness in the largely working-class rural Midwest and so enacts the hyperwhitening, the projection of marked, bad whiteness, discussed above in connection with the analyses of Lawler, (Aaron) Fox, and Hartigan.

50. Chauncey, *Gay New York,* 41.

51. Chauncey, in *Gay New York,* and others reveal the central importance of Harlem in early-twentieth-century gay and lesbian New York, an area that was working class and African American. Gayle Rubin is among the scholars illumining historical patterns of urban location and movement of queer social and sexual activity. See, for example, her "Sites, Settlements and Urban Sex: Archaeology and the Study of Gay Leathermen in San Francisco, 1955–1995," in *Archaeologies of Sexuality,* ed. Robert Schmidt and Barbara Voss (London: Routledge, 2000), 62–88.

52. D. A. Miller, "Secret Subjects, Open Secrets," in *The Novel and the Police* (Berkeley: University of California Press, 1988), 206.

53. Rubin, *Worlds of Pain,* designates two major subgroups within the working class, "hard livers" and the more aspirational "settled livers." Before Rubin, the sociologist Herbert J. Gans had distinguished "routine seekers" and "action seekers" in his influential study of a Boston working-class community, *Urban Villagers: Group and Class in the Life of Italian-Americans* (New York: Free Press, 1962).

54. David Allan Coe on Al Goldstein's *Midnight Blue.* Viewed at http://youtu.be/loXmtX_cJLs (accessed September 27, 2012).

55. See Rich Wiseman, "David Allan Coe's Death Row Blues: Rhinestone Ripoff?," *Rolling Stone,* January 1, 1976, 16.

56. David Allan Coe on Al Goldstein's *Midnight Blue.* Viewed at http://youtu.be/loXmtX_cJLs (accessed September 27, 2012).

57. David Allan Coe on Al Goldstein's *Midnight Blue*. Viewed at http://youtu.be/qlGPsmrZA-Q (accessed September 27, 2012).

58. See verse 2 of "Fuck Aneta Briant," especially, for a profession of need for what is an impressive litany of intimate favors and charms rendered by prison "faggots." On Kunzel's account of mid-twentieth-century prison culture, real homosexuals were distinguished from the men they had sex with (known as wolves or jockers) who took the penetrative role and were understood as heterosexual—but by this time, only *inside* the prison world: *Criminal Intimacy*, 64, 184.

59. Chauncey, *Gay New York*, 119ff. In another context, David M. Halperin uses the term *prehomosexual* in *How to Do the History of Homosexuality* (Chicago: University of Chicago Press, 2002).

60. John Clarke, Stuart Hall, Tony Jefferson, and Brian Roberts, "Subcultures, Cultures, and Class: A Theoretical Overview," in *Resistance through Rituals: Youth Subcultures in Post-War Britain*, 2nd ed., ed. Stuart Hall and Tony Jefferson (New York: Routledge, [1975] 2006), 48 (emphasis in original). Their analysis here is focused on both British and American cultures. Thanks to Rostom Mesli for bringing this passage to my attention.

61. Skeggs, *Class, Self, Culture*, 185, discusses the distinct values of the working vs. middle class on the contemporary political landscape and the nonrecognition of those on the working-class side: "The emphasis on moral authority, produced from recognition politics [to which the middle class has exclusive access], means that many [working-class] values cannot be recognized by the middle-class commentators, those who can only see from their own position and are unable to extend their perspectives."

62. Lawler makes this point about shifting racial ideology in relation to the British context: "Disgusted Subjects," 437.

OUTRO

1. The transwoman character appears in Keith's music video at 1′46″; Rascal Flatts responded positively to listeners' perception of a gay-affirmative message in their song: see http://blog.cmt.com/2009–03–23/rascal-flatts-encourage-gay-fans-to-love-who-you-love/ (accessed September 8, 2012). Thanks to Kate Murphy for bringing the Miranda Lambert track to my attention.

2. The phrase arises in interviews of rural LGBTQ adults in Michigan and Illinois in Emily A. Kazyak, "'There's Still Queer People Here': How Rural Gays and Lesbians Construct Sexual Identities" (PhD diss., University of Michigan, 2010); for comparable findings based on an ethnography of rural LGBTQ youth in Kentucky, see Mary L. Gray, "Introduction: There Are No Queers Here," in *Out in the Country: Youth, Media, and the Queering of Rural America* (New York: New York University Press, 2009), 1–31.

3. Walter Boulden, "Gay Men Living in a Rural Environment," *Journal of Gay and Lesbian Social Services* 12, nos. 3–4 (2001): 67–68.

4. Lamont, *The Dignity of Working Men*.

5. Peterson's analysis notes only that the songs fail to position the working class as an identificatory and action group and does not place their resistance to identity group claims in a larger class-culture context: "Class Unconsciousness in Country Music," 50–56.

6. Halberstam has coined the term *metronormativity* and defined it in terms of a "story of migration from 'country' to 'town,' ... a spatial narrative within which the subject moves to a place of tolerance after enduring life in a place of suspicion, persecution, and secrecy": *In a Queer Time and Place*, 36–37.

7. Skeggs, *Class, Self, Culture*, does not discuss regionalism, but one could argue for the connection. Studies of rural communities attest to the differing mechanisms between social worlds based on knowing and being known by everyone and those based on anonymity: see, for example, Kazyak, "'There's Still Queer People Here'"; Gray, *Out in the Country;* and Boulden, "Gay Men Living in a Rural Environment."

8. Bourdieu, *Distinction*.

9. See, for example, Saez, "Striking It Richer."

References

Abramowitz, Alan, and Ruy Teixeira. "The Decline of the White Working Class and the Rise of a Mass Upper-Middle Class." *Political Science Quarterly* 124, no. 3 (2009): 391–422.

Adair, Vivyan C. "US Working-Class/Poverty-Class Divides." *Sociology* 39, no. 5 (2005): 817–34.

Allegretto, Sylvia A. "The State of Working America's Wealth, 2011." EPI Briefing Paper 292. Economic Policy Institute, Washington, DC, 2011. http://epi.3cdn.net/2a7ccb3e9e618f0bbc_3nm6idnax.pdf.

Balbach, Edith D., Rebecca J. Gasior, and Elizabeth M. Barbeau. "R.J. Reynolds' Targeting of African Americans: 1988–2000." *American Journal of Public Health* 93, no. 5 (2003): 822–27.

Bartels, Larry M. "What's the Matter with *What's the Matter with Kansas?*" *Quarterly Journal of Political Science* 1, no. 2 (2006): 201–26.

Bell, David. "Farm Boys and Wild Men: Rurality, Masculinity, and Homosexuality." *Rural Sociology* 65, no. 4 (2000): 547–61.

Bernstein, Basil B. "Social Class, Language and Socialization." In *Class, Codes and Control*, ed. Basil B. Bernstein, 170–89. London: Routledge and Kegan Paul, 1971.

Bertrand, Michael T. "I Don't Think Hank Done It That Way: Elvis, Country Music, and the Reconstruction of Southern Masculinity." In *A Boy Named Sue: Gender and Country Music*, ed. Kristine M. McCusker and Diane Pecknold, 59–85. Jackson: University Press of Mississippi, 2004.

Bérubé, Allan. *Coming Out under Fire: The History of Gay Men and Women in World War Two.* New York: Free Press, 1990.

Bettie, Julie. "Class Dismissed? *Roseanne* and the Changing Face of Working-Class Iconography." *Social Text* 14, no. 4 (1995): 125–49.

Boulden, Walter. "Gay Men Living in a Rural Environment." *Journal of Gay and Lesbian Social Services* 12, nos. 3–4 (2001): 63–75.

Bourdieu, Pierre. *Distinction: A Social Critique of the Judgement of Taste.* Trans. Richard Nice. Cambridge, MA: Harvard University Press, 1984.

———. "Distinction: A Social Critique of the Judgement of Taste." In *Social Stratification: Class, Race, and Gender in Sociological Perspective*, 3rd ed., ed. David B. Grusky, 870–93. Boulder, CO: Westview, 2008.

———. "The Forms of Capital." Trans. Richard Nice. In *Handbook of a Theory of Research for the Sociology of Education*, ed. John G. Richardson, 241–58. Westport, CT: Greenwood Press, 1986.

———. *Outline of a Theory of Practice*. Trans. Richard Nice. New York: Cambridge University Press, 1977.

———. *Pascalian Meditations*. Cambridge: Polity Press, 2000.

———. *Practical Reason: On the Theory of Action*. Cambridge: Polity Press, 1998.

Bourdieu, Pierre, and Jean-Claude Passeron. *Reproduction in Education, Society, and Culture*. Trans. Richard Nice. Newbury Park, CA: Sage, in association with *Theory, Culture & Society*, Dept. of Administrative and Social Studies, Teesside Polytechnic, [1977] 1990.

Boyd, Nan Alamilla. *Wide-Open Town: A History of Queer San Francisco to 1965*. Berkeley: University of California Press, 2003.

Brooks, David. *Bobos in Paradise: The New Upper Class and How They Got There*. New York: Simon & Schuster, 2000.

Bryson, Bethany. "'Anything but Heavy Metal': Symbolic Exclusion and Musical Dislikes." *American Sociological Review* 61, no. 5 (1996): 884–99.

Bufwack, Mary A., and Robert K. Oermann. *Finding Her Voice: The Saga of Women in Country Music*. New York: Crown Publishers, 1993.

Bunch, Wes. "Lesley Riddle's Music Finally Gaining Recognition." *Kingsport Times-News*, February 21, 2009. www.timesnews.net/article.php?id = 9011949.

Butsch, Richard. "Ralph, Fred, Archie and Homer: Why Television Keeps Recreating the White Male Working-Class Buffoon." In *Gender, Race, and Class in Media: A Text-Reader*, ed. Gail Dines and Jean McMahon Humez, 575–85. Thousand Oaks, CA: Sage, 1995.

Carter, David. *Stonewall: The Riots That Sparked the Gay Revolution*. New York: St. Martin's, 2004.

Chafe, William Henry. *Civilities and Civil Rights: Greensboro, North Carolina, and the Black Struggle for Freedom*. New York: Oxford University Press, 1980.

Chauncey, George, Jr. "Christian Brotherhood or Sexual Perversion? Homosexual Identity and the Construction of Sexual Boundaries in the World War I Era" (1985). In *Hidden from History: Reclaiming the Gay and Lesbian Past*, ed. Martin Bauml Duberman, Martha Vicinus, and George Chauncey Jr., 294–317. New York: New American Library, 1989.

———. *Gay New York: Gender, Urban Culture, and the Makings of the Gay Male World, 1890–1940*. New York: Basic Books, 1994.

Ching, Barbara. *Wrong's What I Do Best: Hard Country Music and Contemporary Culture*. New York: Oxford University Press, 2003.

Christgau, Robert. "Obvious Believers." Review of *Nashville Skyline*, by Bob Dylan. *Village Voice*, May 1969. Reproduced at www.robertchristgau.com/xg/bk-aow/dylan.php.

Clarke, John, Stuart Hall, Tony Jefferson, and Brian Roberts. "Subcultures, Cultures, and Class: A Theoretical Overview." In *Resistance through Rituals: Youth Subcultures in Post-War Britain*, 2nd ed., ed. Stuart Hall and Tony Jefferson, 9–74. New York: Routledge, [1975] 2006.

Clendinen, Dudley. "Floridian: Anita Bryant, b. 1940, Singer and Crusader." *St. Petersburg Times Online*, November 28, 1999. www.sptimes.com/News/112899/news_pf/Floridian/Anita_Bryant_b_1940_.shtml.

Clendinen, Dudley, and Adam Nagourney. *Out for Good: The Struggle to Build a Gay Rights Movement in America*. New York: Simon & Schuster, 1999.

Cowie, Jefferson. *Stayin' Alive: The 1970s and the Last Days of the Working Class*. New York: New Press, 2010.

Crawley, Sara L. "Are Butch and Fem Working-Class and Antifeminist?" *Gender and Society* 15, no. 2 (2001): 175–96.

Cyphert, Dale. "Rhetoric on the Concrete Pour: The Dance of Decision Making." In *Who Says? Working-Class Rhetoric, Class Consciousness, and Community*, ed. William DeGenaro, 144–63. Pittsburgh: University of Pittsburgh Press, 2007.

D'Emilio, John. *Sexual Politics, Sexual Communities: The Making of a Homosexual Minority in the United States, 1940–1970*. Chicago: University of Chicago Press, 1983.

———. "Dade County, USA." *OutHistory*. Article published 2008. www.outhistory.org/wiki/John_D'Emilio:_%22Dade_County,_USA,%22_1977.

DiMaggio, Paul. "On Pierre Bourdieu." *American Journal of Sociology* 84, no. 6 (1979): 1460–74.

DiMaggio, Paul, Richard A. Peterson, and Jack Esco Jr. "Country Music: Ballad of the Silent Majority." In *The Sounds of Social Change: Studies in Popular Culture*, ed. R. Serge Denisoff and Richard A. Peterson, 39–55. New York: Rand McNally, 1972.

Doyle, Patrick. "Exclusive: Merle Haggard on His Kennedy Center Honor, Meeting Obama and Oprah and More." *Rolling Stone Online*, December 28, 2010. www.rollingstone.com.proxy.lib.umich.edu/music/news/exclusive-merle-haggard-on-his-kennedy-center-honor-meeting-obama-and-oprah-and-more-20101228.

Drott, Eric. "What Inclusiveness Excludes." In "Colloquy: Musicology beyond Borders?," ed. Tamara Levitz. *Journal of the American Musicological Society* 65, no. 3 (2012): 825–29.

Duberman, Martin. *Stonewall*. New York: Dutton, 1993.

Duggan, Lisa. *The Twilight of Equality? Neoliberalism, Cultural Politics, and the Attack on Democracy*. Boston: Beacon Press, 2003.

Ehrenreich, Barbara. *Fear of Falling: The Inner Life of the Middle Class*. New York: Pantheon Books, 1989.

———. "The Silenced Majority: Why the Average Working Person Has Disappeared from American Media and Culture." In *Race, Class, and Gender: An Anthology*, 4th ed., ed. Margaret L. Andersen and Patricia Hill Collins, 143–45. Belmont, CA: Wadsworth, 2001.

Ehrenreich, Barbara, and John Ehrenreich. "The Professional-Managerial Class" (pts. 1 and 2). *Radical America* 11, nos. 2 and 3 (1977): 7–31; 7–22.

Elfenbein, Andrew. *Romantic Genius: The Prehistory of a Homosexual Role.* New York: Columbia University Press, 1999.

Ellis, Havelock. *Studies in the Psychology of Sex.* Vol. 2: *Sexual Inversion* [1896]. 3rd ed. Philadelphia: F.A. Davis, 1915.

Ellison, Curtis W. *Country Music Culture: From Hard Times to Heaven.* Jackson: University Press of Mississippi, 1995.

Escott, Colin, with George Merritt and William MacEwen. *Hank Williams, the Biography.* New York: Little, Brown, [1994] 2004.

Faderman, Lillian. *Surpassing the Love of Men: Romantic Friendship and Love between Women from the Renaissance to the Present.* New York: William Morrow, 1981.

———. *Odd Girls and Twilight Lovers: A History of Lesbian Life in Twentieth-Century America.* New York: Columbia University Press, 1991.

Feder, J. Lester. "'Song of the South': Country Music, Race, Region, and the Politics of Culture, 1920–1974." PhD diss., University of California, Los Angeles, 2006.

———. "When Country Went Right." *American Prospect Online,* February 16, 2007. http://prospect.org/article/when-country-went-right.

Feinberg, Leslie. *Stone Butch Blues: A Novel.* Los Angeles: Alyson, [1993] 2003.

Fellows, Will. *Farm Boys: Lives of Gay Men from the Rural Midwest.* Madison: University of Wisconsin Press, 1996.

Fillingim, David. *Redneck Liberation: Country Music as Theology.* Macon, GA: Mercer University Press, 2003.

Fiorina, Morris P., Samuel J. Abrams, and Jeremy Pope. *Culture War? The Myth of a Polarized America.* 3rd ed. Boston: Longman, [2004] 2011.

Foley, Michael S. "A Politics of Empathy: Johnny Cash, the Vietnam War, and the 'Walking Contradiction' Myth Dismantled." *Popular Music and Society* (2013). http://dx.doi.org/10.1080/03007766.2013.798928.

Fonarow, Wendy. *Empire of Dirt: The Aesthetics and Rituals of British Indie Music.* Middletown, CT: Wesleyan University Press, 2006.

Forbis, Wil. "Interesting Motherfuckers: David Allan Coe." *Acid Logic,* January 1, 2006. www.acidlogic.com/im_davidallancoe.htm. Reprinted in Wil Forbis, *Acid Logic: A Decade of Humorous Writing on Pop Culture, Trash Cinema and Rebel Music.* Bloomington, IN: AuthorHouse, 2008.

Fox, Aaron A. *Real Country: Music and Language in Working-Class Culture.* Durham, NC: Duke University Press, 2004.

———. "White Trash Alchemies of the Abject Sublime: Country as 'Bad' Music." In *Bad Music: The Music We Love to Hate,* ed. Charles J. Washburne and Maiken Derno, 29–46. New York: Routledge, 2004.

Fox, Pamela. *Natural Acts: Gender, Race, and Rusticity in Country Music.* Ann Arbor: University of Michigan Press, 2009.

Fraser, Nancy. "Rethinking the Public Sphere: A Contribution to the Critique of Actually Existing Democracy." *Social Text* 25–26 (1990): 56–80.

Frow, John. "Knowledge and Class." *Cultural Studies* 7, no. 2 (1993): 240–81.

Fussell, Paul. "The Life of the Mind." In *Class: A Guide through the American Status System*, 128–50. New York: Touchstone, 1983.

Gans, Herbert J. *Urban Villagers: Group and Class in the Life of Italian-Americans*. New York: Free Press, 1962.

Garber, Marjorie. *Vested Interests: Cross-Dressing and Cultural Anxiety*. New York: Routledge, 1992.

Geary, Daniel. "'The Way I Would Feel about San Quentin': Johnny Cash and the Politics of Country Music." *Dædalus: Journal of the American Academy of Arts & Sciences* 142, no. 4 (2013): 64–72.

Gelman, Andrew. *Red State, Blue State, Rich State, Poor State: Why Americans Vote the Way They Do*. Princeton, NJ: Princeton University Press, 2008.

Gelman, Andrew, Boris Shor, Joseph Bafumi, and David Park. "Rich State, Poor State, Red State, Blue State: What's the Matter with Connecticut?" *Quarterly Journal of Political Science* 2, no. 4 (2007): 345–67.

Giddens, Anthony. "The Class Structure of Advanced Societies." In *Social Stratification: Class, Race, and Gender in Sociological Perspective*, 3rd ed., ed. David B. Grusky, 133–42. Boulder, CO: Westview, 2008.

Gillette, Amelie, et al. "Baseball, Apple Pie, and Kicking Your Fucking Ass: 21 Hilariously Hyperbolic Pro-America Songs." *The Onion*, June 30, 2008. www.avclub.com/articles/baseball-apple-pie-and-kicking-your-fucking-ass-21,2364/.

Gimenez, Martha E. "The Professional/Managerial Class: An Ideological Construct." Unpublished MS. (1977). Reprinted at www.colorado.edu/Sociology/gimenez/work/pmg.html.

Gitelman, Lisa. "Reading Music, Reading Records, Reading Race: Musical Copyright and the U.S. Copyright Act of 1909." *Musical Quarterly* 81, no. 2 (1997): 265–90.

Goldstein, Richard. "My Country Music Problem—and Yours." *Mademoiselle*, June 1973, 114–15, 185.

Gopinath, Gayatri. *Impossible Desires: Queer Diasporas and South Asian Public Cultures*. Durham, NC: Duke University Press, 2005.

Gorman, Thomas J. "Cross-Class Perceptions of Social Class." *Sociological Spectrum* 20, no. 1 (2000): 93–120.

Gray, Mary L. *Out in the Country: Youth, Media, and the Queering of Rural America*. New York: New York University Press, 2009.

Green, Amy. "Even with Fame and Riches, Wilson Says She's Still a 'Redneck Woman.'" *CMA Closeup News*, February 15, 2005. www.gactv.com/gac/nw_cma_close_up/article/0,,GAC_26068_4729456,00.html.

Gregory, James N. *The Southern Diaspora: How the Great Migrations of Black and White Southerners Transformed America*. Chapel Hill: University of North Carolina Press, 2005.

———. "Southernizing the American Working Class: Post-war Episodes of Regional and Class Transformation." *Labor History* 39, no. 2 (1998): 135–54.

Gritzner, Charles F. "Country Music: A Reflection of Popular Culture." *Journal of Popular Culture* 11, no. 4 (1978): 857–64.

Grossman, Maxine L. "Jesus, Mama, and the Constraints of Salvific Love in Contemporary Country Music." *Journal of the American Academy of Religion* 70, no. 1 (2002): 83–115.

Grusky, David B., ed. *Social Stratification: Class, Race, and Gender in Sociological Perspective*, 3rd ed. Boulder, CO: Westview, 2008.

Gussow, Adam. "Playing Chicken with the Train: Cowboy Troy's Hick-Hop and the Transracial Country West." *Southern Cultures* 16, no. 4 (2010): 41–70.

Haggard, Merle, with Tom Carter. *My House of Memories: An Autobiography*. New York: It Books, [1999] 2011.

Halberstam, Judith. *In a Queer Time and Place*. New York: New York University Press, 2005.

Halperin, David M. *How to Be Gay*. Cambridge, MA: Harvard University Press, 2012.

———. *How to Do the History of Homosexuality*. Chicago: University of Chicago Press, 2002.

Harper's Magazine. "Stalking the Virile Female." May 1990, 26–27.

Hartigan, John, Jr. *Odd Tribes: Toward a Cultural Analysis of White People*. Durham, NC: Duke University Press, 2005.

———. *Racial Situations: Class Predicaments of Whiteness in Detroit*. Princeton, NJ: Princeton University Press, 1999.

———. "Who Are These White People? 'Rednecks,' 'Hillbillies,' and 'White Trash' as Marked Racial Subjects." In *White Out: The Continuing Significance of Racism*, ed. Ashley W. Doane and Eduardo Bonilla-Silva, 95–111. New York: Routledge, 2003.

Haslam, Gerald W. *Workin' Man Blues: Country Music in California*. Berkeley: University of California Press, 1999.

Hatten, Robert S. *Musical Meaning in Beethoven: Markedness, Correlation, and Interpretation*. Bloomington: Indiana University Press, 1994.

Himmelstein, Jerome L., and James A. McRae Jr. "Social Conservatism, New Republicans, and the 1980 Election." *Public Opinion Quarterly* 48, no. 3 (1984): 592–605.

Hobsbawm, Eric J. *Primitive Rebels: Studies in Archaic Forms of Social Movement in the 19th and 20th Centuries*. 3rd ed. Manchester: Manchester University Press, [1959] 1971.

———. *Age of Extremes: The Short Twentieth Century, 1914–91*. London: Michael Joseph, 1994.

Horstman, Dorothy. *Sing Your Heart Out, Country Boy*. Rev. and expanded ed. Nashville, TN: Country Music Foundation, [1975] 1996.

Howard, John, ed. *Carryin' On in the Lesbian and Gay South*. New York: New York University Press, 1997.

Hubbs, Nadine. *The Queer Composition of America's Sound: Gay Modernists, American Music, and National Identity*. Berkeley: University of California Press, 2004.

Huber, Patrick. "A Short History of *Redneck:* The Fashioning of a Southern Masculine Identity." In *Southern Cultures: The Fifteenth Anniversary Reader,* ed. Harry L. Watson and Larry J. Griffin, with Lisa Eveleigh, Dave Shaw, Ayse Erginer, and Paul Quigley, 303–27. Chapel Hill: University of North Carolina Press, 2008.

Hunter, James Davison. *Culture Wars: The Struggle to Define America.* New York: Basic Books, 1991.

Jensen, Joli. *The Nashville Sound: Authenticity, Commercialization, and Country Music.* Nashville, TN: Vanderbilt University Press, 1998.

Judge, Mark. "The Decline of Country Music." *Daily Caller,* June 22, 2011. http://dailycaller.com/2011/06/22/the-decline-of-country-music.

Kadi, Joanna. *Thinking Class: Sketches from a Cultural Worker.* Boston: South End Press, 1996.

Kalmijn, Matthijs. "Status Homogamy in the United States." *American Journal of Sociology* 97, no. 2 (1991): 496–523.

Katznelson, Ira. *When Affirmative Action Was White: An Untold History of Racial Inequality in Twentieth-Century America.* New York: W.W. Norton, 2005.

Kazyak, Emily A. "'There's Still Queer People Here': How Rural Gays and Lesbians Construct Sexual Identities." PhD diss., University of Michigan, 2010.

Kennedy, Elizabeth Lapovsky, and Madeline D. Davis. *Boots of Leather, Slippers of Gold: The History of a Lesbian Community.* New York: Routledge, 1993.

Kinsey, Alfred, et al. *Sexual Behavior in the Human Male.* Philadelphia: W.B. Saunders, 1948.

Kleijer, Henk, and Ger Tillekens. "Twenty-Five Years of *Learning to Labour:* Looking Back at British Cultural Studies with Paul Willis." *Soundscapes— Journal on Media Culture* 5 (2003), www.icce.rug.nl/~soundscapes /VOLUME05/Paul_WillisUK.shtml.

Klein, Ezra. Review of *Red State, Blue State, Rich State, Poor State,* by Andrew Gelman, October 13, 2008. http://bnreview.barnesandnoble.com/t5/Reviews-Essays/Red-State-Blue-State-Rich-State-Poor-State-Why-Americans-Vote /ba-p/673.

Klosterman, Chuck. *Sex, Drugs, and Cocoa Puffs: A Low Culture Manifesto.* New York: Scribner, 2003.

Kornheiser, Tony. "Cigarettes and Virile Chicks." *Washington Post,* February 23, 1990, B2.

Krims, Adam. *Rap Music and the Poetics of Identity.* New York: Cambridge University Press, 2000.

Krugman, Paul. "Panic of the Plutocrats." *New York Times,* October 9, 2011. www.nytimes.com/2011/10/10/opinion/panic-of-the-plutocrats.html.

Kunzel, Regina G. *Criminal Intimacy: Prison and the Uneven History of Modern American Sexuality.* Chicago: University of Chicago Press, 2008.

Kusserow, Adrie Suzanne. "De-Homogenizing American Individualism: Socializing Hard and Soft Individualism in Manhattan and Queens." *Ethos* 27, no. 2 (1999): 210–34.

La Chapelle, Peter. *Proud to Be an Okie: Cultural Politics, Country Music, and Migration to Southern California*. Berkeley: University of California Press, 2007.

Lamont, Michèle. *The Dignity of Working Men: Morality and the Boundaries of Race, Class, and Immigration*. Cambridge, MA: Harvard University Press, 2000.

———. *Money, Morals, and Manners: The Culture of the French and American Upper-Middle Class*. Chicago: University of Chicago Press, 1992.

Lareau, Annette. *Unequal Childhoods: Class, Race, and Family Life*. 2nd ed. Berkeley: University of California Press, [2003] 2011.

Lawler, Stephanie. "Disgusted Subjects: The Making of Middle-Class Identities." *Sociological Review* 53, no. 3 (2005): 429–46.

Legendary Performances: Merle Haggard (DVD). Los Angeles: Shout! Factory, 2008.

Leventhal, Stan. "Stand by Your Man: The Rise of Gay C & W Lyrics." *New York Native*, March 15–23, 1982, 23, 31.

Lewis, George H. "The Color of Country: Black Influence and Experience in American Country Music." *Popular Music and Society* 25, nos. 3–4 (2001): 107–19.

Lipsitz, George. *Rainbow at Midnight: Labor and Culture in the 1940s*. Urbana: University of Illinois Press, [1981] 1994.

———. *The Possessive Investment in Whiteness: How White People Profit from Identity Politics*. Rev. and expanded ed. Philadelphia: Temple University Press, [1998] 2006.

Lubrano, Alfred. *Limbo: Blue-Collar Roots, White-Collar Dreams*. Hoboken, NJ: Wiley, 2004.

Lukács, György. *History and Class Consciousness: Studies in Marxist Dialectics*. Cambridge, MA: MIT Press, [1920] 1971.

Lynn, Loretta, with George Vecsey. *Coal Miner's Daughter*. New York: Vintage Books, [1976] 2010.

Malone, Bill C. *Country Music U.S.A.* 2nd rev. ed. Austin: University of Texas Press, [1968] 2002.

———. *Don't Get above Your Raisin': Country Music and the Southern Working Class*. Urbana: University of Illinois Press, 2002.

Mann, Geoff. "Why Does Country Music Sound White? Race and the Voice of Nostalgia." *Ethnic and Racial Studies* 31, no. 1 (2008): 73–100.

Marmot, Michael. *The Status Syndrome: How Social Standing Affects Our Health and Longevity*. New York: Henry Holt, 2004.

McCusker, Kristine M., and Diane Pecknold, eds. *A Boy Named Sue: Gender and Country Music*. Jackson: University Press of Mississippi, 2004.

McDermott, Elizabeth. "Telling Lesbian Stories: Interviewing and the Class Dynamics of 'Talk.'" *Women's Studies International Forum* 27, no. 3 (2004): 177–87.

Mclenon, Andy, and Grant Alden. "Merle Haggard—Branded Man." *No Depression* 48 (November–December 2003). https://archives.nodepression.com/2003/11/branded-man/3/.

Mickler, Ernest Matthew. *White Trash Cooking.* Highlands, NC: Jargon Society, 1986.

Miller, D.A. *The Novel and the Police.* Berkeley: University of California Press, 1988.

Miller, Karl Hagstrom. *Segregating Sound: Inventing Folk and Pop Music in the Age of Jim Crow.* Durham, NC: Duke University Press, 2010.

Mockus, Martha. "Queer Thoughts on Country Music and k.d. lang." In *Queering the Pitch: The New Gay and Lesbian Musicology,* 2nd ed., ed. Philip Brett, Elizabeth Wood, and Gary C. Thomas, 257–74. New York: Routledge, [1994] 2006.

Moss, Kirby. *The Color of Class: Poor Whites and the Paradox of Privilege.* Philadelphia: University of Pennsylvania Press, 2003.

Murphy, Lawrence R. "Cleaning Up Newport: The U.S. Navy's Persecution of Homosexuals after World War I." *Journal of American Culture* 7, no. 3 (1984): 57–64.

Napier, Carson X. Review of *I Love Dixie Blues,* by Merle Haggard and the Strangers with special guests the Dixieland Express. *Ann Arbor Sun* 1, no. 2 (January 11–25, 1974): 17.

Neal, Jocelyn R. "Dancing around the Subject: Race in Country Fan Culture." *Musical Quarterly* 89, no. 4 (2006): 555–79.

Neely, Emily C. "Charline Arthur: The (Un)Making of a Honky-Tonk Star." In *A Boy Named Sue: Gender and Country Music,* ed. Kristine M. McCusker and Diane Pecknold, 44–58. Jackson: University Press of Mississippi, 2004.

Nelson, Heather. "A New Shine: Silver Jews Tunesmith/Poet Moves to Town." *Nashville Scene,* January 13, 2000. www.nashvillescene.com /nashville/a-new-shine/Content?oid = 1183887.

Nestle, Joan. *A Restricted Country.* Ithaca, NY: Firebrand Books, 1987.

———, ed. *The Persistent Desire: A Femme-Butch Reader.* Boston: Alyson, 1992.

Newton, Esther. *Mother Camp: Female Impersonators in America.* Reprint. Chicago: University of Chicago Press, [1972] 1979.

New York Times. "Editorial: The New Resentment of the Poor." August 31, 2011. www.nytimes.com/2011/08/31/opinion/the-new-resentment-of-the-poor.html?_r = 0.

Nystrom, Derek. *Hard Hats, Rednecks, and Macho Men: Class in 1970s American Cinema.* New York: Oxford University Press, 2009.

Ollivier, Michèle. "'Too Much Money off Other People's Backs': Status in Late Modern Societies." *Canadian Journal of Sociology* 25, no. 4 (2000): 441–70.

———. "Modes of Openness to Cultural Diversity: Humanist, Populist, Practical, and Indifferent." *Poetics* 36, nos. 1–2 (2008): 120–47.

Organisation for Economic Co-operation and Development. "The Knowledge-Based Economy." 1996. www.oecd.org/dataoecd/51/8/1913021.pdf.

Ortner, Sherry B. *New Jersey Dreaming: Capital, Culture, and the Class of '58.* Durham, NC: Duke University Press, 2003.

———. *Anthropology and Social Theory: Culture, Power, and the Acting Subject.* Durham, NC: Duke University Press, 2006.

Pecknold, Diane. *The Selling Sound: The Rise of the Country Music Industry.* Durham, NC: Duke University Press, 2007.

Peterson, Richard A. "Class Unconsciousness in Country Music." In *You Wrote My Life: Lyrical Themes in Country Music,* ed. Melton A. McLaurin and Richard A. Peterson, 35–62. Langhorne, PA: Gordon and Breach, 1992.

———. "Understanding Audience Segmentation: From Elite and Mass to Omnivore and Univore." *Poetics* 21 (1992): 243–58.

———. *Creating Country Music: Fabricating Authenticity.* Chicago: University of Chicago Press, 1997.

Peterson, Richard A., and Russell Davis Jr. "The Fertile Crescent of Country Music." *Journal of Country Music* 6 (1975): 19–27.

Peterson, Richard A., and Paul DiMaggio. "From Region to Class, the Changing Locus of Country Music: A Test of the Massification Hypothesis." *Social Forces* 53, no. 3 (1975): 497–506.

Peterson, Richard A., and Albert Simkus. "How Musical Tastes Mark Occupational Status Groups." In *Cultivating Differences: Symbolic Boundaries and the Making of Inequality,* ed. Michèle Lamont and Marcel Fournier, 152–86. Chicago: University of Chicago Press, 1993.

Pew Research Center. "Middle Class, by the Numbers." Pew Research Center, Washington, DC, October 6, 2008. http://pewresearch.org/pubs/983/middle-class-by-the-numbers.

———. "Religious Beliefs Underpin Opposition to Homosexuality." Pew Research Center, Washington, DC, November 18, 2003. www.pewforum.org/2003/11/18/religious-beliefs-underpin-opposition-to-homosexuality/.

———. "War and Sacrifice in the Post-9/11 Era: The Military-Civilian Gap." Pew Research Center, Washington, DC, October 5, 2011. http://pewresearch.org/pubs/2111/veterans-post-911-wars-iraq-afghanistan-civilian-military-veterans.

Prasad, Monica, Andrew Perrin, Kieran Bezila, Steve Hoffman, Kate Kindleberger, Kim Manturuk, Ashleigh Smith Powers, and Andrew Payton. "The Undeserving Rich: 'Moral Values' and the White Working Class." *Sociological Forum* 24, no. 2 (2009): 225–53.

Reardon, Sean F., and Kendra Bischoff. "Growth in the Residential Segregation of Families by Income, 1970–2009." Russell Sage Foundation American Communities Project of Brown University, 2011. http://graphics8.nytimes.com/packages/pdf/national/RussellSageIncomeSegregationreport.pdf.

Reay, Diane. "Dealing with Difficult Differences: Reflexivity and Social Class in Feminist Research." *Feminism & Psychology* 6, no. 3 (1996): 443–56.

———. "Psychosocial Aspects of White Middle-class Identities: Desiring and Defending against the Class and Ethnic 'Other' in Urban Multi-ethnic Schooling." *Sociology* 42, no. 6 (2008): 1072–88.

Rogers, Jimmie N. *The Country Music Message, Revisited.* Fayetteville: University of Arkansas Press, 1989.

Roland, Tom. "John Rich Aghast at Chely Wright Conversation." *GAC Blog*, May 5, 2012. http://blog.gactv.com/blog/2010/05/05/john-rich-aghast-at-chely-wright-conversation/.

Rolling Stone. "100 Greatest Singers of All Time." November 27, 2008. www.rollingstone.com/music/lists/100-greatest-singers-of-all-time-19691231.

Rosenberg, Neil V. *Bluegrass: A History*. Urbana: University of Illinois Press, [1985] 2005.

Rubin, Gayle S. "Sites, Settlements, and Urban Sex: Archaeology and the Study of Gay Leathermen in San Francisco, 1955–1995." In *Archaeologies of Sexuality*, ed. Robert Schmidt and Barbara Voss, 62–88. London: Routledge, 2000.

———. "Thinking Sex: Notes for a Radical Theory of the Politics of Sexuality" (1984). In *Social Perspectives in Lesbian and Gay Studies: A Reader*, ed. Peter M. Nardi and Beth E. Schneider, 100–133. New York: Routledge, 1998.

Rubin, Lillian B. *Worlds of Pain*. New York: Basic Books, 1976.

Saez, Emmanuel. "Striking It Richer: The Evolution of Top Incomes in the United States." July 17, 2010. Update of an article that appeared in *Pathways* (Winter 2008): 6–7. http://elsa.berkeley.edu/~saez/.

Safire, William. "On Language; Virile Women Target Tobacco Men." *New York Times Magazine*, March 11, 1990, 18.

Sample, Tex. *White Soul: Country Music, the Church, and Working Americans*. Nashville, TN: Abingdon Press, 1996.

Savage, Mike. "A New Class Paradigm?" *British Journal of Sociology of Education* 24, no. 4 (2003): 535–41.

Savage, Mike, Gaynor Bagnall, and Brian Longhurst. "Ordinary, Ambivalent and Defensive: Class Identities in the Northwest of England." *Sociology* 35, no. 4 (2001): 875–92.

Savoy, Ann Allen. *Cajun Music: A Reflection of a People*. Vol. 1. Eunice, LA: Bluebird Press, 1984.

Sayer, R. Andrew. *The Moral Significance of Class*. Cambridge: Cambridge University Press, 2005.

Scherman, Tony. "The Last Roundup." *Atlantic* 278, no. 2 (1996): 79–83.

Schulman, Bruce J. *The Seventies: The Great Shift in American Culture, Society, and Politics*. New York: Free Press, 2001.

Scott, James C. *Domination and the Arts of Resistance: Hidden Transcripts*. New Haven, CT: Yale University Press, 1990.

Sennett, Richard, and Jonathan Cobb. *The Hidden Injuries of Class*. New York: Vintage Books, 1972.

Sinfield, Alan. "Private Lives/Public Theater: Noel Coward and the Politics of Homosexual Representation." *Representations* 36 (1991): 43–63.

Skeggs, Beverley. *Class, Self, Culture*. New York: Routledge, 2004.

———. *Formations of Class and Gender: Becoming Respectable*. London: Sage, 1997.

———. "Uneasy Alignments: Resourcing Respectable Subjectivity." *GLQ: A Journal of Lesbian and Gay Studies* 10, no. 2 (2004): 291–98.

Skeggs, Bev, Helen Wood, and Nancy Thumim. "'Oh Goodness I *Am* Watching Reality TV': How Methods Make Class in Audience Research." *European Journal of Cultural Studies* 11, no. 1 (2008): 5–24.

Smith, Thomas Ruys. "'Bring Our Country Back': Country Music, Conservatives, and the Counter-Culture in 1968." *Studies in American Culture* 34, no. 1 (2011): 103–12.

Snibbe, Alana Conner, and Hazel Rose Markus. "You Can't Always Get What You Want: Educational Attainment, Agency, and Choice." *Journal of Personality and Social Psychology* 88, no. 4 (2005): 703–20.

Specter, Michael. "Marketers Target 'Virile Female': R.J. Reynolds Plans to Introduce Cigarette." *Washington Post*, February 17, 1990, A1.

Spencer, Bettina. "Classism in the Court System: Perceptions of Low-Income Rape Victims." Paper presented at the conference "How Class Works," Stony Brook, NY, June 2008.

Spivak, Gayatri, with Ellen Rooney. "'In a Word': Interview." In *The Second Wave: A Reader in Feminist Theory*, ed. Linda J. Nicholson, 356–78. New York: Routledge, 1997.

Steedman, Carolyn Kay. *Landscape for a Good Woman: A Story of Two Lives.* New Brunswick, NJ: Rutgers University Press, 1986.

Stein, Marc. *City of Sisterly and Brotherly Loves: Lesbian and Gay Philadelphia, 1945–72.* Chicago: University of Chicago Press, 2000.

Stewart, Abigail J., and Joan M. Ostrove. "Social Class, Social Change, and Gender: Working-Class Women at Radcliffe and After." *Psychology of Women Quarterly* 17, no. 4 (1993): 475–97.

Stewart, Katie. "Engendering Narratives of Lament in Country Music." In *All That Glitters: Country Music in America*, ed. George H. Lewis, 221–25. Bowling Green, OH: Bowling Green State University Popular Press, 1993.

Streib, Jessi. "Class Reproduction by Four Year Olds." *Qualitative Sociology* 34, no. 2 (2011): 337–52.

Sulzberger, A.G. "In Small Towns, Gossip Moves to the Web, and Turns Vicious." *New York Times*, September 20, 2011. www.nytimes.com/2011/09/20/us/small-town-gossip-moves-to-the-web-anonymous-and-vicious.html.

Tanz, Jason. *Other People's Property: A Shadow History of Hip-Hop in White America.* New York: Bloomsbury, 2007.

Tarradell, Mario. "Country Music Queen Loretta Lynn Sounded Regal during Winspear Opera House Concert." Dallas News.com, January 23, 2012. www.dallasnews.com/entertainment/columnists/mario-tarradell/20120123-country-music-queen-loretta-lynn-sounded-regal-during-winspear-opera-house-concert.ece.

Thompson, Matt. "Shifting Gears: When It Comes to Presidential Elections, There May Be More to the NASCAR Set than Meets the Eye." *American Prospect*, February 1, 2004. http://prospect.org/article/shifting-gears.

Thrall, Jeannie S. "Strategic Parenting: Making the Middle Class through Distinction and Discipline." PhD diss., University of Michigan, 2010.

Turner, Patricia A. "Dangerous White Stereotypes." *New York Times*, August 29, 2011, A23.

Valentine, David. *Imagining Transgender: An Ethnography of a Category.* Durham, NC: Duke University Press, 2007.

Valocchi, Steve. "The Class-Inflected Nature of Gay Identity." *Social Problems* 46, no. 2 (1999): 207–24.

Walker, Karen. "'Always There for Me': Friendship Patterns and Expectations among Middle- and Working-Class Men and Women." *Sociological Forum* 10, no. 2 (1995): 273–96.

Walkerdine, Valerie, and Helen Lucey. *Democracy in the Kitchen? Regulating Mothers and Socialising Daughters.* London: Virago, 1989.

Weavil, Bambi. "In-Depth Interview with Chely Wright: 'It's Really Our Collective Story.'" OutImpact.com, August 21, 2011. www.outimpact.com /entertainment/celebrity-interviews/indepth-interview-chely-wright-its-collective-story/#axzz1VhNyfoPy.

Whitburn, Joel. *The Billboard Book of Top 40 Hits.* 6th ed. New York: Billboard, 1996.

Williams, Roger. *Sing a Sad Song: The Life of Hank Williams.* 2nd ed. Urbana: University of Illinois Press, [1973] 1981.

Williamson, Joel. *The Crucible of Race: Black/White Relations in the American South since Emancipation.* New York: Oxford University Press, 1984.

Williamson, J.W. *Hillbillyland: What the Movies Did to the Mountains and What the Mountains Did to the Movies.* Chapel Hill: University of North Carolina Press, 1995.

Willis, Ellen. "Escape from Freedom: What's the Matter with Tom Frank (and the Lefties Who Love Him)?" *Situations: Project of the Radical Imagination* 1, no. 2 (February 19, 2006): 5–20.

Willman, Chris. "Chely Wright Comes Out, as a . . . Thinker." *Huffington Post,* May 3, 2010. www.huffingtonpost.com/chris-willman/chely-wright-comes-out-as_b_561103.html.

———. *Rednecks and Bluenecks: The Politics of Country Music.* New York: New Press, 2005.

Wiseman, Rich. "David Allan Coe's Death Row Blues: Rhinestone Ripoff?" *Rolling Stone,* January 1, 1976, 16.

Wright, Chely. *Like Me.* New York: Pantheon, 2010.

Zweig, Michael. *The Working Class Majority: America's Best Kept Secret.* Ithaca, NY: Cornell University Press, 2000.

Zweig, Michael, Michael Porter, and Yuxiang Huang. "American Military Deaths in Afghanistan, and the Communities from Which These Soldiers, Sailors, Airmen, and Marines Came." Center for Study of Working Class Life, October 2011. www.stonybrook.edu/workingclass/publications /afghan_casualties.shtml.

Subject Index

Song Index

CPSIA information can be obtained
at www.ICGtesting.com
Printed in the USA
JSHW031900031121
20096JS00003B/170